Drug Trafficking

Drug Trafficking

David L. Bender, *Publisher*
Bruno Leone, *Executive Editor*
Bonnie Szumski, *Managing Editor*
Carol Wekesser, *Senior Editor*

Karin L. Swisher, *Book Editor*

Library of Congress Cataloging-in-Publication Data

Drug trafficking / Karin L. Swisher, book editor.
    p. cm. — (Current controversies)
    Includes bibliographical references and index.
    Summary: Experts debate the following topics: 1) Should drugs be legalized? 2) How has drug trafficking affected American society? 3) Can domestic and international drug trafficking be stopped?
    ISBN 0-89908-576-8 (lib. bdg.) — ISBN 0-89908-582-2 (pbk.)
    1. Drug traffic—United States. 2. Narcotics, Control of—United States. 3. Drug legalization—United States. [1. Drug traffic. 2. Narcotics, Control of. 3. Drug legalization.] I. Swisher, Karin. II. Series.
HV5825.D7769 1991
363.4'5'0973—dc20   91-22022

Printed on
recycled paper

Contents

Chapter 2: Should Drugs Be Legalized?

Yes: Legalizing Drugs Would Solve the Drug Problem

No: Legalizing Drugs Would Be Dangerous

Chapter 3: Is the U.S. War Against International Drug Trafficking Effective?

Yes: U.S. Campaigns Against Drug Trafficking Are Necessary

No: U.S. Campaigns Against Drug Trafficking Should Be Stopped

Chapter 4: How Has Drug Trafficking Affected the U.S.?

Foreword

By definition, controversies are "discussions of questions in which opposing opinions clash" (*Webster's Twentieth Century Dictionary Unabridged*). Few would deny that controversies are a pervasive part of the human condition and exist on virtually every level of human enterprise. Controversies transpire between individuals and among groups, within nations and between nations. Controversies supply the grist necessary for progress by providing challenges and challengers to the status quo. They also create atmospheres where strife and warfare can flourish. A world without controversies would be a peaceful world; but it also would be, by and large, static and prosaic.

The Series' Purpose

The purpose of the Current Controversies series is to explore many of the social, political, and economic controversies dominating the national and international scenes today. Titles selected for inclusion in the series are highly focused and specific. For example, from the larger category of criminal justice, Current Controversies deals with specific topics such as police brutality, gun control, white collar crime, and others. The debates in Current Controversies also are presented in a useful, timeless fashion. Articles and book excerpts included in each title are selected if they contribute valuable, long-range ideas to the overall debate. And wherever possible, current information is enhanced with historical documents and other relevant materials.

Thus, while individual titles are current in focus, every effort is made to ensure that they will not become quickly outdated. Books in the Current Controversies series will remain important resources for librarians, teachers, and students for many years.

In addition to keeping the titles focused and specific, great care is taken in the editorial format of each book in the series. Book introductions and chapter prefaces are offered to provide background material for readers. Chapters are organized around several key questions that are answered with diverse opinions representing all points on the political spectrum. Materials in each chapter include opinions in which authors clearly disagree as well as alternative opinions in which authors may agree on a broader issue but disagree on the possible solutions. In this way, the content of each volume in Current Controversies mirrors the mosaic of opinions encountered in society. Readers will quickly realize that there are many viable answers to these complex issues. By questioning each author's conclusions, students and casual readers can begin to develop the critical thinking skills so important to evaluating opinionated material.

Current Controversies is also ideal for controlled research. Each anthology in the series is composed of primary sources taken from a wide gamut of informational categories including periodicals, newspapers, books, United States and foreign government documents, and the publications of private and public organizations.

Readers will find factual support for reports, debates, and research papers covering all areas of important issues. In addition, an annotated table of contents, an index, a book and periodical bibliography, and a list of organizations to contact are included in each book to expedite further research.

Perhaps more than ever before in history, people are confronted with diverse and contradictory information. During the Persian Gulf War, for example, the public was not only treated to minute-to-minute coverage of the war, it was also inundated with critiques of the coverage and countless analyses of the factors motivating U.S. involvement. Being able to sort through the plethora of opinions accompanying today's major issues, and to draw one's own conclusions, can be a complicated and frustrating struggle. It is the editors' hope that Current Controversies will help readers with this struggle.

Introduction

Much has been said and done to decrease drug use, yet America's intractable drug problem continues to affect all levels of society, from the high echelons of the government to the inner cities. Although the government allocates billions of dollars every year to decrease drug use and stop drug trafficking, addiction and violent crime associated with the drug culture pervade American society. Drug trafficking has been difficult to stop for one reason: The profits generated by the drug-trafficking industry are so immense, they prove motivation to maintain the traffic in illegal drugs despite the costs exacted by law enforcement agencies.

International drug trafficking, the massive, complex system that supplies drugs to the U.S., encompasses the cultivation, manufacture, and distribution of illegal drugs. Drug trafficking is both illegal and highly profitable, grossing approximately $120 billion annually. The drug trafficking chain begins in foreign, usually poor countries in Latin America, Asia, and the Middle East. At each link in the chain of drug production, the profits increase.

Because most drugs follow similar patterns of production and movement, the example of cocaine trafficking can be used to examine the problems involved in stopping drugs. A single coca plant, the plant from which cocaine and crack are derived, begins its journey in remote hills and valleys of Colombia, Bolivia, or Peru. The farmers who grow coca in the remote areas like the Chapare Valley in Bolivia are both isolated and desperately poor. Bolivia's average annual income is $565. These farmers have no plumbing, electricity, or medical care. They have little food beyond what they can grow themselves. Coca brings in three times more money than legal crops such as oranges and coffee. For each sack of dried coca leaves, a farmer can make $20 to $30. For these growers, the economic advantage is clear.

Often the farmers or other local people will convert the dried leaves into coca paste, which is easier to transport than the bulky leaves. The processing is another step in the lengthy profit chain. Once again the local people who are involved in the processing earn more than their usual subsistence income for their involvement in illegal trafficking.

Located deep in the jungles, the coca-processing factories consist of several plastic-lined pits called *pozos*. The dried leaves are placed in a pit and doused with sulfuric acid and diesel fuel. Local peasants stomp on this mixture with their bare feet throughout the night, earning about seven dollars for their work. (In contrast, a usual day's wages ranges from a few cents to about $1.50.) Workers move the stomped coca mixture to smaller pits where more chemicals and finally lime are added to complete the process.

Next, members of powerful drug cartels, large and wealthy criminal organizations, purchase the final product, the coca paste, for about $160 to $200 a kilo. When they transport it to Colombia, they will sell it for about $2,000 a kilo, roughly ten times more than they paid the peasants.

In Colombia, where governmental interference is minimal, the coca paste is refined into powder. This powder is later smuggled into the U.S., the traffickers' most profitable market. Distributors employed by the cartels sell the cocaine to other distributors, who then sell to the pushers, who in turn sell to drug users on the streets. Each time the cocaine changes hands, it is "stepped on" or "cut"—adulterated—with powdered milk, baking soda, or other bland substances. The cocaine is cut to increase the amount of the drug available for sale and thus increase the profit. The Colombians cut the purity down to about 70 percent and the purity declines each time the cocaine changes hands. A kilo of cocaine from Colombia that is first sold in the U.S. for $10,000 will eventually gross more than $250,000 on the street.

> ## "The profitability of drug trafficking is the primary reason it is so difficult to control or eradicate."

These immense profits explain the traffickers' motivation to continue in it, protecting themselves any way they can. To hide profits from U.S. law enforcement, traffickers must either smuggle the money out of the country or "launder" it. Money laundering is a complex process in which drug-related money is sent through real and phony businesses, international money transfers, and deposits into U.S. and foreign banks to conceal the taint of drugs from law enforcement agents. These banks will also reap the profits of drug trafficking. At one time, Miami's banks had a larger cash surplus than all the rest of America's banks combined due to the high volume of drug trafficking and money launder-

ing in that city. The lure of drug profits has tainted the international banking system, corrupted people who work in banking, and taxed the resources of law enforcement agents.

One of the primary reasons drug trafficking has been so profitable is that it is run the same way legitimate businesses are. Drug traffickers, like other savvy businesspeople, assess their market and look for ways to increase it and their profits at the same time. The best example of this is the introduction of crack to the drug users. Crack, a derivative of cocaine, is cheap, smokable, and potent. It is also highly addictive, thereby ensuring that addicts will continue to buy it. When it was introduced in the mid-1980s, crack became instantaneously popular with the drug users and drug traffickers' profits soared.

The profitability of drug trafficking is the primary reason it is so difficult to control or eradicate. Despite the more than $26 billion the Reagan and Bush administrations have devoted to enforcing antidrug laws, drug trafficking continues to plague the U.S. The profits not only motivate the traffickers to remain in the business, but also empower them to defy law enforcement efforts. With more than $100 billion collectively, drug traffickers can utilize ten times the resources of the government's antidrug efforts every year.

Remedies and Solutions

Despite all these hurdles, the nation continues its attempts to eradicate drug trafficking. *Drug Trafficking: Current Controversies* presents articles that discuss drug trafficking's effects on American society and articles that propose remedies and solutions. The violence and corruption that drug trafficking engender provide a strong motive for citizens and governments to find solutions to the problem. While almost everyone agrees that drug trafficking must end, the methods employed to stop it have become a great source of controversy in the United States.

Chapter 1:
Can the War on Drugs Be Won?

Preface

The "war on drugs" describes the measures the U.S. government has taken to reduce the use, transportation, and business of illegal drugs. It utilizes federal, state, and local law enforcement agencies to enforce drug laws and includes policies to relieve both the demand and the supply of drugs. The war on drugs was officially declared in 1971 when President Richard Nixon, in response to rising drug use, declared to Congress that drugs are "America's public enemy No. 1." He declared a "national emergency" and called for a "total offensive" against drugs. Congress responded by pledging $1 billion in funding in 1972 to enforce drug laws and reduce drug use. One year later, four government agencies devoted to enforcing drug laws were reorganized into the Drug Enforcement Administration (DEA). In the same year, Nixon announced, "We have turned the corner on drug addiction in America," although there was little evidence to support his assertion. Funding declined, and little more was actually done about fighting drugs in the 1970s.

The war on drugs was revived in the 1980s as both presidents Ronald Reagan and George Bush expanded government efforts to reduce drug addiction and trafficking. The Reagan administration increased the budget for enforcing

drug laws, and Reagan, like Nixon, called on the Drug Enforcement Administration to reduce the supply of drugs entering the United States. Reagan also passed laws permitting federal agents to utilize the military's intelligence, training, and equipment to locate and intercept drug traffickers. At the same time, state and federal governments instituted laws allowing officials to seize suspected drug traffickers' assets, including houses, boats, cars, and planes. Along with increased laws and law enforcement, the Reagan administration encouraged drug prevention programs like "Just Say No" for school children.

Upon his election in 1988, George Bush adhered closely to Reagan's strategies while initiating policies of his own. On September 5, 1989, Bush announced the creation of the Office of National Drug Control Policy, with the nation's first "drug czar," William Bennett, to unify the government's antidrug efforts. Bush also allocated billions of dollars more to enforce current drug laws, nearly as much per year as was spent during the entire previous decade.

Those who support the drug war argue that it is succeeding. Bennett announced in October 1990 that success in the drug war was in sight and predicted that if law enforcement efforts remain unchanged, drug use could be halved by 1994. Bush concurred, saying, "We're on the road to victory" in the drug war. The assertions of Bennett, Bush, and others that the drug war is successful are based on evidence that casual consumption of marijuana and cocaine has fallen. According to the National Institute on Drug Abuse, annual marijuana use among young adults dipped to 24.6 percent in 1990, the lowest percentage in a decade. Cocaine use among the same group fell to 7.5 percent. In addition, drug-related emergency-room visits and drug overdoses both declined. Jeffrey A. Eisenach, a visiting fellow at the Heritage Foundation, concludes, "If lawmakers continue to improve on current policies, . . . the drug problem can be overcome."

Decreasing Drug Trafficking

Even with these successes, however, the government has had difficulty decreasing drug use and trafficking. Crack, a cheap, easily processed derivative of cocaine, revitalized the drug industry, creating many new addicts and increasing profits for the drug traffickers. Crack's rapid rate of addiction, its price, and its popularity have made the war on drugs more difficult to win. Critics of the war on drugs point out that the number of daily cocaine users jumped from 246,000 in 1985 to 336,000 in 1990, despite the more than $16 billion spent to eliminate drugs from the U.S. in the 1980s. The war on drugs appears to have decreased casual drug use, but hard-core addiction has evaded control and continues to make the drug war difficult to win.

These statistics have led some people to question the war on drugs. Critics maintain that despite the $10 billion the government has allocated to fight the drug war, its efforts are failing. For example, although law enforcement officials reported a 4,000 percent increase in cocaine seizures in the 1980s, the street price of cocaine declined by up to 50 percent in many places, indicating a dramatic rise in cocaine's availability. In addition, U.S. Customs officials estimate that they intercept only 10 percent of the drugs entering the U.S. These critics say that no matter what tactics the government uses, or how much money it spends, attempting to eradicate drug use is futile because Americans will always use drugs.

The war on drugs has been called both necessary and misguided. The articles in the following chapter debate how and whether the war on drugs can succeed in solving America's drug problem.

Can the War on Drugs Be Won?

Yes: The War on Drugs Is Winnable

The War on Drugs Can Be Won
Improved Law Enforcement Can Win the War on Drugs
Community Action Can Win the War on Drugs
Establishing Drug-Free Neighborhoods Can Win the War on Drugs

The War on Drugs Can Be Won

Alfonse D'Amato

About the Author: *Alfonse D'Amato is a Republican senator from New York and a member of the Foreign Operations Subcommittee.*

The country's leading presidential candidate is assassinated. A bomb explodes, killing all 107 people aboard a jetliner. A week later, a judge is murdered. The next day, a half-ton bomb explodes, killing 52 victims in the capital. Another blows up in another city, killing two police officers. Just before a televised speech by the nation's president on the drug crisis, three more bombs explode in one of the country's major cocaine-trafficking centers.

That is the situation in Colombia today. Since its drug barons declared "total and absolute war" on Colombian society in August 1989, hundreds of civilians and officials have been killed, and there have been more than 200 bombings and over $500,000,000 in property damage.

The war on drugs is a war Colombia must win. The fact that Colombia has extradited 10 drug suspects to the U.S. and that its National Police were able to kill one of the leading drug traffickers, Jose Rodriguez-Gacha, on Dec. 15, 1989, shows that it is serious. However, this is not a war that Colombia can win on its own. With its limited resources, that embattled nation is no match for the well-financed armies of the drug traffickers.

President Bush was absolutely right to begin sending Colombia $65,000,000 worth of helicopters, communications equipment, and other assistance in September 1989. He also was right to call for several hundred millions more in economic, military, and law enforcement assistance to the coca-producing countries of Bolivia, Peru, and Colombia. In November 1989, Congress approved this aid package for the Andean nations, and on Dec. 13, 1989, the President signed it into law. Then, in February 1990, he went to Colombia to confer with the presidents of that country, Peru, and Bolivia. At that meeting, they sought ways to increase cooperation against the drug traffickers by targeting their coca crops, drug labs, money laundering, and smuggling organizations.

However, even if everything they agreed upon is undertaken to the fullest, can the drug war be won? The U.S., Latin American nations, and the United Nations all must become energized to prevent the nightmare occurring in Colombia from spreading.

> ## "America's fight against epidemic illegal drug use can not be won on any single front alone."

The U.S. must be prepared to work for the creation of an International Anti-Drug Strike Force to fight the traffickers in Colombia and other drug-producing countries, such as Bolivia and Peru, when their governments ask for such help.

When requested by a foreign government battling the drug cartels, this strike force could help with training, provide additional drug agents, increase intelligence collection capabilities, and, if the host country agreed, even participate in a direct assault against the drug lords.

It is essential that the strike force not be undertaken by the U.S. alone. The advantage of the strike force is that it could provide countries like Colombia with the help they so desperately need without enabling the drug cartels to use all their old propaganda about the "ugly American" and the "Colossus of the North." Instead, the strike force would represent the entire world's condemnation of drug trafficking as the crime against humanity that it is.

In March 1988, more than 60 senators and I introduced legislation to create such an entity. Our bill called for a plan permitting the strike force, at the request of the host government, to eradicate major coca crop concentrations in the Western Hemisphere; patrol the major international transportation corridors through which the illegal drug traffic moves; and arrest the members of the major international drug trafficking organizations involved in producing, transporting, and distributing illegal narcotics.

Public Law 100-690, the final drug bill of 1988, incorporated our ideas and specifically stated that there was a need for an antinarcotics force in the Western Hemisphere. It also called on the UN to explore ways to establish such a force.

On Sept. 28, 1989, the Senate voted on an amendment to the Fiscal Year 1990 Defense Appropriations bill that authorized the use of funds for U.S. participation in an international anti-narcotics strike force. The amendment was passed overwhelmingly by a vote of 95-5. Glad as I am to see that this idea is receiving the attention it deserves, I recognize that the war on drugs never will be won if we focus only on the jungles of Latin America.

The Domestic War

When Drug Enforcement Administration agent Everett Hatcher was murdered in New York in 1989, his wife said: "The loss that we feel is almost unbearable. But even through the grief of our loss, I must ask the question, 'Who really killed Everett Hatcher?' As Pogo said, 'We have met the enemy and he is us.' Middle-class suburban Americans, casual users, dabblers in drugs . . . all of you who fit this description. . . . All of you must accept the blame for the loss of this good, gentle man."

Pres. Virgilio Barco Vargas of Colombia has broadcast the same message: "Those of you who depend on cocaine have created the most vicious criminal enterprise the world has ever

known. . . . There is no home for them. There should be no market for them."

Barco and Mrs. Hatcher are correct. Both the sellers and the users of drugs must be held accountable for their actions. Drug use is not a victimless crime. Every year, 200,000 American babies are born addicted to cocaine. Illegal drugs are causing record homicide and crime rates in every community in this nation.

The words of New York Supreme Court Justice Francis Murphy correctly state the situation: "We hear, but do not listen to the ordinary man and woman. It is they who are the victims of crime, and they in their anguish have something of value to say. . . . They tell us that criminals have taken the city, that crime has beaten government to its knees."

"One approach that will not work is legalization."

To attack this epidemic of crime and drugs, the President has submitted a comprehensive plan to Congress, including more prisons and drug enforcement agents, tougher sentencing for criminals, the Andean initiative, accountability standards for drug treatment programs, and expanded drug prevention efforts in our schools and communities. To increase private sector involvement, he has created a top-level Drug Advisory Council, comprised of 27 distinguished individuals from all sectors of American society, to advise him on new ways to reduce narcotics use.

In 1989, Congress and the President came together and agreed to increase Federal anti-narcotics funding levels for Fiscal Year 1990 to $8,800,000,000, and Congress started work on enacting the President's initiatives. Sadly, it failed to pass his crime and drug treatment proposals and will have to try again. . . .

I also plan to offer legislation providing for the death penalty for major drug dealers. Such a person would be defined as the leader of a criminal enterprise that manufactures or distributes more than 60 pounds of heroin, 300 pounds of cocaine and/or three pounds of crack, or makes $10,000,000 in one year from the manufacture, importation, or distribution of drugs. These traffickers are killing our children by the thousands, destroying lives by the millions, and tearing at the fabric of this nation. Their crimes are so heinous and destructive that I believe they deserve the death penalty.

Drug testing is another legitimate and necessary part of our strategy. The government's program of random testing for those in sensitive positions has caught more than 200 Federal employees who used illegal substances, including 60 air traffic controllers and 42 workers in the nuclear and chemical weapons security program. Any one of these employees could have caused a major disaster. In the U.S. military, a program of drug testing and strict penalties for violations reduced narcotics usage from more than 20% of all personnel to less than five percent.

One approach that will not work is legalization. It was with great sadness and outrage that I learned in December 1989 of Federal District Court Judge Robert Sweet's support for the legalization of crack, heroin, and other illegal drugs. He proposes that the government set the price and the amounts of drugs that could be sold. This immediately opens the door for a black market that would give stronger, cheaper drugs than the government would provide. His proposal, therefore, would lead to continued high levels of drug-related crime.

Legalization Will Not Work

Many of the specifics of Judge Sweet's proposal defy comprehension. He is quoted as saying that "cocaine gives a sense of exhilaration, heroin a glow, a warmth. . . . What then is wrong?" Such statements sound shockingly like an endorsement of drug use and send exactly the wrong message to young people. . . .

Among the disastrous results legalization would lead to are more crime and drug addiction; the destruction of more families; more cocaine babies and others born with birth defects; more drug-related child abuse; more drug-related accidents; more losses in worker productivity; more hospitals overwhelmed with drug emergencies; and more dropouts from our schools.

"To win the war, we ultimately are going to have to focus much more attention on reducing the demand for drugs."

This is not just my opinion. It is the carefully considered judgment of law enforcement and treatment professionals who struggle heroically every day against the drug scourge. John Lawn, former head of the Drug Enforcement Administration, stated: "Anyone who talks in terms of legalizing drugs is willing to write the death warrants for people in the lower socioeconomic classes.". . .

To win the war, we ultimately are going to have to focus much more attention on reducing the demand for drugs and preventing young Americans from ever trying them in the first place. Education and prevention programs that include anti-drug curricula in every school and every grade are an absolute necessity. Congress recently amended the Drug-Free Schools and Communities Act to require local school districts to implement anti-drug education programs for elementary and secondary students, but that is only the beginning. Schools alone can not eliminate tolerant attitudes towards drug use. Reinforcement and support must come from every family and community in this nation.

As President Bush said when he released the nation's first National Drug Control Strategy in September 1989, "America's fight against epidemic illegal drug use can not be won on any single front alone; it must be waged everywhere—at every level of Federal, state, and local government and by every citizen in every community across the country."

Improved Law Enforcement Can Win the War on Drugs

Charles Brandt

About the Author: *Charles Brandt, Chief Deputy Attorney General for Delaware from 1974 to 1976 and past president of the Delaware Trial Lawyers Association, is in private law practice.*

One evening in March 1989, Sgt. Byron Simms and two other undercover Washington, D.C., police officers spotted a flashy new Lincoln illegally parked in one of the city's drug-ravaged neighborhoods. A passenger stepped out, removed a large plastic bag from the trunk, and got back in the car.

Suspecting a drug transaction, the narcotics officers followed the Lincoln to a shopping center. There the suspect, later identified as Gary K. Most, Jr., took the bag into a small grocery.

Within a half-hour, Most returned without the bag. Simms, posing as a shopper, went into the store, where he spotted the bag behind the checkout counter. He questioned the manager and two clerks, who said Most had asked them to keep an eye on it.

When Simms lifted the bag, he felt hard, pebble-like objects inside—"rocks" of crack, experience told him. Sure enough, he pulled out 272 small plastic bags of crack, with a street value of $23,000.

Although Most was sentenced to ten years in prison, in June 1989, the U.S. Court of Appeals overturned the verdict on the ground that his rights had been violated. If one of the clerks had opened the bag and showed the evidence to Simms, that would have been acceptable. But according to the rules of evidence, Simms, trained to recognize criminal behavior and to identify drugs, didn't have the right to pick up the bag in the first place. And so Gary Most went free.

• On February 8, 1989, a federal judge dismissed crack charges against a Jamaican drug dealer because a Denver SWAT [Special Weapons and Tactics] team—carrying a valid search warrant—had failed to knock on the door before battering it down.

• In April 1989, an appellate court in Alaska dropped a charge against a bartender who had sold drugs to undercover state troopers from his jacket hanging some 15 feet from the bar. The court ruled that because the jacket was not within the bartender's reach, the troopers should have gotten a search warrant for the jacket.

• Alabama police were tipped off that a vehicle was transporting guns and drugs. With their own guns drawn, they surrounded the car and noticed a partially smoked marijuana joint on the dashboard. They ordered the occupants to get out. On July 21, 1989, the Alabama Court of Criminal Appeals decided that the police could not have been sure of their informant's reliability, declared the seizure of an automatic pistol and drugs illegal and remanded the case to the lower court—without the key evidence. Of course, minus this evidence, the case probably will never be retried.

> **"Every day in America, drug dealers walk away from their crimes because of legal hair-splitting."**

Every day in America, drug dealers walk away from their crimes because of legal hair-splitting. Police departments, trying to follow court guidelines on proper procedure by studying cases like those above, now find their hands cuffed, their eyes blinded and their ears plugged by the very laws they have sworn to uphold. The sad result is that today, all over the country, drug markets operate flagrantly, protected by rules that exclude authorities better than any steel door.

"Drug markets operate flagrantly, protected by rules that exclude authorities better than any steel door."

Why do we force our cops to stand by impotently, watching criminals ply their trade as if they had diplomatic immunity? The major cause of such rulings that defy common sense is the 1961 Supreme Court case of Mapp v. Ohio. Police had accidentally found pornographic pamphlets and photos in the Mapp house while searching for a bombing suspect. The Supreme Court ruled that since the search was warrantless, evidence of other illegalities discovered had to be excluded in court.

This "exclusionary rule" had its most devastating impact on one area of law enforcement: drug arrests. Before the Mapp decision, a police officer could stop and search a drug dealer or user on suspicion. An anonymous tip from a neighbor was enough to justify a house search warrant. Today, because of the exclusionary rule, there is a barrage of court rulings on proper ways to gather evidence. Police practically need a search warrant to gather enough facts to get one.

On November 1, 1987, for example, a resident of an Atlantic Beach, Fla., apartment complex found a three-year-old boy wandering the parking lot. She called the police. When they questioned the boy, he ran to an apartment, saying, "Mama's in there." The door was ajar and swung open as police knocked. The officers announced their presence. Getting no response, they drew their weapons and entered. They could see marijuana and drug paraphernalia in the bedroom, where the boy's mother and one

David Emory Eason were asleep.

Police then obtained a search warrant for the rest of the apartment, which held even more drugs. Eason was charged with drug possession. But not for long. On June 28, 1989, the District Court of Appeal of Florida dismissed the case because the police had not obtained a search warrant before their initial visit to the apartment.

A Columbia University study compared the number of narcotics-possession arrests during a six-month period just prior to the Mapp decision and the same period the following year. The study found that arrests were cut in half. Furthermore, it noted that "convictions have been harder to obtain since Mapp.". . .

Balancing Act

The exclusionary rule has become the police officer's nightmare. The courts cranked out so many restrictions on police that the 1960s have been called the "criminal-law revolution." It wasn't enough to require a search warrant: the search also had to be limited to a narrowly specified crime, and the warrant had to list facts amounting to "probable cause" for arrest. If the police presented facts suggesting stolen television sets, for example, the warrant would not allow a search for drugs in a desk drawer. Then the courts began to pass judgment on the "reliability" of information that went into the "probable cause" argument. . . .

Defenders of the exclusionary rule say that "police training" on these issues has promoted greater professionalism in police departments. But the price of this noble goal is far fewer drug arrests—and brisk open-air drug markets in every fair-sized city.

I was a prosecutor and Chief Deputy Attorney General for Delaware when many of the present rules were created. I know firsthand how they affected drug enforcement. They constrained the police to operate in slow motion, while drug traffickers picked up frightening speed.

I rode with experienced cops who could tell just by looking at a known dealer whether or not he was carrying drugs. Yet they couldn't search and arrest him. Instead, they could only hope that someday they would be able to get a paid addict to help an undercover cop make a "controlled buy." Even then, in order to protect the informant, weeks would have to pass before an arrest could be made—during which time the dealer would continue to pollute the community with drugs.

Capt. Ronald M. Huston of the Wilmington, Del., police force says that countless criminals walk the streets with impunity, carrying both drugs and guns. One is a major dealer with lavish homes in Delaware and New Jersey. He is known by the federal Drug Enforcement Administration, but is basically untouchable. "Dealers tell us about him, but that's not enough to get a warrant," says Huston. "Unless someone comes forward to wear a body mike, we can't get enough admissible evidence to search him.". . .

In the 1960s, police conduct in some areas of the country against civil-rights demonstrators and minorities enraged the public and justly brought police procedures under scrutiny. But today our drug-plagued society needs to ask: is it the police who pose a threat in our neighborhoods—or the drug dealers carrying attack rifles?

"Our police can't fight drugs if they are hamstrung by laws that defy common sense."

"I don't believe criminal rights are a civil-rights issue," says one black police chief, Reuben Greenberg of Charleston, S.C. "Drug crime mostly affects the poor. They are trapped in their neighborhoods because they can't afford to move. It is their rights I am concerned about, for criminals now have an overwhelming advantage."

Americans did not live in a police state before the Mapp decision. We have other laws to protect citizens from overzealous police. Australia,

Canada, England, France, Japan and West Germany have no exclusionary rules, and they aren't police states. No other democracy protects the rights of criminals over society's right to peace and security—and no other democracy has anywhere near America's drug problem. It is no coincidence that our drug problem greatly worsened after Mapp v. Ohio.

A Ray of Hope

There is a ray of hope, however. In 1984 the Supreme Court created the "good faith" exception to the exclusionary rule. A search warrant that is "largely error-free," but technically imperfect, can provide evidence in court if the police acted in "objectively reasonable reliance" on it. Previously, if an "i" were undotted or a "t" uncrossed, the evidence was thrown out.

Unfortunately, the good-faith rule doesn't apply to searches without a warrant. It cannot be used to justify seizing a hidden machine gun under a raincoat, for example, or cocaine suspected to be in a car—or any of the evidence described in this article.

Clearly, the good-faith exception doesn't go far enough. As Cornelius J. Behan, Baltimore County, Maryland, police chief, asserts, "It is time to revisit the entire area of admissible evidence to see if it is blocking the way to the truth.". . .

Am I suggesting that our cherished Constitutional rights be abrogated? Absolutely not! But the exclusionary rule is a judge-made rule of courtroom evidence, not a Constitutional right. We need to protest the way the Constitution has been nitpicked by judges and the truth banished from courthouses.

American law is dynamic and has always changed with the times. We are in the middle of a drug epidemic. We don't need protection from the cop on the beat—we need protection from criminals. And our police can't fight drugs if they are hamstrung by laws that defy common sense.

Community Action Can Win the War on Drugs

The Lincoln Review

About the Author: The Lincoln Review *is a publication of the Lincoln Institute for Research and Education in Washington, D.C. The institute studies public policy issues that affect the lives of black Americans.*

It is clear that the scourge of drugs, which afflicts all Americans, has had a disproportionate impact upon the black community. In a special section devoted to this problem, *Ebony* (August 1989) states that, "While there are many Whites who use crack, its affordability (a smokable rock of crack sells on the street for between $5 and $20) made it popular with Black, inner-city youths. By the early 1980s, an entire crack-driven subculture, with its underground economy, was mushrooming. Officials of a congressional task force that examined the U.S. drug trade estimate that the enterprise nets close to $150 billion a year. The young mobsters who profit from drug sales flaunt their illegally acquired wealth brazenly. Their flashy displays of such expensive accoutrements as foreign cars, gold jewelry and the latest automatic weapons, help to lure other youngsters into the illicit industry. But the price they pay for such luxury is far greater than the hundreds of dollars that may pass through their hands in a day. These tragic young men and women pay dearly—either through deadly addiction or gangland slayings."

Crack, of course, is only part of the drug plague. Intravenous heroin use has helped the spread of AIDS, and contributed to its disproportionately adverse effects on the black community. According to a study by the American Medical Association, blacks were 37 percent of the AIDS patients who contracted the disease through IV drug abuse. Similarly, 48 percent of those who contracted AIDS by having sex with a drug abuser were black.

The drug economy in black America is conservatively put at between $16 billion and $20 billion annually. Rep. Charles Rangel (D-N.Y.) states: "There is no way of knowing the exact amount, but we know that drug abuse among blacks is disproportionately high. The figure could easily be much higher."

> ## "The scourge of drugs, which afflicts all Americans, has had a disproportionate impact upon the black community."

According to *Ebony* correspondents around the country, "Some blacks make more than $100,000 a week as mid-level suppliers of cocaine. A New York drug kingpin whose empire came crashing down in the summer of 1988 when F.B.I. [Federal Bureau of Investigation] agents and federal marshals seized $20 million in dope and arrested 30 suspects, including his mother and wife, once operated a cocaine and heroin lab that brought in $100,000 a week. There are kids, some as young as eight years old, who are recruited as street lookouts and earn $200 a day and more for alerting pushers that the police are in the neighborhood. In some cases, 'entry-level' positions for teenage dope pushers may pay thousands of dollars a week. A Washington, D.C., woman found $40,000 and two semi-automatic weapons under her young son's bed."

Now, even though the Bush administration has launched a "war on drugs," U.S. officials concede that an all-out effort to get large numbers of addicted people off drugs, whether they are in the inner cities or not, is not being

"The Scourge of Drug Addiction: A Challenge for the Black Community," *The Lincoln Review*, Winter 1990. Reprinted with permission.

planned. That aim, they say, is too complicated and the problems in reaching it too intractable to be achieved in the near future. The true goals of the "war on drugs," one drug-policy aide told *The New York Times*, is to move the nation "a little bit" beyond where current trends would put it anyway.

White House Chief of Staff John H. Sununu says that the anti-drug effort would not "undo all the social problems of the inner cities." But he said he would consider it progress if the plan helped reduce the casual use of illegal drugs and made some headway in reducing habitual use that would "bring some tranquility in terms of the criminal problems that people face in the cities."

Another Senior White House official says that there is little hope for weaning drugs from large numbers of young people who are at the heart of much of the current crisis. Of more concern, he said, "is doing better by the next generation of kids."

The strategy, drafted by William Bennett, [former] director of the National Drug Control Policy, has as one objective a 10 percent reduction in the number of people reporting any use of illegal drugs in the previous month and a 50 percent reduction over 10 years. The goals are less optimistic for what most experts agree is now the worst aspect of the current problem, frequent use of cocaine—particularly crack, its smokable derivative. Over two years, the drug program calls for no reduction at all of people reporting weekly or more frequent cocaine use, but rather only cutting its rate of increase by half.

Social Decay

In the inner cities, drug use is clearly out of control. In Washington, D.C., the infant mortality rate, already among the highest in the U.S., increased by nearly 50 percent in the first half of 1989 because of a surge of babies born to cocaine-addicted women. An estimated 169 babies died before their first birthdays during the first six months of 1989, an infant mortality rate of 32.3 deaths per 1,000 live births, according to preliminary city data. By contrast, the infant mortality rate for all of 1988 was 23.2 deaths per 1,000. "It is like a bomb has gone off," said one city official. "No one in this area knows what to do. I don't know what to do about social pathology and decay in half the city."

Drugs, sadly, are part of a larger social pathology in our inner cities and throughout the larger American society as well. More and more children find themselves in one-parent families and do not receive the care and nurturing which previous generations took for granted. Three reports issued by the U.S. Census Bureau in September, 1989 show that over the past generation, there has been a dramatic change in the American family, marked by a soaring rate of divorce and a sharp increase in single-parent families, as well as a mounting illegitimacy rate.

"The drug economy in black America is conservatively put at between $16 billion and $20 billion."

In 1960, there were 35 divorced people in the nation for every 1,000 married people living with a spouse. By 1988, there were 133. More children are being born out of wedlock. The Census Bureau's Arlene F. Saluter notes: "Childbearing among unmarried women has reached the highest levels ever recorded in the U.S." Current rates are 80.9 per 1,000 unmarried black women and 23.2 per 1,000 unmarried white women between the ages of 15 and 44.

As a result, writes the bureau's Steve W. Rawlings, the proportion of one-parent families has increased dramatically: from 12.9 percent of all families with children in 1970 to 27.3 percent in 1988. Families headed by a single parent made up 21.7 percent of white families with children in 1988, compared with 59.4 percent of black families with children and 33.6 percent of Hispanic families with children.

Professor Glenn Loury of Harvard, who is black, points out that, "The bottom stratum of the black community has compelling problems which can no longer be blamed solely on white racism, and which forces us to confront fundamental failures in black society." The problems of the inner city, he declares, "have taken on a life of their own."

Similarly, columnist William Raspberry, who is also black, says: "We have tended to view everything through the prism of the civil rights assumptions that the absence of the good things is proof of discrimination. Sometimes this assumption is correct. . . . But for today's black underclass, school failure, joblessness, adolescent pregnancy, juvenile crime and drug abuse are due far less to discrimination than to inadequate exertion. . . . The way to inculcate middle-class attitudes in the underclass is to teach their children what the middle class takes for granted: that their fate is in their own hands."

An important study shows that children left to care for themselves after school—whether rich or poor, from single or two-parent homes—are twice as likely to use tobacco, marijuana and alcohol. This study of 5,000 California eighth-graders—said to be the largest focus on these "latchkey children"—found increased risk to children who care for themselves at least one hour a week regardless of the child's sex, race, family income, number of parents at home, academic performance, or involvement in sports and extracurricular activities.

"Drugs . . . are part of a larger social pathology in our inner cities."

The study was funded by the National Institute on Drug Abuse and conducted by the University of Southern California. Professor Jean Richardson, the study's principal investigator, states: "The information related to risk-taking suggests that the self-care situation causes adolescents to perceive themselves as more autonomous, more mature and more able to make decisions that adults may not approve."

Because so many Americans have, in large numbers, abandoned the responsibility of child-rearing, many of our young people are particularly vulnerable to the inducements of the drug culture. . . .

The Moral Compass

What young people, particularly in the inner city, are not learning is the moral compass by which actions and lives are to be judged. Joe Clark, the tough black high school principal from Paterson, New Jersey, who turned a drug-and-crime ridden school around, declares: ". . . in many cases these youths do not learn morality. That is, a sense of fairness to serve as a guide for their actions. The schools should teach them this, if the schools were run with the right intentions, the right spirit. I am not suggesting the removal of the separation of church and state. What I am saying is that education, properly understood and practiced, requires an energetic commitment from teachers and administrators, not only to provide career skills, but also to elevate the mind and the heart to the whole story of life: its wonders and dangers, its joys and sorrows, its struggles and possibilities. The dynamic of right and wrong runs throughout the whole story—from Lexington to Los Alamos, from Hippocrates to Macbeth, from the earliest myths to the headlines of this morning's newspaper—and the truly dedicated teacher cannot help but project the rightness of his or her task, which is the genuine preparation of the next generation for the challenge of life."

One reason for widespread drug addiction is the fertile field we have created. Dr. Robert DuPont, former head of the National Institute of Drug Abuse, states: "Never before in world history has so large a segment of a national population used such a large number of dependence-producing drugs." The reason, DuPont argues, is a shift in values in the U.S. He notes that, "The shift has to do with moving away from centering one's life around values having to do with religion, tradition, family or community, and thinking instead of one's self only. The goal becomes doing what feels right to you. If the purpose of your life is to feel good you are tremendously vulnerable to drugs because they produce good feelings. On the other hand, you might say: 'Wait a minute. I'm here in the world for some purpose larger than my feelings.'. . ."

It is good to fight the war on drugs in Colombia and Peru, and to build more jails for users and dealers. The war on drugs, however, will fail until we recognize that there are causes for the widespread proliferation of drug use beyond what occurs in Washington—or in the drug-producing countries. Politicians cannot win the war against drugs alone and neither can law enforcement officials, although they have a key role to play. Without the active help of committed individuals and of the voluntary sector of churches, schools and civic organizations, long run progress will be difficult to achieve.

At long last, within the black community we can now point to examples of individuals and groups which have entered the fight against drugs.

Taking a Stand

In December 1989, President Bush visited a predominantly black neighborhood in Houston where citizens had joined together to push out drug dealers. The president likened citizen action against illegal drugs to citizens of Eastern Europe seeking democratic reform. "As with the new freedom in Eastern Europe, freedom from drugs isn't something the government can give you," he said. "You've got to take a stand. You've got to take back the streets."

President Bush lauded the efforts of residents of Acres Homes, once the largest unincorporated black community in the South, to retake neighborhoods from drug dealers. More than a year earlier, more than 1,000 residents of the area held a rally in the park that launched the effort to keep dealers out. Bush told several hundred local residents gathered in the park that

their efforts "are a critical part" of his strategy against drugs.

In Washington, D.C., residents of Fairlawn, a working-class neighborhood, have banded together and driven off drug dealers and users. They organized street patrols and reported everything they saw to the police. "We have taken back control of our streets," said James H. Alexander, a resident active in the patrols.

"What young people, particularly in the inner city, are not learning is the moral compass."

Before the patrols began, the situation in the mile-square neighborhood of single-family houses and apartment buildings had reached the point where children could not play outdoors and parents could not go to the store without running a gauntlet of drug hustlers. "You literally had to push past them," Mr. Alexander said. "A bunch of us started talking, and the next thing we called a meeting." The residents formed the Fairlawn Coalition and then donned bright orange baseball caps, equipped themselves with radios and took to the streets. They now have 200 members in their neighborhood of several thousand people. In time, dealers left. Today, children are playing again on the sidewalks and in the yards of Fairlawn.

At San Diego's St. Stephen's Church of God in Christ, recovering addicts have formed a "blockbuster" group that prays together Friday evenings at 8, reports Bishop George McKinney. At 10, they roam the streets until early Saturday morning trying to convince drug dealers and prostitutes that there is a better way.

In Baltimore, about 600 former addicts have joined Bethel A.M.E. [American Methodist Evangelical] Church because of its anti-drug program, says the Rev. Frank Reid III. "We ask all recovering addicts to stand up so that joiners understand they aren't alone," he explains.

"They're not to feel that they're being put on the spot."

"The death of a race" was the theme of the first National Conference on the Black Family/Community and Crack Cocaine. That alarm rang out from Glide Memorial United Methodist Church in San Francisco, among 1,200 church and civic leaders, scholars, and health professionals. "Our lives are at stake," declared the Rev. Cecil Williams, the church's minister and a conference organizer. "Our children's lives are at stake."

The conferees set up a national network in black churches and communities to coordinate drug prevention, intervention and recovery strategies. They proposed saving a generation of besieged young blacks with after-school tutorials, sports activities, expanded job training and scholarships, Big Brother programs, Friday night video/dance parties, peer counseling and programs to improve parenting.

Project A.D.A.M., the Anti-Drug Abuse Movement of the South Carolina Coalition of (100) Black Churches, held walkathons in five cities to spotlight drug abuse. Its "Just Say No" church clubs provide recreational and educational activities to help children between the ages of 7 and 17 build positive self-images and drug-free lives.

"Freedom from drugs isn't something the government can give you. You've got to take a stand."

Father George Clements, pastor of Chicago's Holy Angels Roman Catholic Church, has launched a nationwide campaign to get neighborhood store owners to stop selling glass pipes and other drug paraphernalia. He now seeks a federal law to ban the manufacture and sale of drug equipment.

There have also been effective steps taken against drug users and dealers by a number of courageous public officials in various parts of the country. One of these is Vincent Lane, who became executive director of the Chicago Housing Authority in 1988. One housing project, Rockwell Gardens, was described by EBONY as "the most dangerous CHA development in 1986 and 1987. And in 1988, for every 1,000 Rockwell residents, 54 violent crimes—almost all drug-related—were committed. The buildings were infested with and controlled by gangs."

That was true, EBONY reports, "until Lane, who for 18 years developed and managed his own low-income housing units, busted in with a novel crime-fighting approach called Operation Clean Sweep. The program eventually purged Rockwell buildings of criminals and boosted morale. After that, the crime rate plummeted dramatically in that unit."

Drugs Drive Crime

Mr. Lane states that, "Drugs drive crime, and drug dealers have found a haven for their business in public housing. What we're doing is akin to knocking off the classroom bullies. As a result, there's a sense of renewed community spirit in Rockwell Gardens."

Crime has fallen 36 percent in Chicago's huge violence-plagued Cabrini-Green projects, 32 percent at Rockwell Gardens, and at a similar rate at other CHA buildings. A police task force has secured troubled buildings by surrounding them and occupying hallways. CHA management and security teams gain access to each occupied apartment, ostensibly searching for items in need of repair. "If, by chance, we uncover weapons or drugs," says Lane, "we file a complaint with the police and they go in and arrest the occupant." In some cases, tenants are evicted under federal racketeering laws. Once the building is "swept," legitimate residents above the age of seven are issued photo identification cards that they must show a permanent security staff upon entering the building. "Drug dealers get the message right away," Lane says. "That's why the crime rate goes down instantly."

There are many noteworthy efforts taking place to stem the tide of drugs in the nation's inner cities—but not nearly enough. Consider the case of Ewing Marion Kauffman of Kansas City, Missouri, who owns a majority share in the Kansas City Royals baseball team. In the fall of 1988, he made a deal with some 300 students at Westport High School in Kansas City. He calls his innovative program Operation Choice and it cost him between $5 and $10 million. He promises to pay college tuition and expenses for students who make attendance standards, avoid early parenthood and stay off drugs.

Project Choice was designed "to change the way disadvantaged young people think of their future," according to program director Thomas J. Rhone. "When you show teenagers their potential, their individual pride will manifest itself eventually and they'll begin to understand themselves." Mr. Kauffman says: "I feel terrible about the community's youths. Some don't have parental guidance or the education to make something of themselves. And drug abuse and early parenthood make it pretty difficult for some to overcome their hardships. Project Choice could make a difference."

"Drugs drive crime, and drug dealers have found a haven for their business in public housing."

It is high time that black churches, community groups and others in the voluntary sector entered the battle against drugs. The devastation being inflicted upon the black community by drug abuse can hardly be overstated. People in the Washington, D.C. area, for example, may spend as much on cocaine as they do on food and drink, according to a comparison of regional marketing statistics. The 1988 survey of buying power by Sales and Marketing Management says that with their $67 billion in dispos-

able personal income, residents of the Washington region spent $2.9 billion at eating and drinking establishments and $5.3 billion in food stores. Richard Broughton, a Drug Enforcement Administration intelligence specialist, estimates that illegal drug outlets in the Washington area may do as much as $8 billion a year in sales.

Addicted Babies

Particularly tragic are the increasing numbers of babies born to addicted mothers. During the first three months of 1987 one of every 10 expectant mothers who arrived in labor at Washington, D.C., General Hospital acknowledged that she was using drugs. For the same period in 1989 the ratio increased to one out of every 5 mothers-to-be. More and more, addicted mothers are walking away from the infants, abandoning them to the hospital nurseries. On several occasions during 1989, there was not an acute-care nursery bed to be had between Richmond and Philadelphia.

The psychological impact upon inner-city children is equally devastating. "We're seeing more and more kids who are simply overwhelmed, not unlike people who have experienced shell shock or combat fatigue," says Dr. Marilyn Benoit, director of outpatient psychiatry at Children's National Medical Center in Washington. "They have trouble sleeping. They are distracted. They have panic attacks. They are resigned, distrustful, living for the moment, unable to control their own apprehension."

If the war on drugs is to succeed, it cannot be left to government alone to wage. All of us are under attack, and the front-line is within the nation's inner city and minority communities. It is essential that our churches, civic organizations, schools and the civil rights establishment itself focus their attention upon the greatest danger facing us at the present time—drugs.

Establishing Drug-Free Neighborhoods Can Win the War on Drugs

Charles Murray

About the Author: *Charles Murray, Bradley Fellow at the Manhattan Institute in New York City, is the author of* In Pursuit: Of Happiness and Good Government.

There's something unpleasantly familiar about the debate over the War on Drugs: it bears a strong resemblance to the debate over the war in Vietnam. The sides are divided into hawks who tell us the war is winnable if we just send in a few more divisions, and doves—the legalizers—who think the war shouldn't be fought. The hawks don't want to talk about how much victory will really cost, and the doves don't want to talk about the consequences if their scenarios about the post-surrender future are wrong. Each side includes many who favor their solution less because it promises to work than because of their world view—one that may or may not be relevant. Could it be that we need a different way of looking at the drug problem that yields a different set of solutions?

Let me begin by putting my own biases on the table. In principle, I am a dove. If someone who is high on drugs goes out and robs, rapes, or pillages, he should have the book thrown at him; but it does not follow that the act of taking a drug is in itself something that the government needs to prohibit. I am not persuaded by the To-

Charles Murray, "How to Win the War on Drugs," *The New Republic*, May 21, 1990. Reprinted by permission of *The New Republic*, © 1990, The New Republic, Inc.

ries [conservatives] who want to use the instruments of the federal government to promote virtue. Nor do I worry about the potential costs of legalization, because I don't accept that drug users who find themselves unable to function have thereby earned a legal claim on their fellow citizens' support.

That being said, I cannot bring myself to support a federal law legalizing drugs right now, as a single, isolated change in social policy. For though I am confident that legalization would work in a society where people are held responsible for the consequences of their actions, that's not the way contemporary America works. In the same inner-city areas where the drug problem is worst, I can too easily neglect my children without being called to account, fail to hold a job and still have food to eat and a place to live, or be a vicious nuisance to my neighbors with impunity. These kinds of behavior, which drug addiction often induces, must be subject to social and economic sanctions if legalization is to work. To legalize drugs in America as of 1990 is to give people the right to be responsible for themselves without also obliging them to do so. It is a dangerous mix. Furthermore, I'm a father, and maybe keeping drugs illegal makes it easier for me to keep my children off drugs. On the drug issue, I'm a libertarian who has been willing to sell out.

> ## "It is not necessary that drug abusers become criminals, only that they be made outcasts."

The War on Drugs has made that compromise much harder to live with. The analogy with Vietnam is again apt: the hawks still like to talk about body counts—the number of pounds of cocaine seized, flashy convictions—instead of telling us what ground has been taken and held. The hawks' arguments are still larded with invective—once again, the doves must be cowards. What the public needs to see is some specific, hardheaded analysis of how we can win this war at an affordable price. And that is what the hawks fail to explain.

The *National Drug Control Strategy* produced by William Bennett's office is a case in point. The *Strategy* is written by people who have done their homework—and it is quite modest in the claims it makes about our experience with interdiction, rehabilitation, education, and law enforcement. Then comes the appendix, presenting its quantified two- and ten-year objectives. The ten-year objectives call for 50 percent reductions in a wide variety of important indicators of drug use—an ambitious set of goals indeed. But the goals have no link with the discussion that preceded them.

"Forget about eradicating drug use everywhere."

Interdiction offers a good example. The depressing facts have been well publicized. In 1975 the U.S. Customs Service seized just 729 pounds of cocaine during the entire year, and the price of a pure gram (in 1987 dollars) was $1,200. In 1987 it seized forty-four *tons* of cocaine, and the price of a pure gram was $143, roughly one-ninth of the price twelve years earlier. From 1986 to 1987 Customs' cocaine seizures increased by a prodigious eighteen tons—after which the typical gram of cocaine on the street was purer than it had been a year earlier and still cost the same.

The authors of the *Strategy* obviously had contemplated these figures, and nowhere in the text did the authors claim that increased interdiction efforts would reduce supply on the street. And yet the ten-year objective for the War on Drugs as stated in the appendix is "a 50 percent reduction in estimated amounts of cocaine, marijuana, heroin, and dangerous drugs entering the United States." *How?* Is the goal of a 50 percent reduction just window dressing, complying with a congressional requirement to devise quantified goals? If so, someone should admit that, and then tell us what a reasonable expectation might be. Going by the record so far, the billions being spent on interdiction is money down the drain. . . .

An even more troubling example of the inconsistency between experience and rhetoric in the War on Drugs involves law enforcement. The *Strategy* argues (correctly, I think) that law enforcement has gotten an unfairly bad rap. A substantial body of evidence confirms that enforcement can raise the monetary costs, the search costs, and the risks of punishment involved in using drugs, and thus discourage drug use. The difficulty lies in trying to apply this evidence to the contemporary drug problem. The only large-scale success in drug control that has been claimed involves the stabilization of the heroin user population in the early 1970s, as described recently by James Q. Wilson in an influential article in *Commentary*. I think Wilson is too quick to credit the effect to drug policy—this was the period when cocaine was the chic new drug among the same urban black population that had formerly used heroin. But even accepting Wilson's account, the chief mechanisms for affecting the heroin trade are said to have been a temporary disruption of supply from Turkey and an increased fear of the health risks. The only evidence that raising the criminal risks for small-time dealers and users works is based on small, highly targeted, extremely resource-intensive efforts, in which success lasts for only a few months after the cleanup ends. This doesn't invalidate the theory. Apply the same pressure everywhere, and maybe we would suppress drug use everywhere. But this is where the gap between the conceivable and the possible becomes an abyss.

The Nature of the Problem

A simple exercise will illustrate the nature of the problem. We begin by stipulating that deterrence works if risk is raised sufficiently, and then contemplate the implications of raising that risk. Then we try to plug in some numbers.

According to the 1988 version of the government-sponsored annual survey, 28 million persons used an illicit drug within that year. According to the FBI's [Federal Bureau of Investigation] figures, there were 839,000 arrests for possession of drugs that year—less than 3 percent of all users after taking multiple arrests of the same person into account. In that same year 317,000 persons were arrested for trafficking or manufacture. No one knows what percentage of all dealers this represents. Now fill in the blanks: What percentage of users and how many dealers must we arrest and meaningfully punish to achieve a major reduction in drug use? I am willing to entertain sophisticated answers, ones that incorporate selective arrest strategies and postulate tipping effects and critical masses. I have no trouble believing, given a sophisticated strategy, that the numbers one ends up with can be quite low and still plausibly produce a deterrent effect. I do, however, have a lot of trouble believing that the numbers can plausibly represent anything less than a few million additional arrests per year.

Drug Arrests

Suppose that to drive down drug use substantially it would be necessary to arrest and meaningfully sanction 20 percent of the people who used drugs during the past year, plus triple the arrests and sanctions of drug dealers. That would mean 5.6 million arrests of users and 951,000 arrests of dealers. To put it another way, arrests of drug users alone—forget the dealers— would be almost twice the number of 1988 arrests for the nation's murders, rapes, robberies, burglaries, aggravated assaults, larcenies, and auto thefts combined.

Now let's think for a moment about what we will do with these people. One may again be open to all sorts of creative penalties and still be unable to imagine how the nation's police and courts can cope with the increased flow of traffic that an effective War on Drugs would require. On top of that is the hard truth that an effective deterrent strategy will have to mean incarceration for at least some offenders. If for purposes of illustration we assume that the criminal justice system has to impose some sort of incarceration on 5 percent of the arrested users (which means only 1 percent of all the people who have used drugs during 1988—hardly draconian enforcement) and 75 percent of the arrested dealers, that would come out to a bit less than a million people incarcerated for some period of time. Apart from its sheer size, this number represents more than half again the size of the total 1988 national prison population of 627,000— which was of course already far over the rated capacity of the nation's prisons.

"I am not proposing utopia, but a system that enables people to live the kind of life they choose to live."

The bottom line is self-evidently ridiculous (though it's not so obvious that the percentages that produced it are ridiculous). Suppose, then, that deterrence can be purchased much more cheaply. First we redefine the number of users to include only those who have used drugs during the past month, not the past year. This cuts the target population by almost half, to 14.5 million. Then we assume that all we have to do to achieve a major deterrent effect on drug use is to arrest 5 percent of these recent users and double the current arrests of dealers. Of the persons arrested, we will incarcerate just 2 percent of the arrested users (meaning just one of every 1,000 recent users overall) and 25 percent of the arrested dealers. This is not "strict law enforcement" by any ordinary definition of "strict," and it is not self-evident that such a policy would raise the risks enough to produce deterrence. The point is that even this optimistic scenario implies that the system somehow has to incarcerate almost 173,000 persons in the first year of the policy, plus arrest and meaningfully punish (short of incarceration) another 1.2 million persons. This bottom line too is ridiculous—and deeply unsettling.

I hold no brief for any of these specific numbers. If you're a hawk and you don't like them, change them— but at the end of the line, you have to be able to say, "This will plausibly have a major effect on drug use." I am convinced that punishment can deter drug use, but I cannot figure out how that is to be done in an affordable way, and the hawks have done little to make the case.

Such is the box that I find myself in, perhaps in company with some of my readers. One option, and far from the worst one, is to do nothing more ambitious than we were doing before the War on Drugs began. Drug use in some segments of the population has been dropping for several years. Whatever role the government's drug policy had in this (no one knows), the reductions followed a radical shift in the public perception of drugs. Until the late 1970s, cocaine was still literally fashionable (remember the silver coke spoons worn as jewelry?) among many powerful circles in American society. Since then, drugs have become just as unfashionable in the same circles. Because the opinion leaders don't think it's chic anymore, drug use may well continue to decline no matter what we do.

"The most profoundly important truth about drugs is not that drugs are evil but that drugs are unsatisfying."

But to do nothing ignores the toll that drugs and our drug policy are taking on our country. Things aren't necessarily getting better for everyone equally. There are signs that the drug problem is on its way to becoming a manageable problem for the upper classes but not for the lower ones, in the same way that cigarette smoking has plunged in the upper classes and remained virtually unchanged among the lower ones. And though it's all very well to say things

will heal themselves sometime in the indefinite future, the problems posed right now are severe, and people whose families are at risk need to be able to do something right now.

This brings us to the question that should be the starting point in rethinking the drug problem: *What do we really want to accomplish?* By that, I don't mean the usual goals (e.g., "Reduce by 50 percent the number of adolescents reporting cocaine use in the past month"). Rather, I am asking you to ask yourself what constitutes "success" regarding the drug problem for you and your family. I also ask you to ignore for the moment that you are affluent or an intellectual or otherwise privileged. What is the selfish solution that would work for you, whether or not it rid the entire nation of drugs?

Simple Answers

If you put the goal in this parochial way, some of the answers become relatively simple. Suppose that you are a parent. Your most immediate worry is that your child is going to a school where there is a known drug problem. Step back from the issue, quit brooding about societal ills and complex causes of the national drug problem, and think how absurd it is that the school your child attends has a drug problem. It is not hard for teachers and principals to control schools if they have a free hand to oversee, discipline, suspend, and expel, 1950s-style. Are you willing to give that free hand to your child's school? If yes, then it is easy to run schools so that they have no drug problem, or, more accurately, so that it is no worse than the alcohol problem in the typical 1950s high school.

Consider how drastically the problem of devising good policy changes once the statement of what we are trying to accomplish changes. If I am asked, "Do you have an affordable, practical strategy for reducing adolescent drug use nationwide by 50 percent?" my honest answer must be no. But if I am asked, "Do you have an affordable, practical strategy for sending your child to a school where drugs are not a problem?" my answer is emphatically yes.

The most direct way to achieve this is through a generous, unrestricted voucher program that puts into the hands of parents roughly the current per-pupil costs of public education. Give me the money that my school district currently spends per pupil, do the same for every other parent, and let me choose my own school. If I am really afraid of drugs, I will choose a school with zero tolerance for them—expulsion for the first infraction; frequent, unannounced locker checks; and drug testing. If I am moderately afraid, I will choose a school with a little more relaxed policy. If I am not afraid at all, I will choose a school where the administration cannot touch my child without due process and a search warrant. Wherever I stand on this spectrum, I know how to send my children to a school that is as drug-free as I wish, and I know how to do so without spending any more money on education or the law enforcement system than we currently spend.

Because most parents probably fall in a mainstream "strict" category, a small minority at either end of the spectrum will have to search for other parents who want drug-permissive environments or maximum-security environments. But this is an immeasurable improvement over the current situation, where millions of families cannot find a school run as they wish. What happens to children who have drug problems? Most of the mainstream schools will refuse to admit them, because to do so would be financially ruinous when the parents of the other children hear about it. That's the virtue of the voucher system. On the other hand, schools that specialize in children with drug problems will mushroom when their parents are carrying around vouchers worth three or four thousand dollars.

I began with the school system because it offers a clear example of the policy revisions I have in mind.

Drug Policies

But the school example can be generalized. Translated into a policy goal for the War on Drugs, it would read like this: *National drug policy should make it possible for people to send their children to schools that are as drug-free as they wish, live in neighborhoods that are as drug-free as they wish, and work in workplaces that are as drug-free as they wish; and this should apply to poor people as well as rich people, blacks as well as whites, people who live in cities as well as people who live in small towns.*

Forget about eradicating drug use everywhere. If you could live in a neighborhood, work at a job, and send your children to schools where drugs weren't a problem—and if everyone else could too if they wanted—wouldn't that pretty much give you what you want in the war against drugs? Let me indicate a few of the ways in which this kind of thinking could apply to the workplace and the neighborhood as well as to schools.

> ## "The aim is not to put all the drug dealers in jail, but to enable people to construct neighborhoods that drug dealers will avoid."

Regarding the workplace, the policy goal is to give employers broad latitude in enforcing drug rules that make sense for that business, and the premise is that the vast majority of businesses have the enlightened self-interest to do just that. Part of my policy prescription is for government to refrain from passing laws about who can and cannot require drug tests. Any employer can make its preferred drug-testing policy a condition of employment. Another part of my policy prescription is specifically to exempt drugs from the tangle of law that currently permits an employee to bring wrongful-discharge suits against an employer. If we're serious about conducting a war on drugs, let employers discharge employees (if they wish—not compulsorily) who test positive for drug use without having to worry about a lawsuit.

It is expensive to get rid of employees who are functioning satisfactorily. This provides a built-in safeguard against arbitrary and abusive behavior by employers—not perfect protection, but a lot of protection. The clear incentive for employers is to establish a policy that lets them act quickly and inexpensively when an employee is exhibiting signs of drug use, with stricter (and more expensive) checks in place only where drug use could endanger people or property. Drug policy would be a matter for collective bargaining agreement in unionized workplaces, and of collaborative development between employees and employers in non-unionized industries. My proposition is that it is just as unnatural for a business to suffer from a debilitating drug problem as it is for a school. It is easy to avoid, in ways that huge majorities of workers and employers can agree upon, if the government and courts will let those workers and employers decide on the conditions of employment without interference.

The third sphere within which people should be able to live "as drug-free as they wish"—the neighborhood—would seem to be one place where government enforcement of drug laws is essential unless we want to resort to vigilantism. Nonetheless, bear with me while I postpone calling in the cops and propose a few ways in which we might get to the desired end state without them.

Landlords

One of the greatly maligned forces for social good in this country is landlords. Whatever their faults, landlords have one undoubted virtue: they want responsible tenants. That is, they want tenants who pay their rent on time and don't trash the property. Given their way, they tend to let good tenants be and to evict bad ones, and this is one of the most efficient forms of socialization known to a free society. Actually, the entire process whereby landlords and tenants find each other is much richer in its social functions than this. Entire neighborhoods represent (or once represented) an intricate process whereby that neighborhood evolved a set of norms and attracted a certain kind of person. Expectations

were set up on both sides, and money was often a relatively small part of the discriminating value. In Harlem in the 1940s, for example, the difference between the scruffy, hustling blocks and the exactly neat and orderly working-class blocks was not a vast difference in income among the tenants, but vast differences in norms and values. In the working-class neighborhoods, unless you presented yourself as being a certain kind of person, you weren't going to get in, even if you could pay the rent. In the scruffy neighborhoods, you could get in, but the landlords charged a premium to compensate for the damage they expected you to cause. Economists have technical descriptions for the equilibria that were reached, but the process was not really so different from the way that human beings everywhere have historically tended to stratify themselves not just according to money, but also according to tastes and values.

In the rush to rid society of the socially disapproved reasons for discriminating among applicants, starting with race, we threw out as well all the ways in which landlords performed a neighborhood-formation function. It became almost impossible for a landlord to say, "I'm not going to rent to you because I don't want you living on my property," which is often what neighborhood-forming decisions have to be based on. Then, ensuring that maintaining cohesive neighborhoods in low-income areas became as difficult as possible, we tore down some of those neighborhoods in the name of urban renewal, threw up public housing in the middle of other such neighborhoods, and in a variety of ways made it impossible for neighborhoods to define and defend themselves.

"People should be able to live as drug-free as they wish!"

I realize that getting the government out of the landlord-tenant relationship is an impossibility as of 1990, but a few modest changes might make a big difference. I begin from the observation that the defense of the neighborhood against drugs is a problem especially for black Americans living in urban neighborhoods. The other salient fact is that, in a neighborhood that is already predominantly black, it is difficult for a landlord to discriminate by race. He doesn't get that many opportunities. When a landlord arbitrarily turns down one applicant and chooses another, or when he takes the trouble to evict a tenant (eviction, even without government barriers, is expensive), he is probably doing so for reasons that have nothing to do with race, but a lot to do with trying to get good tenants. Why not free up the housing market in black neighborhoods in the same way that the many "enterprise zone" proposals seek to free up business investment?

"Free up the housing market in black neighborhoods."

I cannot speak to the legal difficulties of drafting the legislation, which might be insurmountable, but the objective is clear enough. In the neighborhoods hardest hit by drugs, make it possible once more for landlords to choose among prospective tenants without having to justify their arbitrariness. If they want to impose a no-drugs rule, they may. If they want to impose a nobody-who-can't-prove-he-has-a-steady-job rule, they may. If they want to impose a no-welfare-mothers rule, they may. If they don't want to rent to you because they don't like your looks, that's up to them. If a tenant violates the terms of the lease, he may be evicted, without the delays that many large cities now superimpose on the terms of the lease. In short, make it possible to make a buck by renting to responsible low-income people. Apply the same freedom to public housing, giving tenant committees wide discretion to screen new applicants and evict existing tenants.

These reforms will permit the creation of neighborhoods of like-minded people in low-income areas. The reason so few white neighborhoods have open-air drug markets is not because police cruisers prowl the streets, but because, for subtler reasons, it would be very foolish for a dealer to set up shop there. For practical purposes, most white neighborhoods already enjoy the same freedoms to form neighborhoods that I propose giving to black neighborhoods. The crazy-quilt of laws and restrictions sometimes gets in the way of middle-class neighborhoods as well, but not often and usually not onerously. The laws and restrictions are really effective in breaking up neighborhoods only when people are poor and where a large proportion of the people rent rather than own. Absent either of those conditions, the attempts of government to interfere with neighborhoods don't work very well, and one or the other is absent in the vast majority of white neighborhoods. Give hardworking, low-income black people the same freedom to segregate themselves into enclaves, using their nonmonetary assets that landlords prize. The aim is not to put all the drug dealers in jail, but to enable people to construct neighborhoods that drug dealers will avoid.

Not Proposing Utopia

This brings us to the question of the underclass. What about the mother who doesn't care what school her children attend? What about the pregnant teenager smoking crack who can't even think far enough ahead to worry about what she's doing to her baby? What about the Uzi-toting young male who has grown up thinking that the way to be a man is to blow away anyone who fails to show him the proper respect? How are school vouchers and a free housing market and employer discretion on drug-testing supposed to do anything for the drug problem in their neighborhoods?

The simplest answer is that maybe it won't do anything at all—but so what? I am not proposing utopia, but a system that enables people to live the kind of life they choose to live. My proposition is that the overwhelming majority of Americans, including the overwhelming majority of low-income black Americans who live in the worst of our inner cities, have sensible preferences about their schools, workplaces, and neighborhoods, and possess the common sense to act on those preferences if we do nothing except make it easier for them to do what they already want to do. I don't know how to turn around the remaining part of the population, but neither do the social engineers. Let us stop fixating on the worst-of-the-worst part of the problem, begin to recognize how badly we have ignored those who are already trying to do everything right, and do the good that we know how to do by helping those who need only a chance. If the result of implementing these policies is to concentrate the bad apples into a few hyper-violent, antisocial neighborhoods, so be it.

In reality, however, I suspect this scenario is too pessimistic. Over a period of time, it seems more plausible that the use of drugs will shrink even among those people who now have the shortest time horizons, the most neglected socialization, and the fewest links with mainstream society. Drug use will drop for essentially the same reason that so many people reading this article have at one time or another taken some kinds of illegal drugs and then stopped with no trouble. It is the reason drug use is dropping in the middle and upper classes. The most profoundly important truth about drugs is not that drugs are evil but that drugs are unsatisfying.

New Options

As matters now stand, the choice perceived by many inner-city youths is limited to the life in their streets, drab and dispiriting, compared with the life they see on their television screens, unimaginably glamorous and unattainable. What they badly need are some options closer to home—a neighborhood a few blocks away, not on the other side of town—where the families have fathers as well as mothers, where the streets aren't strewn with garbage, where the playgrounds are safe from gangs and drug dealers. The people in that nearby neighborhood won't necessarily have much more money, for the kinds of qualities I am talking about do not depend on having much money. They depend on the ability of like-minded people to control and shape their small worlds, Burke's little platoons, to the way of life that they prefer. The price of admission to their worlds is not money, but behavior. I submit that, given this visible alternative, large numbers of the people we currently call the underclass eventually will choose to pay that price in return for admission, for the most basic of reasons: the life that people are living in those other neighborhoods really will be richer, more satisfying, more fun, than the life of a drug addict.

***

> ## "The worst of the drug problem will take care of itself if we let the people who want to avoid drugs do so."

***

All of the effects I have described would probably work better if legalization were added to the package of reforms, but I won't try to make that case here. My more limited point is that the worst of the drug problem will take care of itself if we let the people who want to avoid drugs do so. Enable them to congregate, dominate their neighborhoods, send their children to the same schools. They will set in motion the forces that will bring over a steady stream of converts. To win the war on drugs, it is not necessary that drug abusers become criminals, only that they be made outcasts. In the natural course of events, schools, employees, and communities will do this. Let them.

Can the War on Drugs Be Won?

No: The War on Drugs Is a Failure

The War on Drugs Has Failed
The War on Drugs Should Be Reevaluated
The War on Drugs Cannot Be Won
The War on Drugs Threatens Civil Liberties

The War on Drugs Has Failed

Elaine Shannon

About the Author: *Elaine Shannon is a staff writer for* Time, *a weekly newsmagazine.*

Remember the war on drugs? George Bush waving a plastic bag of crack bought across the street from the White House during a nationally televised speech? The Pentagon planning to station an aircraft carrier off the coast of Colombia to monitor suspected drug smugglers? Candidates for political office proffering urine samples and daring their opponents to do the same? The appointment of combative William J. Bennett as the nation's first drug czar, a post from which he would coordinate an all-out assault on a menace that seemed to threaten the very survival of the U.S.?

Those events now seem like relics of a long-distant past. . . . The war on drugs has become almost an afterthought. Part of the reason is simply that public concern has been diverted by the Persian Gulf crisis and fears of a recession. But there is another sign of the issue's decline: though he sounded a call to arms soon after taking office, the President too has turned his attention elsewhere.

Confident assertions that the U.S. is making great strides in kicking the habit have become conventional wisdom in the drug war's high command. When he resigned as director of the Office of National Drug Control Policy, Bennett proclaimed that success, while not yet achieved, was in sight. He contended that his original goal of cutting drug use in half by 1999 could be achieved five years sooner if the federal, state and local governments maintain their current

efforts.

Bennett's hopeful forecast was shared by the President, who declared earlier this month, "We're on the road to victory." Federal surveys found that "casual" consumption of cocaine and marijuana had fallen, as had emergency-room admissions and deaths from drug overdoses. Federal agents believe cocaine prices have risen because of the pressure international police operations are putting on suppliers.

But how much of the optimistic talk emanating from Washington is warranted and how much of it is hype from an Administration and Congress eager to justify the expenditure of billions of dollars at a time of budget crunches, rising taxes and widespread anger at government? Those on the front line of the war on drugs—the beleaguered law-enforcement officers, the overworked drug counselors, the terrified residents of crack-infested neighborhoods—are far from positive that the "war" is going all that well.

"The war on drugs has become almost an afterthought."

What those on the front line fear most is that Washington is preparing to declare victory and walk away from a battle that it is not winning, but was not serious about waging in the first place. Some critics charge such a turnabout is conceivable only because drug abuse, which continues to rage in poor ghetto areas, has sharply declined within the white middle class. If the Federal Government were to withdraw from the field, it would not be for the first time. In 1973 Richard Nixon announced that the U.S. had "turned the corner on drug addiction." The federal antidrug effort was allowed to shrivel even as Colombia's "cocaine cowboys" were establishing their first beachhead in Miami. Some battlefield reports from the latest round:

Boston. Police are barely holding their own against drug dealers, and a $20 "blow" of crack is still easy to find. "The Federal Government is giving us more lip support than financial support," says William Celester, Boston police commander in Roxbury, Boston's toughest neighborhood. "People tend to believe that if you don't hear about the drug problem, it is somehow subsiding," says Don Muhammad, a minister for the Nation of Islam in Roxbury. "I feel it's going to escalate because of the economy. More people are going to resort to unethical and illegal means of earning a living."

Starr County, Texas. If drug demand is down, says Fred Ball, Drug Enforcement Administration special agent, the smugglers don't seem to know. Starr, along with two neighboring mesquite-covered counties along the Mexican border, has become known as Little Colombia because of high-profile drug smuggling since the federal crackdown in Florida. Officially designated as one of the nation's poorest regions, the area is basking in a cocaine-driven economic boom that has helped fuel a surge in bank deposits. Lavish homes—paid for in cash—have been built fronting the Rio Grande, and luxury cars equipped with cellular telephones dot the unpaved streets of such towns as Roma and Rio Grande City. Hard-pressed lawmen fear that they can do no more than hold the line against the traffickers.

"The best we can do is stick our finger in the hole," says Terry Bowers, a supervisor with the narcotics division of the department of public safety. "We will never be a match for the drug dealers as long as they have unlimited funds and we have to fight budget wars."

Detroit. Dr. Padraic Sweeny, vice chief of emergency services for Detroit Receiving Hospital, is seeing fewer overdoses but more drug-related shootings, stabbings and assaults as street dealers fight over fewer customers. The saddest casualties are children. "We have a whole generation of human beings within this urban area who could be so productive and helpful to humanity but are being lost," says Sweeny. "We have kids 13 and 14 years old who are as hardened as anyone in a penitentiary. Look into their eyes, and you see these cold blank stares, void of most

moral values. The drug trade has shown them that in a little time they can make a lot of money, and they've accepted the violence that goes with it."

"We will never be a match for the drug dealers as long as they have unlimited funds."

Miami. In one of the nation's key drug-smuggling cities, crack addicts are stealing any piece of metal they can to sell for scrap, from awnings to aluminum stepladders. Along State Road 112, only 2% of the lights work, because thieves have ripped off the copper wiring. At one point, Florida had 5,800 addicts begging to get into treatment programs. The number in the autumn of 1990 fell to under 2,000. But experts say that is because many of those who want help most have despaired of getting it and gone back to the street

Los Angeles. Police continue to make drug arrests at a rate of 60,000 a year, roughly the same as in 1988 and 1989. There would be far more if the jails, courts and parole system were not already strained to the breaking point. A 1989 seizure of cocaine at a warehouse in the San Fernando Valley's Sylmar illustrates the size of the problem. Though 21 tons of coke were confiscated, records showed that at least 55 tons, worth $1.1 billion, had passed through the warehouse in the previous three months. According to Deputy Chief of Police Glenn Levant, the raid "made little if any impact on the availability of cocaine that we have been able to measure. There was a big jump in wholesale prices after Sylmar, but in the long term the street price and purity of cocaine remained essentially constant. It didn't make a dent."

Such reports underscore a dismaying fact: for nearly every item of good news on the drug front, there is at least one bad-news bulletin. While the U.S. has made significant progress in curbing casual drug use, it has made far less headway on the problems that most trouble the public, hard-core addiction and drug-related violence. The National Institute on Drug Abuse estimated that the number of current users of illegal drugs had fallen to 14.5 million from 23 million in 1985. But while there was a dramatic decrease in the number of occasional users, the number of people who used drugs weekly or daily (292,000 in 1988 vs. 246,000 in 1985) had escalated as addiction to crack soared in some mainly poor and minority areas. Despite the passage of tough antidrug laws and police dragnets, street crime, much of it drug-related, continues to surge. The nation's violent-crime rate rose 10% in the first six months of 1990. Murders were up 8% in the first six months of the year and armed robbery rose 9%.

Nor, despite increasing vigilance on its borders, has the U.S. been able to stanch the flow of drug imports. Federal drug agents are making impressive cases, last year seizing almost 70 tons of cocaine and more than $1 billion worth of cash and assets—roughly double the Drug Enforcement Administration's 1990 budget of $549 million. A relentless Colombian government campaign has disrupted the Medellín cocaine cartel's refining and transportation operations.

But rival cocaine refiners in Cali and elsewhere have stepped in to fill the void. Raw coca from Bolivia and Peru is plentiful and will remain so. Leaders of the Andean governments have rejected U.S. State Department plans for wholesale eradication, arguing that such an approach would starve and radicalize hundreds of thousands of peasants for whom coca leaves are a valuable cash crop. Moreover, heroin is making a frightening comeback in some areas. Thanks to bumper crops of opium in insurgent-controlled northeastern Burma, Southeast Asian heroin traffickers are flooding New York and New Jersey with moderately priced, high-quality "China White."

According to the DEA, wholesale prices have risen across the nation. But it is not clear whether the increases reflect actual supply shortages or price gouging by traffickers playing on consumer fears. Los Angeles defense attorney David Kenner, who represents many alleged traffickers, maintains that "all the interdiction efforts do is keep profit margins high for the cartels." Robert Bonner, head of the DEA, warns against complacency: "There have been some rays of hope, but I'm not sure we are at the end of the beginning. I think we are still at the beginning."

"Police continue to make drug arrests at a rate of 60,000 a year, roughly the same as in 1988 and 1989."

The U.S. is trying to plug the holes on the Mexican border with radar balloons, aircraft equipped with infrared sensors and ground-implanted motion sensors. But vast stretches of badlands are not constantly under guard. The traffickers, in turn, have proved endlessly inventive. On May 17, Customs agents discovered a 250-ft.-long, 5-ft.-wide concrete-and-steel reinforced tunnel that ran 35 ft. under the border, between a construction-supply warehouse in Douglas, Ariz., and a house in Agua Prieta, Mexico. Agents figure virtually all of Arizona's cocaine supply moved for a time via the passage. . . .

Bennett's successor is Florida Governor Bob Martinez, 55, who was defeated in his bid for a second term. The Republican Governor is known more for a hard-line approach to law enforcement than for progress in education and treatment.

Martinez will inherit an effort that has enjoyed some limited successes. Bennett's supporters credit the drug czar with shaping the national debate on drugs into a more mature and less hysterical discussion. He considers the fact that drugs did not figure in most political races as a plus because "it means the issue is not a political football."

To his credit, Bennett did not fashion a strategy that depended on what he calls "magic bullets." He called for putting steady pressure on every conceivable point, from interdiction abroad to stepped up domestic police work to prevention. His approach won bipartisan support in Congress, which voted a record $10.4 billion for federal antidrug programs. Bennett and congressional Democrats pushed for dramatic increases, to $2.7 billion, in federal spending for drug treatment and education.

But, as Bennett has warned, the war against drugs cannot be won by Washington alone. "If people don't do the right things in their communities," he says, "it's not going to get better, no matter what the Federal Government does." Increased federal funding for treatment has been disappointingly slow to move down to the people who need it. In many cases federal grants have been held up until state legislatures approve new treatment programs and provide matching funds. Services for poor addicts are particularly strained. It may be years before counseling is available to every impoverished drug user who needs and wants it.

"In all too many instances, police crackdowns remain the most visible evidence that the nation is at war on drugs."

The result is that, in all too many instances, police crackdowns remain the most visible evidence that the nation is at war on drugs. Highly publicized police activity in ghettos and barrios has fed the myth that drug abuse is principally a problem of the black and Hispanic underclass. But federal surveys show that 69% of all cocaine users are white, and that two-thirds of all drug users hold jobs. The cocaine epidemic started in the upper middle class in the mid-1970s. It spread to the poor only in the past four years, when dealers started hawking a Caribbean import called crack (or rock) that sold for $10 or $20 a vial, vs. $50 to $100 for a gram of cocaine powder.

Dr. David F. Musto, a psychiatrist and historian at Yale School of Medicine, warns that the myth of drugs as mainly a ghetto habit has an insidious appeal to other Americans: "It allows us to ascribe all the profound social problems of the inner city to one thing—drugs. A lot of people would add, They've brought it on themselves. That lets the rest of us off the hook, free to ignore the deeper problems of unemployment and lack of education." Moreover, says Musto, by pretending that most addicts are dark-skinned and destitute, middle-class Americans can avoid responsibility for confronting the reality of drug abuse among their own families and friends.

Still, the fact remains that the most violent drug dealers inhabit underclass areas, which are not only the source of many customers but are also short on police protection. Many residents of such communities plead for additional police patrols. Says Reggie Walton, a former District of Columbia Superior Court judge who now serves as associate director of the drug czar's office: "I don't want to see people of color disproportionately brought into the criminal-justice system, but the sad reality is that much of the conduct that outrages the citizenry is open-air markets and crack houses, blatantly out in the open. What are the police supposed to do? Turn a deaf ear and a closed eye and walk away? Most people who live in poor communities are decent and have the same right to protection as everybody else."

Recognizing that the war on drugs has singled out the poor, Bennett has urged state and federal authorities to come down harder on middle-class users by suspending driver's and occupational licenses, sending convicted users to boot camp, insisting on drug testing for government contractors. He considers "casual" drug users "carriers" who are even more infectious than addicts because they suggest to young people "that you can do drugs and be O.K." Congress approved Bennett-backed legislation requiring universities that receive federal aid to proscribe drug use and punish offenders.

Ultimately the solution to the drug crisis is to dry up demand. The conventional wisdom is that demand reduction means prevention, which in turn means education. Which means what, exactly? If it were simply a matter of conveying scientifically accurate information on posters and public-service announcements about the dangers of drug use, the national habit would already be history. If it were a matter of poverty, the answer would be better schools and more opportunity. Eliminating poverty is a moral imperative that should need no additional justification. But the vast majority of drug users are not desperately poor; many in fact are fabulously wealthy. Their thirst for drugs springs from some other source.

"The war on drugs is really a battle for hearts and minds, and not merely an issue for police and courts and jails."

The war on drugs is really a battle for hearts and minds, and not merely an issue for police and courts and jails. So far, the antidrug offensive's main accomplishment has been to dissuade some experimenters and weekend users from digging themselves in deeper. The effort has not reached millions of people so bereft of hope that they are willing to risk everything they have, or will ever have, for a few moments of oblivion.

If Washington were really serious about alleviating the drug problem, state and local governments would establish urgent projects to find and deal with addicted mothers of young children and pregnant drug users. Treatment would be made available promptly to every person who wanted it. Federal and state governments would build enough jails, with humane conditions for prisoners, so that judges would no longer feel obliged to turn traffickers out on the streets. There would be many more judges and probation officers to make sure that criminals did their time and stayed clean afterward. U.S. diplomats would no longer cover up for corrupt officials in "friendly" nations. Foreign leaders committed to suppressing drug production would be rewarded with lowered U.S. trade barriers for legitimate exports and economic aid to help peasant farmers switch from coca to legitimate crops.

Such steps would cost additional tens of billions of dollars and take many years to achieve significant results. Implementing them would also require a new kind of leadership in Washington, one that is patient enough to pursue a steady and determined policy instead of gyrating from cries of alarm to premature claims of success.

The War on Drugs Should Be Reevaluated

Steven Wisotsky

About the Author: *Steven Wisotsky is professor of legal studies at Nova Law School in Fort Lauderdale, Florida, and the author of several articles on America's drug problem. He is also the author of the book,* Beyond the War on Drugs.

The Reagan and Bush administrations have acted aggressively in mobilizing the agencies of the federal government in a coordinated attack on the drug supply from abroad and the distribution of drugs within the United States. The War on Drugs, empowered by Congress with an ever stricter set of police powers and punishments, has attained a vast global scale that includes the largest increase in law-enforcement personnel in American history; involvement of the FBI [Federal Bureau of Investigation], the CIA [Central Intelligence Agency], NASA [National Aeronautics and Space Administration] spy satellites, and the military; a projection of U.S. law-enforcement power on the high seas and in foreign nations: a breathtaking expansion of repressive laws that include pre-trial detention and mandatory life sentences for some drug offenders; urine testing for civil-service and private-sector workers; and dragnet enforcement techniques such as bus boardings and roadblocks directed against the public. Perhaps most tellingly in an age of budget deficits and Gramm-Rudman constraints, total federal spending on the War on Drugs rose from approximately $1 billion to $9 billion during the 1980s.

Reprinted from Stephen Wisotsky's *Beyond the War on Drugs* with permission of Prometheus Books, Buffalo, New York.

The crackdown has not been without results. By nearly every bureaucratic standard, the War on Drugs is a huge success. It has set new records in every category of measurement—drug seizures, investigations, indictments, arrests, convictions, and asset forfeitures.

Despite the administration's accumulation of impressive statistics, domestic marijuana cultivation took off, and the black market in cocaine grew to record size. In a 1985 National Household Survey, more than 22 million Americans reported having tried cocaine; roughly 5.8 million reported having used it during the month preceding the survey.

As if to mock the aggressive efforts of the War on Drugs, the rapid increase in supply and decline in price occurred in the face of President Reagan's doubling and redoubling of the federal anti-drug enforcement budget. Resources specifically devoted to interdiction rose, military assistance rose, personnel levels at DEA [Drug Enforcement Administration] rose, and substantial amounts of military equipment were sent to Colombia, Bolivia, and other Latin American governments for use against trafficking operations there.

"Despite the administration's accumulation of impressive statistics, domestic marijuana cultivation took off."

Commenting in 1987 on the interdiction budget, the Office of Technology Assessment concluded:

> Despite a doubling of federal expenditures on interdiction over the past five years, the quantity of drugs smuggled into the United States is greater than ever. . . . There is no clear correlation between the level of expenditures or effort devoted to interdiction and the long-term availability of illegally imported drugs in the domestic market.

The social "return" on the extra billions spent during the 1980s has been a drug-abuse problem of historic magnitude, accompanied by a drug-trafficking parasite of international dimensions.

Thus it is not simply that the War on Drugs has failed to work; in many respects it has made things worse. In this country it has spun a spider's web of black-market pathologies, including roughly 25 percent of all urban homicides, widespread corruption of police and other public officials, and street crime by addicts. It has promoted subversive alliances between Latin American guerrillas and traffickers. Some Latin American and Caribbean nations have been effectively captured by drug traffickers; where capture is incomplete, intimidation reigns.

Laws of Supply and Demand

Of course, these pathologies were foreseeable. They are a function of money. Drug law yields to a higher law: the law of the marketplace, of supply and demand. The naive attack on the drug supply by aggressive enforcement at each step—interdiction, arrest, prosecution, and punishment—results in a "crime tariff," reward for taking the risk of breaking the law. The criminal law thereby maintains inflated prices for illegal drugs in the black market.

For example, an ounce of pure pharmaceutical cocaine at roughly $80, just under $3 a gram, becomes worth about $4,480 if sold on the black market at $80 a diluted gram (at 50-percent purity). The crime tariff is thus $4,400 an ounce. This type of law enforcement succeeds to the extent (probably slight) that demand is elastic or sensitive to price. But because the crime tariff is paid to lawbreakers rather than the government, it pumps vast sums of money into the black market—more than $100 billion a year by government estimates. The flow of these illegal billions through the underground economy finances or supplies the incentives for the pathologies described above: homicides, street crime, public corruption, and international narco-terrorism. If these phenomena were properly costed out, one might well conclude that the War on Drugs makes a net negative contribution to the safety, well-being, and national security interests of the American people.

Confronted by these threatening developments, both the public and the politicians predictably react in fear and anger. The specter of uncontrolled and seemingly uncontrollable drug abuse and black-marketeering leads to frustrated reaction against the drug trade. The zeal to "turn the screw of the criminal machinery" leads directly to the adoption of repressive and punitive measures that aggrandize governmental powers at the expense of individual rights.

The War on Drugs has substantially undermined the American tradition of limited government and personal autonomy. Since the early 1980s, the prevailing attitude, both within government and in the broader society, has been that the crackdown on drugs is so imperative that extraordinary measures are justified. The end has come to justify the means. The result is that Americans have significantly less freedom than they did only five or six years ago. What is truly frightening is the high level of public consent; according to the polls, a majority of the public is willing to sacrifice personal freedoms in order to wage the War on Drugs.

> ## "The War on Drugs has substantially undermined the American tradition of limited government and personal autonomy."

Election-year politics in 1988 continued to ratchet the War on Drugs machinery tighter and tighter. On March 30, 1988, Attorney General Edwin Meese sent a memorandum to all United States Attorneys encouraging the selective prosecution of "middle- and upper-class users" in order to "send the message that there is no such thing as 'recreational' drug use. . . ." At about the same time, former Customs Commissioner William von Raab's "zero tolerance" initiative was begun to punish drug use in order to reduce "the demand side of the equation." This means the seizure and forfeiture of the cars, planes, or boats of persons found in possession of even trace amounts of illegal drugs. These forfeited assets in effect represent fines far greater than would ordinarily be imposed for drug possession; but as civil forfeiture is *in rem* (that is, a procedure against a thing as opposed to against a person), no conviction or prosecution is required at all.

Zero Tolerance

Some examples: The Coast Guard boarded and seized the motor yacht Ark Royal, valued at $25 million, because ten marijuana *seeds* and two stems were found aboard. Public criticism prompted a return of the boat upon payment of $1,600 in fines and fees by the owner. The fifty-two-foot Mindy was impounded for a week because of cocaine dust in a rolled-up dollar bill. The $80 million oceanographic research vessel Atlantis II was seized in San Diego when the Coast Guard found .01 ounce of marijuana in a crewman's shaving kit. It was returned also. But a Michigan couple returning from a vacation in Canada lost the wife's 1987 Cougar when Customs agents found two marijuana cigarettes in her husband's pocket. No charges were filed, but the car was kept by the government. In Key West, Florida, David Phelps, a shrimp fisherman, lost his 73-foot shrimper to a Coast Guard seizure because 3 grams of cannabis seeds and stems were found aboard. Legally, the boat is forfeitable whether or not Phelps had any responsibility for the drugs—though the 1988 Act softened the law somewhat by creating an exemption for innocent owners.

On April 19, 1989, Bush called upon the House and Senate to vote promptly on a bill providing for capital punishment when a death results from drug dealing, or when a law-enforcement officer is killed in the course of a drug-related crime. Congress complied. Other strong measures were debated and rejected. In June the administration declared its goal of a "drug-free America," and Congress wrote that into law in the 1988 Act, setting 1995 as the tar-get date.

At the same time that anti-drug extremism began to rise, a movement began in the opposite direction. Respected journalists and other opinion leaders began to break ranks with the War on Drugs. Today, a significant body of opinion has emerged, outside the academic community, that is opposed to the War on Drugs. The opposition transcends the liberal/conservative split. Traditionally, conservatives have advocated strict law enforcement, and liberals have been identified with a permissive approach to the drug issue. Now respected conservative spokesmen also have begun to dissent from the War on Drugs. Clearly, the challenge to the monopoly status of the War on Drugs is gaining ground. The Drug Policy Foundation and the Criminal Justice Policy Institute, drug policy reform organizations, have been established in Washington to promote the cause of rationality in drug control. The dissent has also begun to spill over to the political sector, at home as well as abroad. Nothing approaching this level of opposition has been seen or heard since the War on Drugs started.

"Uncritical acceptance of the War on Drugs is no longer possible."

What accounts for this trend? Negative experience almost certainly plays the central role. There is little doubt that the perception that the War on Drugs is a failure at controlling drug supply, drug money, and drug violence has spread significantly. Uncritical acceptance of the War on Drugs is no longer possible. The perception that it has negative side-effects and breeds crime, violence, and corruption has spread even to the comic pages of the daily newspapers. But the question remains: What should be done now?

One historically tested model of exploring policy reform is the appointment of a National

Study Commission of experts, politicians, and lay leaders to uncover facts, canvass a full range of policy options, and recommend further research where needed. The model of the National Commission on Marihuana and Drug Abuse in the early 1970s deserves serious consideration. At the very least, a national commission performs a vital educational function: public hearings and attendant media coverage inform the public, bringing to its attention vital facts and a broader array of policy options. The level of public discourse is almost certain to be elevated.

> ## "The result of drug enforcement is a black market estimated by the government to be over $100 billion a year."

The overriding goal of such a commission should be to develop policies directed toward reducing both drug abuse and the black-market pathologies resulting from the billions in drug money generated by drug law enforcement. In pursuit of these goals, the commission's study might benefit from adherence to the following five points.

1. *Define the drug problem*

What exactly is the problem regarding drugs in the United States? The lack of an agreed-upon answer to this question is one of the primary sources of incoherence in present law and policy. People now speak of "the drug problem" in referring to at least five very different phenomena: (1) the mere use of any illegal drug; (2) teenage drug use; (3) the abuse of illegal drugs, that is, that which causes physical or psychological harm to the user; (4) drug-induced misbehavior that endangers or harms others, such as driving while impaired; and (5) drug-trafficking phenomena (crime, violence, and corruption) arising from the vast sums of money generated in the black market in drugs. This confusion in the very statement of the problem

necessarily engenders confusion in solving it.

2. *Set specific goals*

A creative definition or redefinition of the drug problem would of itself carry us toward a (re)statement of goals. Rational policy-making is impossible without a clear articulation of the goals to be achieved. Part of that impossibility arises from the inconsistencies between goals. For example, pursuit of the goal to attack the drug supply creates a crime tariff that makes pursuit of the goal to suppress drug money more or less impossible. Instead, the result of drug enforcement is a black market estimated by the government to be over $100 billion a year, money that gives rise to homicidal violence, street corruption by addicts, corruption of public officials, and international narco-terrorism. It is therefore essential to distinguish between problems arising from drugs and problems arising from drug money.

3. *Set realistic and principled priorities based on truth*

The suppression of drugs as an end in itself is frequently justified by arguments that drugs cause addiction, injury, and even death in the short or long run. Granted that all drug use has the potential for harm. But it is clear beyond any rational argument that *most* drug use does not cause such harm and is, like social drinking, without lasting consequence. Drugs are not harmful per se.

Benign Neglect

Accepting the truth of that premise means that not all drug use need be addressed by the criminal law, and that society might actually benefit from a policy of benign neglect respecting some forms of drug use. I have in mind the Dutch model, where nothing is legal but some things are simply ignored, cannabis in particular. The benefit to the Dutch has been declining rates of cannabis smoking throughout the 1980s, despite its relatively free availability. The Dutch claim that by stripping cannabis of the allure of forbidden fruit, they have succeeded in making it boring. But in the United States there are approximately a half million arrests a year for marijuana, almost all for simple possession or petty sale offenses. Depending upon the age of consent chosen, most of these arrests could be eliminated from the criminal justice system, thereby achieving a massive freeing of resources for the policing of real crime.

Five Distinctions

Because we live in a world of limited resources, it is not possible to do everything. It is therefore both logical and necessary to make distinctions among things that are more and less important. I have in mind at least five basic dichotomies: (1) drug use by adults (low priority) versus drug use by children (top priority); (2) marijuana smoking (low priority) versus use of harder drugs (higher priority); (3) private use of drugs at home (no priority) versus public use of drugs (high priority); (4) drug consumption (low priority) versus drug impairment (high priority); (5) occasional use (low priority) versus chronic or dependent use (higher priority).

From these general criteria for drug policy, I would recommend to the national commission five specific goals for an effective, principled drug policy:

(1) Protect the children. This priority is self-evident and needs no discussion. I would simply add that this is the only domain in which "zero tolerance" makes any sense at all and might even be approachable if enforcement resources were concentrated on it as a top priority.

(2) Get tough on the legal drugs. It is common knowledge that alcohol (100,000 annual deaths) and tobacco (360,000 annual deaths) far exceed illegal drugs as sources of death, disease, and dysfunction in the United States. Everyone knows that alcohol and tobacco are big business—the advertising budget alone for alcohol runs about $2 billion a year—and, what is worse, the federal and state governments are in complicity with the sellers of these deadly drugs by virtue of the billions in tax revenues that they reap.

I am not suggesting prohibition of these drugs. That is wrong in principle and impossible in practice, as experience teaches. Nonetheless, there are more restrictive measures that can and should be undertaken. One is to get rid of cigarette vending machines so that cigarettes are not so readily available to minors. A second is to require or recommend to the states and localities more restrictive hours of sale. A third is to levy taxes on these products consistent with their social costs—billions of dollars in property damage, disease, and lost productivity. These costs should be financed largely by the buyers; at present prices, society is clearly subsidizing them by providing police, fire, and ambulance services for road accidents; Medicare and Medicaid reimbursement for therapy, surgery, and prosthesis or other medical care; and many other hidden costs effectively externalized from the smoker or drinker to society as a whole. Such taxes would have the additional salutary effect of reducing the consumption of these dangerous products to the extent that demand is elastic.

"The current administration's goal of a drug-free America is both ridiculous . . . and wrong."

---

(3) Public safety and order. Here we need policies directed toward protection of the public from accident and injury on the highway; in the workplace; and from unruly disruptions in public streets, public transport parks, and other gathering places. Programs specifically tailored to accomplish this more focused goal make a lot more sense than futile and counterproductive "zero tolerance" approaches. Street-level law-enforcement practices need to be reviewed to see to what extent they may actually encourage hustling drugs in the street to avoid arrests and forfeitures that might follow from fixed points of sale.

Driving and workplace safety require more knowledge. Nothing should be assumed. Drug use, as the examples of Air Force pilots' use of amphetamines and Sigmund Freud's use of cocaine show, does not automatically mean impairment. Even with marijuana there is ambiguous evidence as to motor coordination. Responsible research is required.

Public Health

(4) Protect public health. The emphasis here is on the word "public." Policy should be directed toward (a) treatment of addicts on a voluntary basis and (b) true epidemiological concerns, such as the use of drugs by pregnant women and the potential for transmission of AIDS by intravenous drug users. Addiction treatment is now shamefully underfunded, with months-long waiting lists in many cities.

Purely individualized risks are not in principle a public health matter and are in any case trivial in magnitude compared to those now accepted from alcohol and tobacco. Francis Young of the DEA found no known lethal dose of marijuana. Even with cocaine, which has lethal potential, fewer than 2,000 deaths annually result from the consumption of billions of lines or puffs every year. In any event, harmfulness is not the sole touchstone of regulation.

(5) Respect the value of individual liberty and responsibility. The current administration's goal of a drug-free America is both ridiculous—as absurd as a liquor-free America—and wrong in principle. A democratic society must respect the decisions made by its adult citizens, even decisions perceived to be foolish or risky. After all, is it different in principle to protect the right of gun ownership, which produces some 10,000 to 12,000 homicides a year and thousands more nonfatal injuries? Is it different in principle to protect the right of motorcyclists, skydivers, or mountain climbers to risk their lives? Is it different to permit children to ride bicycles that "cause" tens of thousands of crippling injuries and deaths a year? To say that something is "dangerous" does not automatically supply a reason to outlaw it. Indeed, the general presumption in our society is that competent adults with access to necessary information are entitled to take risks of this kind as part of life, liberty, and the pursuit of happiness. Why are drugs different?

Only a totalitarian government would legislate these matters. After all, if the government is conceded to have the power to prohibit what is dangerous, does it not then have the power to compel what is safe? More specifically, if one drug can be prohibited on the ground that it is dangerous to the individual would it then not be permissible for the government to decree that beneficial doses of some other drug must be taken at specified intervals?

"Apart from the unique problem posed by drugs in the ghettos, anti-drug hysteria is far too common."

The freedom of American citizens has already been seriously eroded by the War on Drugs. More civil liberties hang in the balance of future legislation and executive actions. Is the defense of Americans from drugs to be analogized to the defense of the Vietnamese from communism? Was it necessary to destroy the city of Hue in order to save it? The national commission should give serious weight to this value in its policy recommendations.

4. *Focus on the big picture*

Present drug policy suffers from a kind of micro-think that borders on irresponsibility and is sometimes downright silly. This typically manifests itself in proud administration announcements or reports to congressional committees of a new initiative or accomplishment without regard to its impact on the bottom line. The examples are endless—a joint strike force with the government of the Bahamas; a shutdown of a source of supply; the Pizza Connection case, the largest organized crime heroin-trafficking case ever made by the federal government; a new bank secrecy agreement with the Cayman Islands; a new coca-eradication program in Bolivia or Peru; and so on. But none of these programs or "accomplishments" has ever made any noticeable or lasting impact on the drug supply. Even now, as the Godfather of Bolivian cocaine resides in a Bolivian prison, is there any observable reduction in the supply of cocaine? There must be insistence that enforcement programs make a difference in the real world.

The whole drug-enforcement enterprise needs to be put on a more businesslike basis, looking to the bottom line and not to isolated "achievements" of the War on Drugs. In fact, the investor analogy is a good one to use: if the War on Drugs were incorporated as a business enterprise, with its profits to be determined by its success in controlling drug abuse and drug trafficking, who would invest in it? Even if its operating budget were to be doubled, would it be a good personal investment? If not, why is it a good social investment? This kind of hardheaded thinking is exactly what is and has been lacking throughout the War on Drugs. No attention has been paid to considerations of cause and effect, or to trade-offs, or to cost-benefit analyses. New anti-drug initiatives are not subjected to critical questioning: What marginal gains, if any, can be projected from new programs or an additional commitment of resources? Conversely, how might things worsen?

"There is a paradox here: the use of less legal force may actually result in producing more control over the drug situation."

It is important to abjure meaningless, isolated "victories" in the War on Drugs and to focus on whether a program or policy offers some meaningful overall impact on the safety, security, and well-being of the American people. In this respect, does it really matter that the DEA doubled the number of drug arrests from 6,000 to 12,000 during the 1980s? Or that the Customs Service dramatically increased its drug seizures to nearly 200,000 pounds of cocaine? Or that a kingpin

like Carlos Lehder Rivas was convicted and imprisoned for life plus 135 years? Might it not be that the resources devoted to those anti-drug initiatives were not merely wasted but actually counter-productive?

Similarly, it is critical to pay scrupulous attention to cause and effect. Throughout the War on Drugs, administration officials have been making absurd claims about the effects of anti-drug policies. In 1988, President Reagan asserted that the War on Drugs was working. His evidence? Marijuana smoking was down to 18 million persons a year and experimentation with cocaine by high-school seniors in the University of Michigan survey declined by 20 percent. This is the classic fallacy of *post hoc, ergo propter hoc.*

Declining Drug Use

The same University of Michigan survey shows that marijuana consumption peaked in 1979, three years before the War on Drugs even began. Cocaine is purer, cheaper, and more available than ever before. Yet the 1988 National Institute of Drug Abuse Household Survey showed "current" (past month) use of cocaine down by 50 percent, and past-year use down from 12.2 million to 8.2 million, or roughly one-third. The survey reports that past-month use of all illicit drugs "continued a downward trend which began in 1979 and accelerated between 1985 and 1988." The decline is substantial—from 23 million in 1985 to 14.5 million in 1988.

That decline obviously occurred before the user-accountability crackdown of 1988. If use is down, it is not because of successful law enforcement. Most categories of drug use are down and will likely continue to go down as people become more educated and more concerned about health and fitness.

But the trend is much broader, encompassing cigarettes and liquor as well as illegal drugs. One important factor is the aging of the baby boom generation. That demographic bulge leaves fewer young people behind and thus contributes to the aging of the population as a whole. An older population is simply one that is less likely to use party drugs. Another probable cause is the resurgence in the 1980s of a post-hippie work ethic and careerism among the young, a preoccupation with getting and spending. Drugs don't fit so well into the style of the late 1980s.

To attribute these changes to law enforcement is at the least unprofessional. The liberalization of marijuana laws in California, Oregon, Maine, and elsewhere in the early 1970s produced no observable rise in consumption (either new users or increased frequency) of marijuana compared to other states. The connection between law and individual behavior at this level is remote. Government policies are no more responsible for the current decline in drug use than they were for the boom in the 1970s and early 1980s. Drug use will almost certainly continue to decline in the 1990s, no matter what law enforcement does, for roughly the same reasons that cigarette smoking and drinking of hard liquor have declined— without any change in law or law enforcement.

"The War on Drugs has produced a siege mentality."

---

5. *Substitute study for speculation*

The War on Drugs has produced a siege mentality. Senators from large states speak of invasions and national security threats. To a large extent, anxieties are focused on the sordid crack scene of the inner cities and revulsion at tragedies like cocaine babies. The fundamental fact of life is that the crack scene grew up and flourished under the regime of the War on Drugs. The war zone created by the confrontation between cops and crack dealers is hardly an advertisement for continuing the present approach. On the contrary, the ugliness of the crack scene confirms the folly of the War on Drugs, since law enforcement is the only thing that props up the price high enough to make it more worthwhile than selling apples or pencils. The sale of drugs is the only industry in the in-

ner cities; and the pathology we see there is a magnification of the pre-existing pathologies of the unwed mother and the unemployed single male through the lens of the money to be made dealing drugs. In short, drug money, rather than drugs, is the root of the evil.

Anti-drug Hysteria

Apart from the unique problem posed by drugs in the ghettos, anti-drug hysteria is far too common, even among professionals who should know better. A former director of the National Institute of Drug Abuse claimed that without the War on Drugs to restrain the people, we would have 60 million to 100 million users of cocaine in this country. This is extremely unlikely. But rather than trading assertion and counter-assertion, the real question is epistemological: How does the director know what he "knows"? Clearly, there is no empirical basis for his claim. It must therefore be an expression of fear or perhaps a political maneuver, but clearly something other than a statement of fact. Why would the director of the public agency most responsible for informing the public on drugs take that tack? Whatever his reasons, wild speculation is not the path to informed judgment and intelligent, workable policy. Why not truly confront the question of what less-restricted availability of cocaine would mean in terms of increased drug use, taking account of both prevalence and incidence?

There are a number of ways in which this might be done if we truly want to know the answers. One way is to do market research. A standard technique of market research is to conduct surveys and ask people about what they desire in a product in terms of price, quality, and other features. How much will they buy at various prices? The same techniques are adaptable, *mutatis mutandis*, to illegal drugs.

What about the effects of the drug? Is cocaine addictive? Longitudinal studies should be encouraged. Household Surveys by the NIDA register only gross numbers and do not track users. (They do not even cover group quarters, such as college dormitories and military barracks, where drug use may be higher than average.) At present we have almost no real-world knowledge of the experience of past and present cocaine users, except those unrepresentative few who come forward as former or recovering addicts. Even the NIDA has conceded that we lack any estimate of the relative proportions of addictive use versus experimental or other nonconsequential use in the total population of cocaine users. Isn't that critical information in regulating the drug?

"We have a lot to learn from the Dutch."

Drug users should be systematically interviewed, but they will be loath to step forward in the current climate of repression. Useful experiments might also be performed using volunteers from the prison population (for example, those serving life sentences without parole) and perhaps volunteers from the military services. How would people behave and how would their health fare with abundant access to cocaine? Would it be used widely or intensively or both? Finally, comparative studies from countries such as Holland can tell us a great deal about the effects of more freely available cannabis and heroin. We have a lot to learn from the Dutch.

A Paradox

There is a paradox here: the use of less legal force may actually result in producing more control over the drug situation in this country. Consider the analogy of a panic stop in an automobile. In a typical scenario, a driver observes a sudden obstruction in the road and slams on the brakes in order to avoid a collision. If too much force is used on the pedal, the sudden forward weight transfer will very likely induce front-wheel lockup. At that point, the car starts skidding out of control. If the driver turns the wheel left or right, the car will simply keep on skidding forward toward the very obstacle that the driver is trying to avoid. In this moment of panic, the "logical" or instinctive thing to do is to stomp the brake pedal even harder. But that is absolutely wrong. The correct thing to do to stop the skid is to modulate the brake pressure, releasing the pedal just enough to permit the front wheels to begin rolling again so that steering control is restored. Thus, the correct and safe response is counter-intuitive, while the instinctive response sends the driver skidding toward disaster.

The War on Drugs Cannot Be Won

Doniphan Blair

About the Author: *Doniphan Blair, a free-lance writer, filmmaker, and graphic designer, currently resides in Oakland, California.*

It's been over a year since the Bush administration declared war on drugs, and the front-line reports are still not promising victory. In 1989, hard-core drug use remained stable in American high schools, while drug production doubled worldwide according to recent State Department and government-funded studies. Meanwhile, the strategy of the Drug War has been attacked by a wide variety of professionals—from economists and police officers to psychologists. Although only a few dissenters have seriously discussed or even referred in passing to legalization (mostly from the political right—Milton Friedman, George Schultz, and William F. Buckley—as well as Judge Robert Sweet, Representative George Crockett, and Mayor Kurt Schmoke), most maintain that Drug War policy is seriously flawed or "modestly reworked Richard Nixon" at best.

Naturally, the Bush administration disagrees. Reiterating his commitment to current tactics, President Bush proclaimed that there would be "no shift in philosophy or emphasis from the first plan" when he unveiled his second Drug War budget on January 25, 1990. [Former] Drug Czar William Bennett, in particular, takes umbrage with Drug War defeatism and never tires of repeating that "the scourge is beginning to end." As evidence, he cites the decade-long decrease in casual use, the increase in arrests, the massive cocaine seizures of fall 1989, and the

Doniphan Blair, "Drug War Delusions." This article first appeared in the September/October issue of *The Humanist*, and is reprinted by permission.

recent "surrender" of the Colombian cartels. Even Charles Rangel, head of the House Committee on Narcotics and occasional administration critic, agrees: "If we really declare war—and all we've had is a war of words, we really haven't put the resources there . . . we can win."

Unfortunately, eradication and interdiction are futile, according to Robert Stutman, retired head of the New York office of the Drug Enforcement Administration [DEA]. Indeed, the Andean nations (Bolivia, Colombia, and Peru, in particular) cannot afford aggressive eradication—environmentally, economically, or politically. Defoliation poisons the land, and the projected U.S. aid of $450 million hardly compensates for a crop worth at least four times that amount. Military intervention does little more than force peasants into local insurgencies. For its own political reasons, the United States refrains from pressuring certain governments or prosecuting certain individuals. There have been no sanctions against Pakistan, whose $5 billion a year drug industry feeds a third of America's estimated 500,000 to one million heroin addicts, and Manuel Noriega's cocaine connection was well known to the CIA [Central Intelligence Agency] years before an invasion was mounted to facilitate his arrest.

> ## "American policy directly inspires drug use and the narcotics industry."

Even if the political will did exist, the sheer scope of the elimination strategy is a logistical nightmare. Heroin is difficult to interdict, say DEA officials, because of the variety of countries and smuggling routes involved. Realistically, the goal of destroying millions of acres of crops across three continents, sealing thousands of miles of border, and arresting hundreds of thousands of traffickers and dealers is technically infeasible. Especially intimidating is the fact that seizures and arrests have little long-term effect.

Product and personnel are quickly replaced by a highly capitalized industry that can easily develop new smuggling routes and methods and enlist new members. Despite the crackdown in Colombia initiated by President Virgilio Barco after the assassination of presidential candidate Carlos Galan, and despite the U.S. confiscation of almost 35 metric tons of cocaine in September 1989, the DEA admits that trafficking returned to near-normal levels by the end of October 1989. Seizures have risen over 4,000 percent since 1980, but the inflation-adjusted street price of cocaine is down more than 50 percent in many places.

"Demand is the determining factor of the drug market."

Economists point out that it is illogical to attempt financial disincentives at both ends of the drug pipeline. Even if enforcement could deflate growers' prices while inflating street costs, users would make do with less and pay more, thereby stimulating the black market. And if interdiction was completely successful, addicts would simply transfer their needs to more available substances. Aside from pharmaceuticals and American-made drugs such as amphetamines and PCP, there are hundreds of chemicals—from typewriter correction fluid to industrial solvents—that are currently used as intoxicants. These substances are much more toxic than organically derived drugs.

Demand is the determining factor of the drug market, just as it is in any other industry. According to the 2,000-plus police chiefs in 49 states who are diverting scarce resources to programs such as Drug Abuse Resistance Education (DARE), education is more cost effective than police work. Although President Bush finally conceded its importance at the Cartagena summit in February 1990, and although 30 percent of his $10.6 billion Drug War budget is earmarked for education and treatment, much of the remaining 70 percent attacks the most appropriate agency for effecting "demand reduction": the individual.

Incarceration, the only rehabilitation program universally available on demand, is not designed to promote the self-esteem, autonomy, and job skills needed for rehabilitation. "The best predictor of success is whether the addict has a job," says Dr. Charles Schuster, director of the National Institute of Drug Abuse. Even if drugs were not available in most prisons, isolation from drugs is no longer considered the critical factor. Dr. Herbert Kleber, assistant to William Bennett, believes that addiction stems more from the environment than the actual biochemical effect of the drug. Although Bennett has advocated incarceration over treatment, the prison setting contradicts Kleber's thesis of positive environmental "habilitation."

Whether in jails or clinics, addicts cannot be sequestered indefinitely. When they return to the streets, independence—not obedience—is more likely to help them withstand the powerful peer pressures and environmental cues that trigger relapse. "Subjects who are able to stop were less conforming and more independent," writes Donald Forgays in a NIDA monograph. Self-managed cures work well, he claims, despite their denigration by the rehab establishment. Of course, the 50 to 85 percent dropout rates of most rehab clinics indicate that all treatment depends upon self-motivation. The discipline and self-comprehension required for long-term sobriety cannot be coerced. Individuals must take responsibility for their own rehabilitation, according to Alcoholics Anonymous, one of the best-known and most successful programs, and one essentially based upon self-management.

Hope for an Instant Cure

Nevertheless, numerous scientists and citizens continue to hope for a magic bullet. Bush's Drug War budget allocated almost $400 million for researching psychotherapeutic drugs or antagonists, even though researchers admit that most users would not administer them voluntarily. Addicts want to get high—not destroy their capacity for pleasure, as many of these drugs threaten to do. Although it may be useful for the first dark nights of detoxification, pharmaceutical intervention also violates the individual's mental sovereignty.

Restricting free will or the capacity for pleasure also blocks the addict's ability to enjoy non-drug gratification, one of the basic objectives of rehabilitation. Counterattractions, as they were called by the temperance movement, are considered by many to be the best hedge against addiction or relapse. This parallels standard Marxist analysis: improve the quality of life—that is, liberate the masses—and drug demand would disappear.

"The United States holds the world record in per capita drug consumption."

Unfortunately, no one really knows what causes drug use, Dr. Kleber contends. "The person may be susceptible for psychological, biological, or socioeconomic factors, and for a combination of them. My guess is that in the United States, for example, two-thirds of the population is susceptible." Socioeconomic factors include both social deprivation and drug availability, but neither of these explains the addiction of the middle class, which finances the majority of America's $50 billion to $150 billion a year drug habit. While the biological disease argument has been fashionable since the 1950s, the latest neurological research focuses on the fuzzy world of human endorphin and enkephalin production, which is also controlled by psychological mood swings.

Despite continued research into genetic "predispositions" to addiction, the determining factor of drug use seems to be psychological. "Physical and psychic dependence characterize the addicted state," write George Koob and Floyd Bloom of the Scripps Clinic. "These two defini-tions are virtually inseparable when one attempts to identify the molecular and cellular elements of drug dependence." The drug's effect is also influenced by the user's limbic (automatic) nervous system, which produces tolerance as it resists the high, and the user's cortical (controllable) nervous system, which actually participates in the high (a process which must reverse during rehabilitation).

The user's selection of his or her drug of choice keys off innate temperament, according to some researchers, while the drug high itself only amplifies or diminishes preexisting mental states in most usage. Morphine, for example, still permits the perception of relatively slight sensation; it is only the relationship to feeling that is altered. The neurological connection further responsibilizes the addict, but it also reaffirms that overcoming automatic drug desire requires the strengthening of the controllable nervous system.

But there is another uncontrollable biological factor: heredity. Some scientists find a powerful genetic argument in the molecular similarity of human enzymes and hormones to certain drugs. Endorphins and enkephalins, for example, resemble opiates. "Our nervous system . . . is arranged to respond to chemical intoxicants in much the same way it responds to rewards of food, drink, and sex," explains UCLA researcher Ronald Siegel. "Intoxication is the fourth drive." This drive can be observed in the spinning games of children or the ritual drug use of primitive groups. "Experimentation with psychoactive substances by adolescents should be considered within the general framework of developmental processes (natural thrill-seeking) rather than as an indication of psychosocial pathology," according to researchers at Tel Aviv University. Nevertheless, no one is suggesting that prolonged or obsessive drug abuse is normal.

The American Malaise

Although addiction rates are high in Bogota, Zurich, and Bangkok, the United States holds the world record in per capita drug consumption. Undoubtedly, this phenomenon is related to America's obsession with instant gratification and consumerism, as well as its disposable income, its overreliance on medicine, and the alienation, pressure, and loss of values common to modern civilization. Still, there is ample evidence to suggest a more serious, specifically American malaise.

Most addictive behavior emerges during the turmoil of adolescence, when individuals are obliged to develop new relationships to themselves, their peer groups, and their society. Contemporary American adolescents mature younger, participate in fewer transitional rituals, and must integrate into a diverse, complex, and confusing society. Consequently, they may be more tempted to cling to adolescent ideals, childhood fantasies, or infantile obsessions.

Although psychological problems are generally precipitated by physical or emotional trauma, extreme contradictions between ideals and reality can lead to intellectual trauma. Veterans of the Vietnam War experienced the highest historical levels of post-traumatic stress syndrome because of the degree to which U.S. activities and rationales violated their ideals. Similarly, impoverished Americans have difficulty reconciling the image of their country's wealth and ethical tradition—with which the media bombards them daily—to the reality they find on the streets.

"If addicts must assume responsibility in order to rehabilitate, it is only logical that society must do so."

According to ex-CIA station chief John Stockwell, U.S. covert activities in Vietnam, Cambodia, Indonesia, Latin America, and elsewhere have led to the deaths of up to 6 million individuals. Such tragedies are devastating enough without tacitly or overtly claiming that they are morally correct. The truths that the founding fathers held to be self-evident cannot simultaneously be proclaimed and contravened without causing the socially derived schizophrenia observed by many researchers in totalitarian regimes. In addition, as recent events in the Soviet Union illustrate, a society's openness also highlights its moral hypocrisy. Meanwhile, in the United States, almost twice as many blacks are in jail as are attending college—a situation that would lead to a de facto genocide if the Bush administration's program of more arrests and increased prison sentences is successfully prosecuted.

The American Dream

The same expectations that make children sensitive to the nonloving actions of their parents make Americans, of any race or class, especially prone to ethical trauma. As an individual's financial and legal power, education, or access to information increases, the more contradictions he or she would tend to perceive, both psychologically and politically. In order to maintain the all-powerful illusion of the American Dream without admitting its errors or correcting them, Americans gravitate toward apathy and dysfunctional solutions (defending the Constitution by violating it, as with Oliver North, or attempting to adjust the conflicting ethical relationships with drugs).

In addition to a background of mixed ethical signals, American policy directly inspires drug use and the narcotics industry—economically, legally, psychologically, and morally. First of all, residents of disenfranchised communities—in the inner city or the Third World—naturally see drugs as a profitable commodity or cash crop. They need only look to America for their basic business education or to learn how a people in less dire financial straits accommodates ethical considerations. In addition to the traditional inequities of the industrialized nation-developing nation relationship, the United States continues to export illegal pharmaceuticals, insecticides, weapons, and cocaine manufacturing chemistry back to South America (the DEA finally moved to block suspected precursor chemical shipments on February 6, 1990) and continues to profit from the laundering of narcodollars.

"The United States will eventually be obliged to address its drug problem through freedom and honesty."

Secondly, by repeating all the historical mistakes of Prohibition, the legal response has escalated the Drug War. Over the past ten years, the street price of marijuana has risen up toward $300 an ounce and coke has become the proletariat's drug of choice as law enforcement pushed the industry toward more compact, transportable, and profitable drugs as well as better marketing (the improved packaging and large discounts of crack). Consequently, the fantastic sums of money and lengthy jail sentences involved have devalued life and spawned a murder rate inconceivable in the marijuana trade. Thirdly, there is the psychological ambiance. "Nothing can stand in the way of freedom's march," President Bush has proclaimed, and North American drug users and South American drug traffickers have taken him as much at his word as the citizens of Eastern Europe. They don't have to read John Stuart Mill's defense of opium use in On Liberty to recognize that regulating a population's bloodstream violates obvious principles of liberty, privacy, and the pursuit of happiness. Current efforts to increase testing and search and seizure fly in the face of long trends toward liberalization as well as the recent revolution in acceptable personal behavior. Moreover, testing further impugns the authority of the individual, who is held responsible anyway for errors committed while sober.

Finally, the moral ascendency of drug prohibition is called into question by the massive, socially sanctioned consumption of tobacco, alcohol, and prescription drugs, with related mortalities soaring over 400,000 per year. While some 3,500 individuals overdosed on cocaine in 1989 the pharmaceutical Darvan, no more effective than aspirin, killed over 1,000 people (after first addicting them). On the other hand, heroin, the most effective pain reliever known to science, is prohibited even for terminally ill patients. These discrepancies imply that the criterion for illegality is nothing more than a puritan taboo against excessive pleasure and that the obsessive demonization of illegal drugs is simply a cover-up for the rampant abuse of legal drugs and intoxicants.

The Scapegoat Syndrome

Object elimination encourages denial. By focusing on the objects of the Drug War (the drugs and the drug traffickers), it is easier to deny responsibility for the causes of the drug problem. Ironically, the scapegoat syndrome is equally evident in the rationales of individuals using the drugs as of those calling for increased drug repression. But if addicts must assume responsibility in order to rehabilitate, it is only logical that society must do so as well. Indeed, America appears to be evolving toward increased social and individual accountability in most other quarters. If these traditions continue to grow, the United States will eventually be obliged to address its drug problem through freedom and honesty, rather than by trimming back on those qualities so essential to democracy.

The bottom line should be that intrinsic contradictions in American society foster drug use, and that societal honesty and individual liberty—of which legalization is but a part—foster drug avoidance and rehabilitation.

The War on Drugs Threatens Civil Liberties

Edward M. Kennedy

About the Author: *Edward M. Kennedy, a U.S. senator from Massachusetts since 1962, has been influential in passing civil rights legislation. He served as the assistant majority leader from 1969 to 1971. Kennedy serves on the armed services, judiciary, labor and human resources, and joint economic committees. He is also the author of* Decisions for a Decade *and* In Critical Condition.

It is in times of great unrest that constitutional protections are most at risk, and therefore most important. I want to address the role of the Constitution in one of the most unsettling challenges confronting contemporary society—the nation's battle against drugs.

We call it a war, but it is a lopsided war; a war in which we depend too much on police, courts, and prisons to wage battles that others should be fighting, too.

Law enforcement has an indispensable role to play in combating drug abuse. But it cannot do the job alone. Enduring victories will not be gained until students are persuaded that drugs are harmful, until communities create a climate in which drugs are unacceptable, and until drug treatment is available to all who want to kick their habit.

Excessive reliance on criminal law to solve this deeply rooted social problem is not only doomed to failure, it threatens to distort our criminal justice system.

We are willing to spend vast resources building prisons to warehouse drug offenders. We are

Edward M. Kennedy, "Fight Evil, Forget Freedom," *Human Rights*, Fall/Winter 1990. Reprinted with permission.

willing to expend the time of clogged courts to administer assembly-line justice to a mushrooming rag-tag army of addicts. Yet we are unwilling to invest commensurate resources in the treatment and education programs that could stop these crimes from happening in the first place.

We are fighting a war on drugs in which the two principal weapons are a blank check policy for law enforcement and a bankrupt policy for prevention, education, and treatment of drug abuse. These priorities are unacceptable.

Inevitably, our distorted battle plan in the war on drugs has begun to undermine the freedoms in the Bill of Rights. As the goal of a drug-free America continues to evade us, the nation as a whole, egged on by irresponsible public officials, seems increasingly willing to wage war on the Constitution as well—and we must not let that happen.

"The war on drugs has begun to undermine the freedoms in the Bill of Rights."

The Fourth Amendment guarantees the right to be free from unreasonable searches and seizures. It is an inherently American right, born of colonial anger over the abusive tactics of King George. As Justice Brennan wrote, quoting Justice Brandeis, "The Fourth Amendment rests on the principle that a true balance between the individual and society depends on the recognition of 'the right to be let alone—the most comprehensive of rights and the right most valued by civilized men.'"

What we see now, however, is the emergence of a "drug exception" to the Fourth Amendment.

Drug courier profiles, traditionally and appropriately used with other evidence of criminality, are now employed by overzealous officials as the sole basis for stopping individuals on suspicion. It's doubtful that experts or anyone else can tell us, with an acceptable degree of certainty, what a drug dealer looks like. The potential for abuse and bias stemming from racial and other stereotyping is obvious. The war on drugs must never become a war on black Americans, Hispanic Americans, poor Americans, or any other class of Americans.

Drug courier profiles are also being used as a pretext for another troubling practice in law enforcement. A police officer approaches a citizen on a hunch or because the individual matches one aspect of the profile. Lacking the reasonable suspicion required by the Constitution, the officer asks "consent" for a pat-down or more intrusive search.

Few citizens, law-abiding or not, feel free to refuse the officer's request or to challenge his badge and authority. Even in ordinary times, police questioning may be seen as threatening—even by law-abiding citizens. But these are not ordinary times, and in communities across the country such actions are acquiring the whiff of police state tactics.

More and more courts today, influenced by the drug scare in the same way that courts in the McCarthy era were influenced by the Communist scare, have stretched the Fourth Amendment beyond acceptable limits to accommodate this practice. The Reagan-Bush judiciary is routinely upholding the legality of searches involving citizens who fit no profile at all, people who are stopped simply at random in bus, train, or airplane terminals.

The Fourth Amendment is also being challenged by the unthinking resort to random drug testing. The technique is appropriate when based on reasonable suspicion, such as after a worksite accident. But random testing of individuals not engaged in safety-sensitive activities is a degrading invasion of privacy and should not be permitted.

Right of Due Process

The war on drugs is also exerting pressure on the Fifth Amendment right to due process. Overreliance on criminal sanctions to deal with drug abuse has stretched the resources of the legal system to the breaking point. As a result, individual cases are receiving less and less consideration—and defendants are receiving less and less due process.

"The Constitution is perfectly capable of accommodating the legitimate interests of law enforcement."

Recently, officials in the Department of Housing and Urban Development launched a nationwide strategy to seize public housing units where drug dealing has allegedly occurred. Nothing wrong with that, you say? Yes, there is. The plan called for eviction of residents without notice, without even an opportunity to be heard.

A federal court in Richmond declared the tactic flatly unconstitutional. But the administration refused to be deterred. It announced that drug evictions would go forward in other cities—as though due process means less for Chicago or Boston than it does for Richmond.

Eventually, a nationwide restraining order was obtained. The HUD procedures were revised, and lawful seizures have been carried out. But the lesson of that sorry episode is clear. The Constitution is perfectly capable of accommodating the legitimate interests of law enforcement—but end runs around the Bill of Rights are unacceptable, and it is irresponsible for any administration committed to the rule of law to try them.

If the Fourth and Fifth Amendments have sometimes fallen victim to the war on drugs, so has the Sixth Amendment. The ABA [American Bar Association] deserves great credit for its leadership in defending the right to counsel. But the lawyer-client relationship is under attack on several fronts. Pretrial seizures of assets, for example, are occurring under circumstances that undermine a defendant's right to have the lawyer of his choice.

In turn, this abuse is having a significant impact on public defenders. Yet their needs continue to be ignored. The president's most recent national drug strategy requested additional funds for almost everyone in sight—the FBI [Federal Bureau of Investigation], the Drug Enforcement Administration, the U.S. Attorneys' offices, and even the National Park Rangers—but not one penny for public defenders.

The IRS [Internal Revenue Service] is getting into the act as well. It is threatening civil and criminal actions against attorneys who refuse to disclose the identities of clients who pay in cash. Forcing lawyers to break the attorney-client privilege is wrong. Defense lawyers serve a vital role in our adversarial system of justice. We must not permit the war on drugs to degenerate into a war on lawyers.

Finally, I cite the Eighth Amendment and its ban on cruel and unusual punishment. In the drug war, excessive punishment is becoming the order of the day. Mandatory minimum sentences are proliferating, with profound consequences for prison crowding. The sweeping feel-good death penalty legislation that recently passed the Senate included the unprecedented expansion of the death penalty to drug crimes that do not result in death.

A Paper Tiger

As an antidrug strategy, the death penalty is a paper tiger. It looks tough. It sounds tough. But it isn't tough. Capital punishment is full of sound and fury, but it signifies nothing. Demagoging the death penalty is no answer to the drug epidemic.

Not everyone agrees that the death penalty is cruel and unusual punishment and therefore unconstitutional. Certainly, the Supreme Court does not agree, although I hope one day it will. But we need not subscribe to that view to be concerned that executing a defendant who has not killed is an excessive punishment.

"Demagoging the death penalty is no answer to the drug epidemic."

Resorting to the death penalty raises equal protection concerns as well. Study after study presents compelling evidence that race discrimination permeates capital sentencing decisions throughout the country. Discrimination is unacceptable in any context, but nowhere is it more intolerable than in the awesome determination of who shall live and who shall die.

In sum, in ways both obvious and subtle, key parts of the Bill of Rights—the Fourth, Fifth, Sixth, and Eighth Amendments—are under siege.

Ironically, the part of the Bill of Rights that this administration tries hardest to honor is wrongly honored. The Second Amendment does not prohibit Congress or the states from imposing reasonable restrictions on the sale of assault rifles, Saturday Night Specials, or any other firearms.

It is time to end the arms race on our city streets. And the way to begin is to do all we can to take these weapons out of the hands of drug traffickers and other criminals. . . .

Our constitutional rights do not contribute to the drug problem, and compromising them will not solve it. We do not need to trample the Bill of Rights to win the war on drugs.

Chapter 2:
Should Drugs Be Legalized?

Preface

Drug laws in the United States have undergone many changes in the last hundred years. In the nineteenth and early twentieth centuries, for example, cocaine and opium were not only legal but were widely used. Small amounts of cocaine were part of the recipe for the beverage Coca-Cola, and laudanum, derived from opium, was a common sedative and sleep aid. Public concern about the dangers of drug addiction, however, began to spread as doctors and private citizens began to understand more about the seriousness of addiction to these drugs. In response to this growing public concern, the government passed the first national drug law, the Pure Food and Drug Act, in 1906. The act required the accurate labeling of patent medications containing opium and certain other drugs. Although these drugs were still legal, manufacturers were required to notify the public of the presence of these drugs in their products.

In response to growing public antipathy to drug use and drug addiction, the government passed the Harrison Narcotics Act (HNA) in 1914. The act completely banned the sale of substantial doses of opium and coca, the source of cocaine. The HNA still permitted the import and export of the drugs for medical purposes, but the government regulated and taxed the drugs. Initially, the HNA permitted doctors to prescribe drugs to addicts to maintain their addiction. Later, as increased knowledge about drug addiction reduced the number of casual drug users, the public pressured the government to stop doctors from prescribing drugs for addicts. Eventually, the government acquiesced to public demands and completely banned coca and opium.

Drug trafficking became a problem in the years that followed the Harrison Narcotics Act. Smugglers secretly began bringing opium, heroin, and cocaine into the U.S. to sell to addicts. In 1918, a special committee studied the effects of the HNA and found that drug smuggling from Mexico and other drug-producing countries into the U.S. had increased. An article in the *Illinois Medical Journal* in 1926 addressed the HNA saying, "Instead of stopping the traffic, those who deal in dope now make double their money from the poor unfortunates upon whom they prey." Some people began to question the effectiveness of laws banning certain drugs, despite public support for those laws.

Although the committee found that the HNA was ineffective, the public continued to support the government's policy of creating and enforcing strict drug laws. In 1924, Congress banned heroin entirely, and in 1937 the government passed the Marihuana Tax Act. This act required those who used marijuana to obtain a special license. However, since licenses were not available to private citizens, the act effectively banned marijuana. In addition, the act imposed heavy penalties on drug smugglers, culminating in the 1956 U.S. Narcotic Drug Control Act, which permitted the death penalty for selling heroin to minors. The act was passed in response to increased heroin trafficking and addiction in America's major cities. However, heroin was not the only drug Americans were using.

Beginning in the mid-1960s, the popularity of drugs such as marijuana, hallucinogens, and opiates increased dramatically. In response, President Richard Nixon declared drugs "America's public enemy No. 1," and Congress then devoted $1 billion to stopping drug trafficking. Nixon's methods included increased enforcement of drug laws, but drug use continued to rise.

By the early 1980s, more than 25 percent of young adults were using marijuana on a fairly regular basis. In response to this, the Reagan administration began to increase funding to enforce drug laws both against users and against drug smugglers and sellers. The government's concerns intensified with the rising use and availability of crack, a highly addictive, cheap, smokable version of cocaine. The Reagan administration took, and the Bush administration continues to take, a hard stance against drugs, devoting more money and strengthening laws to address the problem of drug trafficking.

However, many experts have denounced these increased efforts as ineffective. According to lawyer James Ostrowski, drug-trafficking profits from black-market sales have increased as a result of drug laws. Increased risk of arrest and the possibility of drug seizures encourage traffickers to increase their prices. Drug-related crimes such as murder, including the executions of debt-ridden drug addicts and the assassinations of police informants, are on the rise. In addition, armed robberies committed by addicts to

finance their addiction have increased. Rising crime rates, the ballooning costs of enforcing drug laws, and the continued and widespread availability of illegal drugs have caused some people to advocate the legalization of drugs.

Benefits Of Legalization

These advocates claim many immediate benefits from legalizing drugs. They contend that first, legalization would relieve the financial burden of enforcing drug laws. Second, drug-related murders and robberies would decrease, since legalization would end street sales of drugs and make them cheaper. Finally and most importantly, supporters claim, legalizing drugs would end drug trafficking. Federal judge Robert Sweet, the district judge for the southern district of New York says, "I have come to the conclusion that we must abolish the prohibition of drugs. . . . Prohibition policies only fuel the engine of drug abuse."

Opponents of legalization scoff at these optimistic claims, arguing instead that legalizing illegal drugs will only exacerbate the nation's drug problem by making drugs more widely available. One opponent of legalization, University of Delaware professor of criminal justice James A. Inciardi, believes that legalization would cause drug use to skyrocket in minority communities, where drugs are most available. Former director of the Office of National Drug Control Policy, William Bennett, argues that legalizing drugs would not eliminate the black-market traffic in drugs. Instead, he contends, drug traffickers would offer even more dangerous, still-illegal drugs for addicts to consume. He also maintains that drug traffickers desperate for profits would sell more forcefully to children too young to purchase drugs legally. These critics contend that drugs must remain illegal.

Legalization and prohibition of illegal drugs provide the focus for the following chapter. The articles debate the merits of both prohibition and legalization in an effort to provide a solution to the nation's intractable drug problem.

Should Drugs Be Legalized?

Yes: Legalizing Drugs Would Solve the Drug Problem

Legalizing Drugs Will Solve America's Drug Problem
Drugs Should Be Legalized
Legalizing Drugs Can Reduce Drug Abuse
Prohibiting Illegal Drugs Has Failed
Legalizing Drugs Would Have Many Benefits

Legalizing Drugs Will Solve America's Drug Problem

James Ostrowski

About the Author: *James Ostrowski is a Buffalo, New York, attorney and former vice chairman of the New York County Lawyers Association Committee on Law Reform.*

Most of the serious problems that the public tends to associate with illegal drug use in reality are caused directly or indirectly by drug prohibition. Let's assume the war on drugs was given up as the misguided enterprise it is. What would happen? The day after legalization went into effect, the streets of America would be safer. The drug dealers would be gone. The shootouts between drug dealers would end. Innocent bystanders no longer would be murdered. Hundreds of thousands of drug "addicts" would stop roaming the streets, shoplifting, mugging, breaking into homes in the middle of the night to steal, and dealing violently with those who happened to wake up. One year after prohibition was repealed, 1,600 innocent people who otherwise would have been dead at the hands of drug criminals would be alive.

Within days of prohibition repeal, thousands of judges, prosecutors, and police would be freed to catch, try, and imprison violent career criminals who commit 50 to 100 serious crimes per year when on the loose, including robbery, rape, and murder. For the first time in years, our overcrowded prisons would have room for them. Ultimately, repeal of prohibition would open up

75,000 jail cells. The day after repeal, organized crime would get a big pay cut—$80,000,000,000 a year.

How about those drug dealers who are the new role models for the youth of inner cities, with their designer clothes and Mercedes convertibles, always wearing a broad, smug smile that says crime pays? They snicker at the honest kids going to school or to work at the minimum wage. The day after repeal, the honest kids will have the last laugh. The dealers will be out of a job. The day after repeal, real drug education can begin and, for the first time in history, it can be honest. There will be no more need to prop up the failed war on drugs.

"Drug prohibition has been an extremely costly failure."

The year before repeal, 500,000 Americans would have died from illnesses related to overeating and lack of exercise, 390,000 from smoking, and 150,000 from drinking alcohol. About 3,000 would have died from cocaine, heroin, and marijuana combined, with many of these deaths the result of the lack of quality control in the black market. The day after repeal, cocaine, heroin, and marijuana, by and large, would do no harm to those who chose not to consume them. In contrast, the day before prohibition repeal, all Americans, whether or not they elected to use illegal drugs, were forced to endure the violence, street crime, erosion of civil liberties, corruption, and social and economic decay triggered by illegal drug use.

Today's war on drugs is immoral as well as impractical. It imposes enormous costs on large numbers of non-drug-abusing citizens in the failed attempt to save a relatively small group of hard-core drug abusers from themselves. It is immoral and absurd to force some people to bear costs so that others might be prevented from choosing to do harm to themselves. This crude utilitarian sacrifice—so at odds with traditional

American values—never has been, and never can be, justified. That is why the war on drugs must end and why it *will* be ended once the public comes to understand the truth about this destructive policy.

"Each dollar spent on drug enforcement yields seven dollars in economic *loss*."

What about the economic impact of prohibition? First, take a common estimate of annual black market drug sales—$80,000,000,000. Because the black market price of drugs is inflated, at the very least, 10-fold over what the legal price would likely be, 90%, or about $70,000,000,000, constitutes an economic loss caused by prohibition. That is, the drug user and his dependents are deprived of the purchasing power of 90% of the money he spends on illegal drugs without any *net* benefit accruing to the economy as a whole. The added expenditure by the drug user pays for the dramatically increased costs of producing and selling illegal drugs. Large amounts of land, labor, and capital, not required in the legal drug market, are utilized in the illicit one. The high prices users pay for illegal drugs compensate dealers for their expenditure of these resources, as well as for the risk of violence and imprisonment they face. In a world of scarce prison resources, sending a drug offender to prison for one year is equivalent to freeing a violent criminal to commit 40 robberies, seven assaults, 110 burglaries, and 25 auto thefts.

Ironically, the economic loss to users under prohibition frequently is cited as a justification for prohibition. However, this harm is a major cost of prohibition, to be held against it in the debate over legalization. The total cost of drug-related law enforcement—courts, police, prisons, on all levels of government—is about $10,000,000,000 each year. In a sense, each dollar spent on drug enforcement yields seven dollars in economic *loss*. That is, prohibition takes $10,000,000,000 from taxpayers and uses it to raise $80,000,000,000 for organized crime and drug dealers, impoverishing many users in the process. To pay for expensive black market drugs, poor users then victimize the taxpayers again by stealing $7,500,000,000 from them.

This $80,000,000,000 figure does not include a number of other negative economic consequences of prohibition that are difficult to estimate, such as the lost productivity of those who die as a result of prohibition, those in prison on drug convictions, and users who must "hustle" all day to pay for their drugs; the costs imposed by organized crime activities funded by narcotics profits; government and private funds spent on prohibition-related illnesses such as AIDS, hepatitis, and accidental overdose; and the funds spent on private security to fight drug-related crime.

Another financial toll merits special mention—the negative impact of prohibition on the economic viability of inner cities and their inhabitants. Prohibition-related violence and property crime raise costs, make loans and insurance difficult or impossible to secure, and make it difficult to attract skilled workers. Prohibition lures some workers away from legitimate businesses and into the black market, where salaries are astronomically higher. As long as a black market in illegal drugs thrives in the inner cities, it is difficult to see how they ever can become economically viable.

Laws Are Ineffective

The fatal flaw in the policy of prohibition is that those who need to be protected most—hard-core users—are those least likely to be deterred by laws against drugs. For these individuals, drug use is one of the highest values in life. They will take great risks, pay exorbitant prices, and violate the law in pursuit of drugs. Further, it is naive to think that prohibition relieves prospective or even moderate drug users of the need to make responsible decisions with respect to illegal drugs. It is too easy and inexpensive to obtain a few batches of crack or heroin to claim that prohibition obviates individual choice. Consumer preference—not law enforcement—is the likely explanation for the existence of 20,000,000 marijuana smokers, but only 500,000 heroin users. If 20,000,000 people sought heroin, the black market would meet that demand, perhaps with synthetic substitutes, just as it met the enormous demand for alcohol in the 1920's. Prohibition is a comforting illusion at best.

"Governmental intrusions into our most personal activities are the natural and necessary consequence of drug prohibition."

Perhaps the most telling indicator of the ineffectiveness of U.S. drug laws is their failure to reduce the overall use of illegal substances. On a per capita basis, the use of narcotics was no more prevalent before prohibition than it is today, and the use of cocaine is more widespread than when it was legally available. In 1915, the year the first national control laws became effective, there were about 200,000 regular narcotics users and only 20,000 regular cocaine users. Today, there are about 500,000 regular heroin users and 2,000,000 regular cocaine users. (Opium and morphine essentially have been driven out of circulation by the more profitable heroin. Prohibition has not reduced use, but it has made narcotics more powerful.) Thus, with a population more than twice what it was in 1915, the percentage of Americans using narcotics has remained the same, while cocaine use has increased by more than 4,000%. Seventy years of intensive law enforcement efforts have failed to reduce drug use measurably.

The failure of drug control should not be surprising. During Prohibition, drinkers switched from beer and wine to hard liquor, often of dubious quality, resulting in a drastic increase in deaths from alcohol poisoning. Whether Prohibition actually reduced total consumption is disputed, but it *is* known that its repeal did not lead to an explosive increase in drinking. More recently, in those states that have decriminalized marijuana, no substantial increase in use has occurred. When the Netherlands decriminalized marijuana in 1978, use actually declined.

Common sense indicates that illegal drugs always will be readily available. Prison wardens cannot keep drugs out of their own institutions—an important lesson for those who would turn this country into a prison to stop drug use. Police officers regularly are caught using, selling, and stealing drugs. How are these people going to lead a war on drugs?

Drug money corrupts law enforcement officials. Corruption is a major problem in drug enforcement because drug agents are given tremendous power over desperate people in possession of large amounts of cash. Drug corruption charges have been leveled against FBI agents, police officers, prison guards, U.S. Customs inspectors, even prosecutors. In 1986, in New York City's 77th Precinct, 12 police officers were arrested for stealing and selling drugs. Miami's problem is worse. In June, 1986, seven officers there were indicted for using their jobs to run a drug operation that used murders, threats, and bribery. Add to that two dozen other cases of corruption in the last three years in Miami alone. We must question a policy that so frequently turns police officers into criminals.

Civil Liberties Threatened

Drug hysteria also has created an atmosphere in which long-cherished rights are discarded whenever narcotics are concerned. Urine-testing, roadblocks, routine strip searches, school locker searches without probable cause, preventive detention, and nonjudicial forfeiture of property are routine weapons in the war on drugs. These governmental intrusions into our most personal activities are the natural and necessary consequence of drug prohibition. It is no accident that a law review article entitled "Crackdown: The Emerging 'Drug Exception' to the Bill of Rights" was published in a law journal in 1987. Explaining why drug prohibition, by its very nature, threatens civil liberties, law professor Randy Barnett notes that drug offenses differ from violent crimes in that there rarely is a complaining witness to a drug transaction. Because sales are illegal, but their participants are willing, the transactions are hidden from police view. Thus, to be at all effective, drug agents must intrude into the innermost private lives of *suspected* drug criminals.

"Because there is no quality control in the black market, prohibition also kills by making drug use more dangerous."

Dangerous precedents are tolerated in the war on drugs, but they represent a permanent increase in government power for all purposes. The tragedy is how cheaply our rights have been sold. Our society was once one in which the very thought of men and women being strip-searched and forced to urinate in the presence of witnesses was revolting. That now seems like a long time ago. All of this stems from a policy that simply does not work, since it is prohibition itself that causes the very problems that make these extreme measures seem necessary to a befuddled public.

In spite of the greatest anti-drug enforcement effort in U.S. history, the drug problem is worse than ever. What should be done now—get tougher in the war on drugs, imprison middle-class drug users, use the military, impose the death penalty for drug dealing, shoot down unmarked planes entering the U.S.? The *status quo* is intolerable, as everyone agrees. However, there are only two alternatives—further escalate the war on drugs or legalize them. Once the public grasps the consequences of escalation, legalization may win out by default.

Escalating the war on drugs is doomed to fail,

as it did under Pres. Richard M. Nixon, Gov. Nelson A. Rockefeller in New York, and Pres. Ronald Reagan. It is confronted by a host of seemingly intractable problems: lack of funds, prison space, and political will to put middle-class users in jail, and the sheer impossibility of preventing consenting adults in a free society from engaging in extremely profitable transactions involving tiny amounts of illegal drugs.

Yet, none of these factors ultimately explains why escalating the war on drugs wouldn't work. Failure is guaranteed because the black market thrives on the war on drugs and benefits from any intensification of it. At best, increased enforcement simply boosts the black market price, encouraging suppliers to supply more drugs. The publicized conviction of a dealer, by instantly creating a vacancy in the lucrative drug business, has the same effect as hanging up a help-wanted sign saying, "Drug dealer needed— $5,000 a week to start—exciting work."

Furthermore, there is a real danger that escalating the war on drugs would squander much of the nation's wealth and freedom, causing enormous social disruption. No limit is yet in sight to the amount of money and new enforcement powers that committed advocates of prohibition will demand before giving up on that approach.

Drug Crusades

As author Thomas Sowell writes, "policies are judged by their consequences, but crusades are judged by how good they make the crusaders feel." So, the question must be: do drug laws cause more harm than good? Drug laws greatly increase the price of illegal substances, often forcing users to steal to get the money to obtain them. Although difficult to estimate, the black market prices of heroin and cocaine appear to be about 100 times greater than their pharmaceutical prices. For example, a hospital-dispensed dose of morphine, a drug from which heroin is derived relatively easily, costs only pennies; legal cocaine costs about $20 per ounce. It frequently is estimated that at least 40% of all property crime in the U.S. is committed by drug users so they can maintain their habits. That amounts to about 4,000,000 crimes per year and $7,500,000,000 in stolen property.

"Drugs motivate some people— those who most need protection from them—more than any penalties a civilized society can impose."

Supporters of prohibition traditionally have used drug-related crime as a simplistic argument for enforcement: stop drug use to halt such criminal acts. They even have exaggerated the amount of such crime in the hopes of demonstrating a need for larger budgets and greater powers. In recent years, however, the more astute prohibitionists have noticed that drug-related crime is, in fact, drug-*law*-related. Thus, in many cases, they have begun to argue that, even if drugs were legal and thus relatively inexpensive, users still would commit crimes simply because they are criminals at heart. The fact is, while some researchers have questioned the causal connection between illegal drugs and street crime, many studies over a long period have confirmed what every inner-city dweller already knows: users steal to get the money to buy expensive illegal drugs. Moreover, prohibition also stimulates crime by criminalizing users of illegal drugs, thus creating disrespect for the law; forcing users into daily contact with professional criminals, which often leads to arrest and prison records that make legitimate employment difficult to obtain; discouraging legitimate employment because of the need to "hustle" for drug money; encouraging young people to become criminals by creating an extremely lucrative black market in drugs; destroying, through drug crime, the economic viability of low-income neighborhoods, leaving young people fewer alternatives to working in the black market; and removing the settling of drug-related disputes from the legal process, creating a context of violence for the buying and selling of narcotics.

In addition, every property crime committed by a drug user is potentially a violent one. Many victims are beaten and severely injured, and 1,600 are murdered each year. In 1988, a 16-year-old boy murdered 39-year-old Eli Wald of Brooklyn, father of a baby girl, taking $200 to buy crack. Another New York City crack user murdered five people in an eight-day period to get the money to buy crack.

Prohibition also causes what the media and police misname "drug-related violence." This is really *prohibition*-related violence, and includes all the random shootings and murders associated with black market transactions—rip-offs, eliminating the competition, and killing informers and suspected informers. The President's Commission on Organized Crime estimates a total of about 70 drug-market murders yearly in Miami alone. Based on that figure and FBI data, a reasonable nationwide estimate would be at least 750 such murders each year. Recent estimates from New York and Washington suggest an even higher figure. Those who doubt that prohibition is responsible for this violence need only note the absence of violence in the legal drug market. For example, there is no violence associated with the production, distribution, and sale of alcohol. Such violence was ended by the repeal of Prohibition.

Health and Social Consequences

Because there is no quality control in the black market, prohibition also kills by making drug use more dangerous. Illegal drugs contain poisons, are of uncertain potency, and are injected with dirty needles. Many deaths are caused by infections, accidental overdoses, and poisoning. At least 3,500 people each year will die from AIDS caused by using unsterile needles, a greater number than the combined death toll from cocaine and heroin. These casualties include the sexual partners and children of intravenous drug users. Drug-related AIDS is almost exclusively the result of drug prohibition. Users inject drugs rather than taking them in tablet form because tablets are expensive; go to "shooting galleries" to avoid arrests for possessing drugs and needles; and share needles because these implements are illegal and thus difficult to obtain. In Hong Kong, where needles are legal, there are *no* cases of drug-related AIDS.

As many as 2,400 of the 3,000 deaths attributed to heroin and cocaine use each year—80%—actually are caused by black market factors. For example, many heroin deaths are the result of an allergic reaction to the street mixture of the drug, while 30% are caused by infections. The attempt to protect users from themselves has backfired, as it did during Prohibition. The drug laws have succeeded only in making use much more dangerous and in driving it underground, out of the reach of moderating social and medical influences.

"The law simply cannot deter millions of people deeply attracted to drugs."

Drug prohibition has had devastating effects on inner-city minority communities. A poorly educated young person in the inner city now has three choices—welfare, a low-wage job, or the glamorous and high-profit drug business. It is no wonder that large numbers of ghetto youth have gone into drug dealing. How can a mother maintain authority over a 16-year-old son who pays the rent out of his petty cash? How can a teacher persuade students to study hard, when dropouts drive BMW's? The profits from prohibition make a mockery of the work ethic and of family authority.

A related problem is that prohibition also forces users to come into contact with people of real criminal intent. For all the harm that alcohol and tobacco do, one does not have to deal with criminals to use those substances. Prohibition drags the drug user into a criminal culture.

Once accustomed to breaking the law by using drugs and to dealing with criminals, it is hard for the user, and especially the dealer, to maintain respect for other laws. Honesty, respect for private property, and similar marks of a law-abiding community are further casualties. When the huge illicit profits and violence of the illegal-drug business permeate a neighborhood, it ceases to be a functioning community. The consequences range from the discouraging of legitimate businesses to disdain for education and violence that makes mail carriers and ambulance drivers afraid to enter housing complexes.

Drug Switching

Drug switching is another issue that any regime of control must face. What is the point of attempting to limit access to certain drugs, when the user merely turns to other, more dangerous ones? For example, opium use in China may or may not have been reduced vastly, but tranquilizers and sedative pills have been used widely in China, and they are easily available on the market. Furthermore, two-thirds of all Chinese men now smoke cigarettes. Examples of drug switching abound. When narcotics first were outlawed, many middle-class users switched to barbiturates and later to sedatives and tranquilizers. The laws did nothing to terminate this group of addicts—they simply changed the drug to which the users were addicted. Marijuana smoking first became popular as a replacement for alcohol during Prohibition. Similarly, it is common for alcoholics trying to stay sober to take up smoking instead. Recently, it has been reported that some intravenous heroin users have switched to smoking crack to avoid the risk of AIDS.

In both America and England, narcotics use peaked and then declined long before national prohibition was adopted. Today, in spite of the availability of alcohol, problem drinkers are considered to compose only about 10% of the population. In spite of the fact that marijuana can be purchased on virtually any street corner in some cities, only about 10% of the population has done so in the last month, according to the National Institute on Drug Abuse. Significantly, the figures for cocaine are quite similar, despite the drug's reputation for addictiveness. About 20,000,000 have tried the drug, but only 25% of that number have used it in the last month and only about 10% are considered addicts. It bears remembering that, for cocaine, the sample population is drawn from that segment of the population already interested enough in drugs to break the law to obtain them. Thus, an even lower percentage of repeat users could be expected from the overall population under legalization. These numbers support Stanton Peele's claim in the *Journal of Drug Issues* that "cocaine use is now described [incorrectly] as presenting the same kind of lurid monomania that pharmacologists once claimed only heroin could produce."

Drugs have a direct, powerful effect on human consciousness and emotions. Drug laws, on the other hand, have only an occasional impact on the user. For the many users who continue to take drugs even after being penalized by law, the subjective benefits of drugs outweigh the costs of criminal penalties.

"Legalization has been justified on both philosophical and pragmatic grounds."

Even without criminal sanctions, many users continue to take drugs despite the severe physical penalties these substances impose on their bodies. Again, they simply consider the psychic benefit of drug use more important than the physical harm. The fact is, drugs motivate some people—those who most need protection from them—more than any penalties a civilized society can impose, and even more than what some less-than-civilized societies have imposed. The undeniable seductiveness of drugs, usually con-

sidered a justification for prohibition, thus actually argues for legalization. The law simply can not deter millions of people deeply attracted to drugs; it only can increase the social costs of drug use greatly.

As for drug sellers, they are simply more highly motivated than those who are paid to stop them. They make enormous profits—much more than they could make at legal jobs—and are willing to risk death and long prison terms to do so. They are professionals, on the job 24 hours a day, and able to pour huge amounts of capital into their enterprises. They are willing to murder competitors, informers, and police as needed.

Drug Dealers' Advantages

Drug dealers have 10 times as much money to work with as do those attempting to stop them. Drug enforcement suffers from all the inefficiencies of bureaucracies, while dealers are entrepreneurs, unrestrained by arbitrary bureaucratic rules and procedures. They do what needs to be done based on their own judgment and, unlike drug enforcers, are not restrained by the law. The public has the false impression that drug enforcers are highly innovative, continually devising new schemes to catch dealers. Actually, the reverse is true. The dealers, like successful businessmen, are usually one step ahead of the "competition."

Legalization has been justified on both philosophical and pragmatic grounds. Some argue that it is no business of government what individuals do with their bodies and minds. I take no position on this philosophical issue. Rather, I argue on purely practical grounds that drug prohibition has been an extremely costly failure. I challenge advocates of prohibition to rise above the level of platitudes and good intentions and to present hard evidence that prohibition, *in actual practice*, does more good than harm.

Drugs Should Be Legalized

John Clifton Marquis

About the Author: *John Clifton Marquis is a missionary priest assigned to Our Lady of Victory Parish in Compton, California.*

The United States' federal, state, county, and city governments have spent the last 50 years writing and enacting antidrug laws with increasingly severe punishments for offenders. These laws are false gods promising a salvation they cannot produce. Every year, they demand more adoration from their devotees: more time, more money, more people, more resources. And yet, no matter how punitive the sanctions (including the death penalty itself), the drug-providing business has only escalated; indeed, ballooned. This is simple, historical fact.

Drug laws are a moral issue. Fifty years of drug legislation have produced the exact opposite effect of what those laws intended: the laws have created a tantalizingly profitable economic structure for marketing drugs. When law does not promote the common good, but in fact causes it to deteriorate, the law itself becomes bad and must be changed.

The undeniable result of current U.S. drug laws is the certainty that drugs will be very, very expensive. The corollary to that "given" is that people will commit many and violent sins to control the money that is to be made.

The moral issue here is to do the very best that can be done to give the community maximum control over drug availability and consequent drug use. Society cannot cure every drug abuser or alcoholic; that is a given. But the community can create a social condition in which in-nocent people do not become victims and where health-care professionals have a better opportunity (with more funds and people available) to serve the healing process of the drug abusers.

The moral principle involved here is very old and very sure: pick the lesser of two evils. Drug abuse is bad. It is a patent evil to the person abusing drugs and to everyone connected with him or her. But drug abuse is a problem that church and society can tackle and, in many cases, cure or control. In practice, our communities have the spiritual and psychological tools at hand. However, most do not have sufficient human and economic resources to use those tools effectively to help the people who desperately need them. The overwhelming majority of these resources are mainlined into a self-abortive policing effort that, by its very nature, cannot succeed.

Drug use and abuse clearly are serious problems. Yet a more intrusive and caustic moral illness results from the presence of drugs in the United States: greed. Greed is a much more subtle evil than the immaturity that leads to substance abuse. Like a cancer, it produces ancillary evils as destructive as its root. The people of the United States know by daily experience the destruction and havoc wreaked upon their lives by drug providers. This is the moral evil that must be erased.

> **"Fifty years of drug legislation have produced the exact opposite effect of what those laws intended."**

I am painfully aware that, for many millions of U.S. citizens, the very mention of completely legalizing drugs sounds like a form of blasphemy. That is why I deliberately described current U.S. drug laws as false gods. They are the blasphemy. They are the idolatrous Frankenstein that elected officials have created. They make the

John Clifton Marquis, "Drug Laws Are Immoral," *U.S. Catholic*, May 1990. Reprinted with permission.

drug trade incredibly lucrative. Neither police action nor the appointment of drug czars will faze the drug lords. As a nation, the United States may well arrest and convict thousands of dealers. Law enforcement agencies can incarcerate them all at disastrous cost to the public. For the kind of economic profit illegal drugs provide, however, there will always be other losers to take their places. The kingpins will go on.

Moral leaders have no alternative but to choose between authentic morality, which produces good, and cosmetic morality, which merely looks good. Drug laws look good! But the tragic flaw of cosmetic morality, like all other forms of cosmetics, is that it produces no change of substance.

"Lawmaking is not now, and never has been, the magic formula for goodness."

Proponents of cosmetic morality would rather look good than pay the tough, personal price of doing good. Authentic morality knows its limitations in the human condition and does all it can for the common good.

Some people are convinced that any and every problem can be solved with just a little more firepower. Yet the United States already has the third highest rate of incarceration in the world, following only South Africa and the Soviet Union. Continued enforcement of drug laws may make us number one. Funds needed for education and health care will be stripped away to maintain police agencies and prisons. U.S. liberties and judicial process are endangered because of a growing mania to win in court one way or another. Authentic moral leaders cannot afford the arrogant luxury of machismo, with its refusal to consider not "winning." Winning, in the case of drug abuse, is finding the direction and methods that provide the maximum amount of health and safety to the whole society without having a cure that is worse than the disease.

The fact is that the United States never had organized crime until Prohibition. Illegal (and thus very expensive) alcohol created a new economic market with hoodlums machine-gunning one another to death over profits. The percentage of U.S. citizens who drank hard liquor actually increased after alcohol was outlawed. When alcohol became legal again, the now-organized crime syndicate simply picked up the drug trade.

The standard argument against the legalization of drugs (all drugs, across the board) is: "It will make people, especially young people, think drugs are good." The people involved in drug dealing and drug using already think they are good. They are acquiring the money or pleasure so highly prized by the U.S. culture. At this point, what is imperative for leaders in the United States to realize is how young people think about good and bad. As a culture, U.S. youth do not equate illegal with immoral. Within their culture (and their experience of what adults have been doing with laws for the last generation), illegal simply means "harder to get," "forbidden fruit," or "adult toy." The United States has some laws for the protection of human life and other laws for the execution of human life. What does that teach young people about law? Law may very well have been a teacher of good and bad for Saint Paul and Saint Thomas Aquinas, but it is hardly that for U.S. youth.

Another Popular Argument

Another popular argument (and gross misconception) is that legal drugs will be too available. The reality is that U.S. grade schools and prisons are two of the hottest areas of drug trade. How much more available can the stuff become?

Legalizing all drugs in the United States would have one immediate and dramatic effect: it would render them cheap. In today's market, a kilogram of illegal heroin or illegal cocaine has a street value of several million dollars. A kilogram of illegal marijuana has a street value of about a quarter of a million dollars. A kilogram of legal cocaine would be worth perhaps a couple of hundred dollars, and a kilogram of legal marijuana would be priced with expensive tobacco. As long as drugs are illegal, the obscenity of the pricing structure will perdure. Legal drugs do not drug lords make. Legal drugs eradicate the reason for violence to control the trade.

There is no doubt that some people will abuse legal drugs; this happens with legal alcohol. It is also a sad human fact that some very sober and reasonable people drive cars recklessly; gamble away their hard-earned money; use their gift of sexuality promiscuously or violently; use the gift of speech to spread slander, calumny, and gossip; and go on to do a great variety of inappropriate and sinful things. Human nature is, after all, wounded by the reality of sin. But lawmaking is not now, and never has been, the magic formula for goodness.

The problems, hurts, and difficulties that will definitely result from legalized drugs will be far, far less numerous and less destructive to the whole society than the theft, bribery, violence, murder, mayhem, and self-degradation that are daily bread in the United States today. U.S. citizens must have the integrity and the painful honesty to keep in the forefront of their minds that they are not preventing addiction to crack or any other drug at this time. The current methods are not working. Humility, not arrogance, will help society find the best way to reach its goal, which is the common good.

The authentic definition of humility is truth.

Humility is never as immediately invigorating as machismo. Humility forces one to accept and live with limitations. Humans cannot have a perfect world. But they certainly can have a good world. U.S. citizens have to choose between looking good and doing good, between authentic morality and cosmetic morality. They must have the integrity and the fortitude—the guts—to choose the lesser of two evils. Then they will have the strength to work hard for the common good.

Legalizing Drugs Can Reduce Drug Abuse

Ethan A. Nadelmann

About the Author: *Ethan A. Nadelmann is an assistant professor of politics and public affairs at Princeton University's Woodrow Wilson School of Public Policy in Princeton, New Jersey.*

Legalization—I much prefer the term "decriminalization" or "normalization"—means different things to different people. To some it simply means taking the crime, and the profit, out of the drug business. For some, it's a rallying cry, in much the same way that "repeal prohibition" was used, 60 years ago, for bringing people together from across the political spectrum.

That's why one day my allies on a panel may be William F. Buckley, George Shultz, or economist Milton Friedman, and on the next day it may be Ira Glasser of the American Civil Liberties Union.

Legalization also refers to a framework of analysis—in particular, cost-benefit analysis. If we look at the current drug prohibition policies and determine, as best we can, their costs and benefits, and then compare them with the costs and benefits of alternative options, it seems to many of us that the best mix ends up looking a lot more like legalization than it does like the current situation.

Finally, legalization implies degrees of emphasis rather than absolutes. For example, alcohol is legal, but it is not legal to drive under the influence of alcohol or to sell it to children. Conversely, we speak about cocaine and the opiates as *il*legal, but in fact doctors can prescribe these drugs.

Baltimore Mayor Kurt Schmoke has suggested that if we are going to have a "War Against Drugs," it is a war that should be headed not by the Attorney General or even by a Drug Czar, but by the Surgeon General. In other words, drug policy should not rely first and foremost on criminal justice sanctions but on public health approaches, combined with some degree of respect for the rights of adult American citizens to make their own choices—even bad ones.

Personally, when I talk about legalization, I mean three things: The first is to make drugs such as marijuana, cocaine, and heroin legal—under fairly restricted conditions, but not as restricted as today. Second is a convergence in our substance abuse policy. We need a policy that is tougher on alcohol and especially tougher on tobacco—not with criminal laws so much as with other measures that would make them less available and less attractive. And at the same time be tough on marijuana, cocaine, and heroin as well, but while relying far less on criminal sanctions.

And third is to more intelligently manage our resources—to stop pouring the billions of dollars that we are now spending on law enforcement approaches down the drain and put them into drug treatment and drug abuse prevention instead.

"Legalization implies degrees of emphasis rather than absolutes."

Drug treatment is certainly no panacea. Most people who go into it end up backsliding. But it does help some people: It makes them less likely to die from overdoses and less likely to steal or commit other crimes. The evidence shows that it is worth doing, both for society and for drug abusers themselves. Even without coercing people into treatment, there are already waiting lines for the available treatment facilities.

Reprinted with permission from Ethan A. Nadelmann, "Should Some Illegal Drugs Be Legalized?" *Issues in Science and Technology*, vol. 6, no. 4, Summer 1990. Copyright © 1990 by the National Academy of Sciences, Washington, D.C.

More important, though, than drug treatment is drug abuse prevention. And here I am talking not so much about K-12 drug education but about "nonspecific" services such as prenatal and postnatal care, Head Start programs, inner-city education, and job training. These approaches are not just things in which the United States lags behind most other advanced industrial democracies in providing, they also seem to be the best drug prevention approaches ever developed—if you evaluate them in terms of producing non-drug-abusing, productive, tax-paying citizens down the road.

These are not just the decent and humane things to do. They also turn out to be, dollar for dollar, a lot more cost-effective than building more jails.

The Solution Becomes the Problem

Fundamentally, we need to consider legalization because the criminal justice approaches of the past have failed, and those of the present and future are likewise largely doomed to failure. This has nothing to do with squabbles between law enforcement agencies, or corruption in Third World countries, or whether or not we have a Drug Czar, or whether or not his name is William Bennett. Rather, it reflects the nature of the commodity, the nature of the market, and the lucrativeness of it all.

Criminal justice approaches have not only failed to solve the problem, they have made matters far worse. Most of what people identify as part and parcel of the drug problem are in fact the results of drug prohibition, just as when people talked about the alcohol problem 60 years ago, most of what they identified were the results of alcohol prohibition.

Let's look very quickly at some of these approaches: international enforcement, interdiction, and domestic enforcement (of high-level traffickers as well as their street-level sellers).

Can we keep drugs from being exported to the United States? No, we can't. These drugs can be grown virtually everywhere, and to try preventing export from any one place results in "push down, pop up."

Push down heroin coming out of Turkey, and it pops up in Mexico. Push it down in Mexico, and it pops up in Southeast Asia. Push down there and it comes from South*west* Asia. We have pushed down in so many places that it pops up virtually everywhere now. The United States is a multi-source heroin-importing country. The same is true with regard to marijuana and cocaine.

Another reason is that international law enforcement has but a tiny effect on the ultimate domestic price of drugs. Even if you double, triple, or quadruple the foreign price, it has almost no impact on the streets.

And finally, this is a business from which hundreds of thousands, if not millions, of people in Latin America and Asia are earning a very good living. The drugs are usually indigenous to their areas—opium in parts of Asia, for example, cannabis in Jamaica and parts of Africa, and coca that goes back thousands of years in Latin America—and cause few local problems. Moreover, they appear to bring in much more money than any alternative would provide.

"We need to consider legalization because the criminal justice approaches of the past have failed."

Thus if you spray Latin American peasants' drug crops and try to persuade them to grow macadamia nuts instead, they respond by hiding their crops. And if you go down there, as William Bennett's people have done, and say, "Don't you understand how immoral you are being? You are poisoning the youth of America," the peasants are unimpressed. "Don't lecture us about morality," they say. "Our moral obligation is to do the best we can for ourselves, our families, and our communities. If that means selling this drug, which is native to our country anyway, then so be it." And they might well add another point: "While you *Nortamericanos* are talking to us about morality, your trade representatives are going around the world shoving down tariff barriers so that your farmers can export more tobacco. Are you so much on a moral high ground?"

Costs of Enforcement

What about interdiction? I don't know anybody who believes anymore that it makes a difference. Drugs can come into the country in any which way, and in small amounts—arriving by boat, plane, and car, hidden in flowers, chocolates, and statues. Looking for drugs is like looking for a needle in a haystack.

Interdiction *has* worked somewhat with respect to marijuana. But the success has proven counterproductive. The Coast Guard found that as it realized a few successes in interdicting marijuana, the drug lords seemed to be switching to cocaine. And why not? It is less bulky, less smelly, more compact, and more lucrative. This pretty much parallels the responses of bootleggers during prohibition, who switched from beer to hard liquor.

The other consequence of the marijuana interdiction "success" was to transform the country into perhaps the number-one producer of marijuana in the world. Some people think that the United States now produces the world's best marijuana, in fact, and that if the dollar were to drop lower, we would become a major exporter of marijuana.

What about domestic enforcement? If you go after the big drug traffickers—the people who most profitably and egregiously violate the drug laws—it makes little difference. Every time you arrest Mr. Number One, there is Mr. Number Two to fill his shoes. Indeed, it is often from Number Two that the police get the information to arrest Number One.

Similarly, with street-level enforcement, you can clean up some neighborhoods—at least for a while—but can you, for very long, keep drugs out of the hands of people who really want them? You have the same push-down, pop-up ef-fect on the streets as there is on the global scale. Push down on 102nd Street and guess what pops up on 104th Street?

Now, law enforcement does accomplish some things. It reduces availability a little, increases the price, and deters some people. But the costs and other negative consequences of continuing to focus on criminal justice end up making a lot of things much worse.

Consider the direct costs. In 1987, we spent something like 10 billion dollars just enforcing drug laws. It may be close to 20 billion. Drug-law violators—and here I am not talking about drug-*related* crimes but drug-law violations such as possession, dealing, distribution, and manufacturing—are the number-one cause of imprisonment in New York state prisons, in Florida prisons, and as far as I know, in other state prisons as well. They accounted for about 40 percent of all felony indictments in the New York City courts in 1989 and for over 52 percent in Washington, D.C.—quadruple what it was in 1985.

"Looking for drugs is like looking for a needle in a haystack."

When cops say that the urban criminal-justice system is becoming synonymous with drug enforcement systems, they are increasingly correct. In the federal prisons, 40 percent of the people there are there on drug-law violations; between three-quarters of a million and a million people were arrested in 1989 on drug charges. We now have one million people behind bars in the United States, practically double what the number was just 10 years ago. And a rapidly rising percentage of them are there for violating drug laws.

But although the direct costs are enormous, the indirect costs are far more severe. Drug prohibition is responsible for all sorts of violence and crime—from street-level theft to high-level corruption—that seemingly have little to do with drugs per se.

Consider this: Tobacco is at least as addictive as heroin and cocaine, but have you ever worried about being mugged by a tobacco addict? Of course not, because it is cheap—too cheap, in my view. Heroin and cocaine cost much more to buy, even though they don't cost much more to produce. They are expensive because they are illegal, and addicts are obliged to raise the income, typically illegally, to pay for them. That would change under a maintenance system, or other forms of drug legalization, in which the prices were lower.

"Drug prohibition is responsible for all sorts of violence and crime."

And the systemic violence of the drug-crime connection would also change. There would be far less need for illicit drug traffickers, and thus far fewer occasions for them to settle disputes among themselves by shooting one another, shooting cops and innocent bystanders (including kids) along the way.

Another cost, not much talked about, is the impact of prohibition on drug quality. Simply stated, drugs are more dangerous because they are illegal. Just as tens of thousands of people died or were blinded or poisoned by bad bootleg liquor 60 years ago, perhaps the majority of overdose deaths today are the result of drug prohibition.

Ordinarily, heroin does not kill. It addicts people and makes them constipated. But people overdose because they don't know what they are getting; they don't know if the heroin is 4 percent or 40 percent, or if it is cut with bad stuff, or if it is heroin at all—it may be a synthetic opiate or an amphetamine-type substance.

Just imagine if every time you picked up a bottle of wine, you didn't know whether it was 8 percent alcohol or 80 percent alcohol, or whether it was ethyl alcohol or methyl alcohol. Imagine if every time you took an aspirin, you didn't know if it was 5 milligrams or 500 milligrams.

Life would be a little more interesting, and also a little more dangerous. Fewer people might take those drugs, but more would get sick and die. That is exactly what is happening today with the illicit drug market. Nothing resembling an underground Food and Drug Administration has emerged to regulate the quality of illicit drugs on the streets, and the results are much more deadly.

A Moral Argument

My strongest argument for legalization, though, is a moral one. Enforcement of drug laws makes a mockery of an essential principle of a free society—that those who do no harm to others should not be harmed by others, and particularly not by the state. The vast majority of the 60 to 70 million Americans who have violated the drug laws in recent years have done no harm to anybody else. In most cases, they have done little or no harm even to themselves. Saying to those people, "You lose your driver's license, you lose your job, you lose your freedom," is, to me, the greatest societal cost of our current drug prohibition system.

Prohibiting Illegal Drugs Has Failed

Jann S. Wenner

About the Author: *Jann S. Wenner is the founder and publisher of* Rolling Stone, *a bimonthly magazine chronicling rock music and popular culture.*

Despite decades of interdiction and enforcement efforts that have cost billions of dollars, there are more drugs and more blood on the streets than ever before. Our courts and prisons are crowded beyond capacity, corruption is rampant at home and governments abroad are under siege.

With all the hysteria and hypocrisy about drugs, we have ignored the clear lessons of history. Prohibition financed the rise of organized crime and failed miserably as legal and social policy. Likewise, the war on drugs has created new criminal conspiracies, and yet another moral crusade has failed miserably.

The latest round of anti-drug hysteria has created a climate akin to the anti-Communist witch hunts of the McCarthy era. Douglas Ginsburg, a conservative legal scholar from Harvard University, was forced to withdraw from consideration for the Supreme Court after admitting he had smoked marijuana. The constitutional guarantee against unreasonable search and seizure is being breached routinely. President Bush's drug czar, William Bennett, has encouraged schoolchildren to turn in friends and family suspected of taking drugs.

The urge to use some form of mind-altering substance is ingrained in human nature. Trying to legislate it out of existence can only lead us to grant to government powers it should not have in a free society.

Jann S. Wenner, "Drug War: A New Vietnam?" *The New York Times,* June 23, 1990. Copyright © 1990 by The New York Times Company. Reprinted by permission.

The arguments against legalization are tired and invalid. Legalization does *not* imply governmental approval of drug use. It would not increase availability or result in a massive wave of new addicts. Legalization *would* eliminate the inner-city violence associated with competitive drug dealing and allow billions of dollars to be rechanneled for treatment, anti-drug education and economic assistance.

Despite Richard Nixon's attempts to eradicate marijuana production and consumption, about 60 million Americans have smoked pot and 21 million now smoke it regularly. Eleven states have decriminalized personal use, and not a single death has been attributed to a marijuana overdose. Yet as late as 1988, the Government was spending an estimated $986 million for anti-marijuana enforcement. That same year 391,600 people were arrested for marijuana offenses.

Attempts to control cocaine have likewise failed. In a textbook case of innovative marketing, cocaine — once the drug of the elite—trickled down to the poor in the form of crack. Even though cocaine prices fell in the 80's, consumption increased so greatly that crack profits made the drug barons of Latin America among the richest men in history.

> ## "The latest round of anti-drug hysteria has created a climate akin to the anti-Communist witch hunts."

The war on drugs, as well intentioned as it might be, has now become the problem. Allowing this underground market to continue, according to Federal Judge Robert Sweet, "creates an economic incentive for drug sellers to increase the use of drugs." Moreover, if we eliminated the crime premium, the price would fall. If we cut out the illegal traffickers, the spiral of crime would end.

Would legalization produce a flood of new addicts? With crack, which is abhorred by society at large, this question is simply irrelevant. In the areas where a large market for crack already exists, legalization would not increase availability in the least.

If the legalization of drugs results in a few more abusers, let us accept the consequences. Most middle-class Americans have access to a social safety net that includes family, employers and social services, as well as health insurance, education and treatment facilities.

"The urge to use some form of mind-altering substance is ingrained in human nature."

In the ghettos, where the drug war is being waged, things are far more desperate. Real wages for poor black men dropped 50 percent during the 1970's. Approximately one-third of black men from poor areas are arrested on drug charges by the age of 30. Nearly one in four black males between the ages of 20 and 29 is in prison, on probation or parole or awaiting trial.

The Administration's response to the plight of the poor has been far from ministerial. Its drug strategy calls for an increase in law-enforcement officers and a huge increase in prison space. The 1990 drug-war budget of $9.5 billion allots $1.5 billion for prisons—a 100 percent increase—and $876 million for the military's involvement.

The residents of inner cities don't need more police officers or prison space. They need opportunity and equality. Spend the billions that will result from a drug-peace dividend on education, job assistance, child care and economic redevelopment.

Bloodshed

Legalizing drugs would also eliminate the bloodshed associated with all levels of drug dealing and smuggling. Federal judges would find some 15,000 fewer cases a year on their dockets, which is a small fraction of the burden that would be lifted from state and local courts. And since nearly 50 percent of all Federal prisoners are serving time for drug-related offenses, the national prison crisis would be eased.

In addition, the risk of death by overdose, hepatitis, AIDS and other illnesses resulting from the use of street drugs would be greatly reduced. Eliminating the black market in illegal drugs would dry up an estimated $50 billion to $60 billion a year in profits for organized crime.

In 75 years of trying, the Government has failed to control drugs through prohibition. We are now spending nearly $10 billion a year on the drug war. With the military and the Central Intelligence Agency wading into an escalating, hopeless war, perhaps the history lesson can begin. Like Vietnam, the drug war is a quagmire, a conflict that is tearing apart the fabric of our country. There is no light at the end of the tunnel.

Drug Prohibition

We have to admit that we are wrong about drug prohibition. Perhaps then we can behave as a kinder, gentler and more mature society.

Legalizing Drugs Would Have Many Benefits

Tibor R. Machan and Mark Thornton

About the Authors: *Tibor R. Machan is a professor in the philosophy department and Mark Thornton is a professor in the economics department, both at Auburn University in Auburn, Alabama.*

Americans are growing increasingly skeptical of the government's claims about winning the war against drugs. Should this war be supported because a smaller percentage of teenagers use marijuana, or should it be opposed because a larger percentage of teenagers and young adults use cocaine and crack? Should people be optimistic when multi-billion dollar shipments of cocaine are confiscated, or pessimistic that seizures continue to increase yet have such little impact on price and consumption? We argue that drug prohibition was doomed to failure and that the best alternative is an immediate return to complete legalization of such drugs.

One of the clearest lessons from history is that suppression of voluntary trade only drives the market underground and adds a criminal element. We claim that the trade and use of drugs should not be prohibited and must be dealt with by means of education, character building, willpower, and social institutions, without benefit of force of arms. Unfortunately this proposition is no longer obvious in our "free" society—perhaps due to the widespread conviction that individual responsibility is merely a relic of ancient philosophy and religion.

Tibor R. Machan and Mark Thornton, "The Re-legalization of Drugs," *The Freeman*, April 1991. Reprinted by permission.

The war on drugs received several major increases in funding during the 1980s, and the U.S. military is now heavily involved in drug-law enforcement. Despite these increased resources we are no closer to success with drug prohibition than socialism is at creating a "new economic man." The fact that a full array of illegal drugs is available for sale throughout the Federal prison system, the Pentagon, and in front of the Drug Enforcement Administration building in Washington, D.C., demonstrates that little has been accomplished.

One lofty goal of drug prohibition was to prevent crime by removing access to mind-altering drugs. The great American tragedy is that prohibition has created a vast new area of criminal activity—crimes such as robbery, burglary, and prostitution committed in order to pay for the high prices of illegal drugs. It is well documented that drug users commit crimes to pay the high prices brought on by prohibition and that wealthy addicts do not.

The rate of crimes with victims increased during the alcohol prohibition of the 1920s only to decline rapidly in 1933, the year Prohibition was repealed. Crime continued to decline until the mid-1960s and has been increasing ever since. The prison population increased by 35 percent between 1984 and 1988. During that period the "criminals on parole" population increased by over 50 percent! More innocent bystanders are being killed, more school systems are infected, and more neighborhoods are destroyed by the growing problems of prohibition.

> **"Americans are growing increasingly skeptical of the government's claims about winning the war against drugs."**

The 1990 arraignment of Mayor Marion Barry was a spectacular media event, but drug prohibition has been corrupting the political process for a very long time. This corruption is not confined to the United States. A look around the globe shows that countries that produce, process, and sell illegal drugs are also afflicted with corrupt political systems—consider Southeast Asia, Lebanon, Mexico, South America.

Drug Deaths Skyrocket

The government recently reported with great pride that a smaller percentage of teenagers are regular marijuana smokers. What was left out of that press release is that consumption of virtually every other type of drug has increased and that the number of reported deaths associated with illegal drug use continues to skyrocket. New types of drugs such as smokable cocaine and synthetic opiates are being introduced onto the streets at an alarming rate. The switch from marijuana to the more potent and dangerous drugs is directly attributable to the enforcement of drug laws.

Prohibition forces black market suppliers to take precautions against detection. This ever present profit-making incentive takes on several forms such as:

1. Producing only the most potent form of a drug.
2. Switching from low potency drugs, such as marijuana, to high potency drugs, such as cocaine and heroin.
3. Inventing and producing more potent drugs, such as "designer drugs," which are synthetic opiates thousands of times more potent than opium.

These results have been labeled accurately in the popular press the "Iron Law of Prohibition."

The history of drug prohibitions reveals that black markets produce low quality, high potency, and extremely dangerous products. The most powerful weapon of these black marketeers is not the gun, but the ability to stay at least one step ahead of law enforcement.

The population of the United States is growing older and more affluent. Normally these demographic changes would reduce drug use and addiction. Even habitual heroin users stabilize their habits and mature out of addiction if they survive the war on drugs. However, these beneficial trends have been far outweighed by the increased severity of the effects of prohibition. In fact, we would be surprised if prohibition actually did work. Any law or program that undermines individual responsibility and liberty has little chance of enhancing a democratic and free market society.

Most Americans agree that prohibition is not working—the dispute is over what to do about it. Many argue that we don't have the right people in charge, but we have been changing the guard (and the law) now for over 150 years. Others argue that we just haven't done enough, but things have only become worse as we devote more of our resources and surrender our liberties to this cause. The support for prohibition rests on the fact that people cannot contemplate the obvious alternative—legalization.

Legalization has many obvious benefits. Lower prices would mean that drug users would no longer have to resort to crime to pay for their habits. With the tremendous profits gone, corruption of public officials would be reduced, and because Americans constitute a bulk of world consumption, political corruption worldwide would be reduced.

"The great American tragedy is that prohibition has created a vast new area of criminal activity."

Government budgets at the Federal, state, and local levels could be cut as entire programs are dismantled. However, one thing legalization would *not* do is balance government budgets. There is no way that tax rates on drugs could be raised high enough to offset the more than $300 billion Federal deficit. Furthermore, high tax rates would encourage the black market to continue, people would still commit crimes to pay the high prices, and politicians would still be involved in corruption.

Legalization will create jobs in the private sector. People will be employed making heroin, cocaine, and marijuana for "recreational" and "legitimate" users. All of these products have legitimate uses and may have as-yet-undiscovered uses. Marijuana (hemp) will be a valuable (and environmentally safe) source of products such as paper, fiber, fuel, building materials, clothing, animal and bird food, medicine and medicinal preparations, and a protein source for humans. It can be grown in a variety of climates and soil types and grows well without chemical fertilizers or pesticides.

"Most Americans agree that prohibition is not working."

The repeal of drug prohibitions will allow police, courts, and prisons to concentrate on real criminals while at the same time greatly reducing the number of crimes committed to pay for drugs. No longer will judges be forced to open prison doors because of overcrowding. The courts and police will be better able to serve and protect—crime will pay a lot less! Street gangs will deteriorate without their income from illegal drug sales.

The people involved and methods of producing and selling drugs will change dramatically. The current dealers of drugs will not survive in a competitive marketplace. Large companies will produce and distribute these drugs on a national scale. In such an environment the drugs will be less potent and less dangerous. Consumers will be safer and better informed—changes in the product will be consumer-driven. The producers will face many legal constraints such as negligence and product liability laws. The threat of wrongful death suits and class action lawsuits will also constrain their behavior. . . .

Constructive debate can overcome political and ideological maneuvering only if people clearly understand the differences between prohibition and legalization. Prohibition is simply a piece of legislation enforced by use of law officers, guns, and prisons. Prohibition is *not* drug education, drug treatment centers, rehabilitation centers, self-help programs such as Alcoholics Anonymous, religion, family, friends, doctors, help hot lines, and civic organizations. "Just Say No" does not have to leave because we say goodbye to prohibition.

In discussing the problems of drug abuse many people feel that legalization would only reduce the prices of drugs and therefore only increase the amount and severity of drug abuse. People would be smoking marijuana in McDonald's, the school bus driver would be shooting up heroin, and airplane pilots would be snorting cocaine before takeoff. This confusion results from a failure to distinguish between prohibition and private contractual regulations. . . .

While we haven't examined all aspects of prohibition and legalization, enough of the issues have been discussed to refute many of the myths of legalization and to make the question of quantity consumed a non-issue. Re-legalization is the admission of government's failure in pursuit of a lofty goal, not a ringing endorsement of drug abuse.

Legalization has been labeled immoral by prohibitionists, but nothing could be further from the truth. Reliance on individual initiative and responsibility is no sin. It is not only the key to success in the battle against drug abuse, it is also a reaffirmation of traditional American values. How can someone make a moral choice when one is in fact forced into a particular course of action? How is the fabric of society strengthened when we rely on guns and prisons to enforce behavior rather than letting behavior be determined by individual responsibility and family upbringing?

The sooner we move toward re-legalization, the sooner we can begin the process of healing the scars of prohibition, solving the problems of drug abuse, and curing this nation's addiction to drug laws.

Should Drugs Be Legalized?

No: Legalizing Drugs Would Be Dangerous

Drugs Should Not Be Legalized

Edwin J. Delattre

About the Author: *Edwin J. Delattre is John M. Olin scholar in applied ethics at Boston University's School of Education and the former president of St. John's College in Annapolis, Maryland and Santa Fe, New Mexico.*

How wonderful it would be if a scourge like substance abuse could be easily remedied. In practice, the problems are rather more grim and complicated.

Let's suppose that we legalize *all* currently illegal drugs and narcotics, including ice, blotter drugs, heroin and so on. Asian and Central American cartels, plus the manufacturers of illegal synthetic drugs in the United States, can introduce new free-base drugs into the market at least annually. We would have to continue to legalize whatever they manufacture in order to keep pace with them.

We do not have reliable rehabilitation methods for all such drugs and narcotics. There is, for example, no pharmacological equivalent for crack or ice of methadone treatment for heroin addiction—although there is some promising research with antidepressants and chemical blockers. That is why our drug control policy stresses treatment and rehabilitation *research* as well as rehabilitation programs. Still, legalize everything, and we will be legalizing what we cannot presently treat.

So, supposing we legalize only what we *can* treat. The traffickers will step up the pace of sales in what remains illegal—*unless*, of course, we try to tax the sale of the drugs we legalize.

Put a tax on legal drugs, and the cartels will undersell the government; they can manufacture and distribute the drugs more cheaply than government or private sector manufacturers and distributors in the United States can—and still make impressive profits. We could undersell the cartels by subsidizing the cost of production and distribution, but that would use up all the money for rehabilitation, and more.

The criminal drug interests worldwide are ruthless, and they will not give up their share of profitable markets just because something or other is legalized. These are people who murder newborn babies, eviscerate them, fill their bodies with heroin and have them carried across international borders in the arms of women who pretend to be nursing them. They also operate multibillion-dollar businesses in the criminal diversion of legalized prescription drugs. That's where valium, percodan and all the other uppers and downers you can buy on the street come from. Legalization has not eliminated such criminal markets.

"Legalize everything, and we will be legalizing what we cannot presently treat."

Make crack legal, and the traffickers will sell—as they now sell in many cities—crack laced with speed. Make crack laced with speed legal, and they will sell crack laced with insecticides. The cartels will offer progressively more exotic and dangerous combinations—like the rocks of half crack, half smokable heroin that are now becoming fashionable among many users in America. Furthermore, they will sell drugs 24 hours a day, seven days a week, in any amount, in any intensity, in any combination, to any buyer of any age, and often on credit. Legal government "pharmacies" cannot compete with that.

Legalize drugs for adults, and the cartels will market harder to children. They will tell the children, "It's OK to use drugs—after all, they're

Edwin J. Delattre, "Drug War Blasts Blowing in Our Ears," *The Washington Times*, November 23, 1990. Reprinted by permission of the Boston University *Daily Free Press*.

legal for grownups." To prevent that, perhaps drug legalization proponents would legalize drugs for children—and alcohol, too. Then we can try to rehabilitate them. Certainly, it will be much more difficult to mount successful antidrug education programs if drugs are legal—or to sustain any social pressure against them.

The worst shortcoming of rehabilitation as a remedy, of course, is that many people with drug and narcotic habits who need treatment, do not *want* it. Though they harm themselves and others, they *like* drugs, and they have no intention of changing their habits.

Many addicts know that rehabilitation involves agony, and they want no part of it. Even many of the users who *do* seek treatment are impulsive and never stay with it. Some women and girls who bear drug-exposed babies are in this group, and legalization offers no protection to these children—before they are born or afterward.

What about safety in the streets? Actually, when drug markets start to shrink, competitive drug wars for turf and market share tend to get worse, not better. The homicide rate often rises; so do drive-by shootings and other varieties of violent crime for profit.

Notably, "supply side" and "demand side" do not mean what some legalization advocates think they mean. They equate supply side with criminal justice and military efforts and demand side with rehabilitation and education efforts.

Rehabilitation Programs

In fact, rehabilitation programs are designed partly to help people who deal drugs as a way of supporting their own drug habits to get out of trafficking. Rehabilitation applies to both the supply *and* demand sides.

Likewise, comprehensive drug education programs are not designed only to prevent children and youths from *using* drugs; they also mean to keep them from *dealing* drugs and to escape recruitment into drug-trafficking gangs. This is essential, because most urban gangs that traffic

drugs will not allow their younger members to use drugs. Drug consumption makes for unreliable behavior and is therefore bad for business.

Similarly, law enforcement efforts to make users accountable are intended to reduce demand. The expenses of many law enforcement programs are demand-side expenses—user accountability programs are one more method of trying to give people incentives to seek rehabilitation.

"Legalize drugs for adults and the cartels will market harder to children."

And law enforcement expenses do not necessarily drop when previously illegal substances and activities are legalized. Alcohol is legal, but 23,000 Americans die in alcohol-related traffic accidents annually. Law enforcement expenses to try to prevent drunken driving, and to pick up the pieces, help victims, arrest violators, file reports and testify in court after accidents are enormous.

The same thing would be true for legalized drugs, just as it already is for legalized gambling. The most notable lesson of legalized gambling is that when gambling is legalized, illegal gambling increases. Why? Because more people become gamblers in legal lotteries, casinos and the like, and then they learn that you can gamble with illegal bookies on credit and without paying taxes on winnings.

In America, we legalized heroin distribution clinics from 1914 until 1925 in order to accomplish exactly what legalization advocates want to accomplish now. Heroin was legalized even when alcohol was illegal. The experiment did not work.

Reasoning responsibly about what we ought to do is very demanding business—and it takes a lot more homework than drug legalization proponents have yet been willing to give it.

The Arguments for Drug Legalization Are Flawed

Charles Colson

About the Author: *Charles Colson is a contributing editor to* Christianity Today, *a bimonthly evangelical magazine. He served as special counsel to former president Richard Nixon from 1969 to 1973.*

There's a certain relish to be found in arguing with one's ideological opponents; but it becomes awkward when you find yourself disagreeing with people you greatly admire and with whom you usually agree.

I have felt this awkwardness recently. First, with William F. Buckley; I can count on one hand the number of times I've disagreed with Bill in the quarter-century that we've been friends. Then with Milton Friedman, my economic guru during my years in politics. And with George Shultz, a much-respected colleague when we served together in the White House.

And day by day, it seems the momentum gathers. The issue, of course, is legalizing drugs. Proponents want them decriminalized and sold, like alcohol, under strict licensing.

Their arguments have a surface appeal:

We are losing the war on drugs. True. We *are* losing the drug war—in spite of the fact that we've conducted costly and celebrated prosecutions like the "pizza connection" case. We've beefed up border patrols and police squads, spent billions, and even managed to bring narco-terrorist Manuel Noriega to the U.S. for trial.

These are impressive efforts. Yet cocaine,

Charles Colson, "Half-Stoned Logic," *Christianity Today,* March 5, 1990. Reprinted with permission.

crack, and their ilk flow more freely than ever through American streets and into American veins. But does that mean we should surrender? We were losing World War II until the battle of Midway, but no one suggested handing the keys to the Pentagon over to the Japanese.

Legalization will drastically reduce crime. Perhaps it would put some organized crime out of business. But consider the fact that the vast majority of today's offenders have drug histories. Can we assume that people stoned on illegal drugs would behave differently from people stoned on legal drugs?

Legalization will put the drug lords out of business. Now here's an idea we all would love. But would legalization do that? The cartels would still control production and prices; and if, as proponents urge, drugs are sold under license and prohibited to minors, there would still be a healthy black market.

Alcohol and nicotine are legal and they kill more people than drugs do. True; drunk drivers kill 100,000 U.S. citizens a year, and smoking claims 350,000 lives. But does permitting two killers justify legitimizing a third, more lethal assassin?

Statistics tell us that of all users of alcohol, 10 percent become addicts. For cocaine it is *70 percent.* Laboratory monkeys, allowed all the cocaine they want without threat of punishment (in other words, it was "legal"), self-administer the drug by pressing a feeder bar so obsessively that they forgo food, water, sleep, and sex. They just keep pressing the bar to get the white powder—until they die of exhaustion.

"For government to legitimize drugs would be for government to abandon its most fundamental duty."

Prohibition didn't work, either. Prohibition was not the result of Victorian-era prudes trying to force their piety on an unwilling society. Rather, it was the response to an enormous public-safety and health crisis. In the new industrial era, thousands of drunken workers were being killed or maimed each year, while the tavern trade spawned prostitution rings, spreading venereal diseases that then, like AIDS today, had no known cure.

And Prohibition worked: per-capita alcohol consumption declined, industrial safety dramatically improved, and the spread of VD slowed. Not until 1970 did per-capita alcohol consumption again reach pre-Prohibition levels.

All of these are, of course, pragmatic issues about which advocates and critics of legalization can argue indefinitely. But the immediate debate should turn on deeper, moral issues. These should be of particular concern to Christians.

Abandoning Our Future

First, government's primary duty—at least from a Judeo-Christian perspective—is to restrain evil and promote order. No one, including Bill Buckley or Milton Friedman, could argue that drugs are benign. They destroy individual lives and create chaos for society through soaring crime, lost productivity, and staggering welfare costs. For government to legitimize drugs would be for government to abandon its most fundamental duty.

Second, laws have moral consequences. The old canard "you can't legislate morality" is a dangerous myth. The law is a body of rules regulating human behavior, which reflects society's view of right and wrong. Statutes prohibiting murder, for example, reflect the moral judgment that human life has intrinsic dignity. The law both reflects moral values and is a moral teacher.

This leads to a third crucial issue: decriminalization would destigmatize the use of drugs. Human behavior is profoundly influenced by societal attitudes that reject particular actions as wrong. Government cannot nod yes to drugs

and urge its citizens to "just say no." To so undercut its efforts at anti-drug education would be fatal, for ultimate victory over drugs will come *only* when we curb demand.

"Decriminalization would destigmatize the use of drugs."

Our responsibility to ourselves and our posterity is to envision greater possibilities for our society and strive toward those, making whatever sacrifices that are necessary. Our vision should not be of a half-stoned society that crassly sanctions immorality; it must be of a society in which our children and grandchildren can live free of the drug curse. That's a goal worth fighting for, win or lose.

There is one final image of drug abuse that proponents of legalization rarely mention. They argue for what has become that most sacred of American rights: individual freedom. Since people have the right to choose their own behaviors, why not allow mature adults to choose to use drugs if they want? "It is absurd that Americans should be forced to pay for a war on drugs just to keep people from choosing to harm themselves," writes one decriminalization supporter.

No one who has seen a crack baby, addicted to drugs in its mother's womb, could accept the idea that drug abuse is a victimless crime. These infants, filling neonatal intensive-care units across the country, weigh two or three pounds. Their skin is so sensitive they cannot be held. Many have violent seizures, their twig-like arms and legs twitching convulsively. Often they must be calmed with sedatives—because all they do is cry. What government with any claim to moral authority would sanction substances that so cruelly destroy the generation that holds its future?

Drug Legalization Is Too Risky

Harold J. Dwyer Jr.

About the Author: *Harold J. Dwyer Jr. is rector in the Episcopal Church of the Trinity, Coatsville, Pennsylvania, a member of the Addictions & Recovery Committee of the diocese of Pennsylvania, and chair of the Coatsville Drug Task Force.*

A mood of frustration and fear is becoming more prevalent in U.S. society with each passing week. This mood, a response to the plague of drugs which seems to be destroying our people, has engendered a reaction that is likely to be even more destructive than the drugs we all fear.

From the floor of Philadelphia's City Council to the office of the mayor of Baltimore, as well as in scientific journals and church periodicals, we are barraged by the prophets of failure who would have us believe the only solution to our drug crisis is to sound a retreat. Some proposals call for a brief tactical regrouping, a legalization of "less harmful" drugs and controlled distribution of others. More libertarian schemes suggest the legalization of any and all substances. What these ideas have in common is the suggestion that since there has been no clear example of the effectiveness of current criminal justice approaches to the drug problem, it is time to throw in the towel.

A typical argument of this type is found in an article by Ethan A. Nadelmann, which appeared in the September 1989 issue of *Science* magazine:

> Drug legalization increasingly merits serious consideration as both an analytical model and a policy option for addressing the drug problem. Criminal justice approaches to the drug problem have proven limited in their capacity to cur-

Harold J. Dwyer Jr., "Wage War on Drugs with New Weapons," *The Witness*, June 1990. Reprinted with permission.

tail drug abuse. They also have proven increasingly costly and counterproductive. Drug legalization policies that are wisely implemented can minimize the risks of legalization, dramatically reduce the costs of current policies and directly address the problems of drug abuse.

The article presents a simple idea, one with which few people would have difficulty. The criminal justice approach has not been effective in the elimination of drug abuse in our society. This fact should not surprise us since drug abuse is, in fact, a health-care problem, not just a criminal problem. The crimes connected with the use of illegal drugs are only a portion of the destructive effects of the drug problem. In fact, studies indicate that some of the most "expensive" drugs, in terms of cost of abuse-related accidents, health complications, and lost time on the job, are the already legal drugs—alcohol and nicotine.

> ## "The war on drugs will not be won by making drugs more available."

If we admit the cost of these legal substances, and if we acknowledge that we cannot in any way predict the effect of increased consumption that might result from the legalization of other drugs, dare we add more substances to the list of chemicals to which people might become legally addicted? The history of the abuse of prescription drugs obtained through legitimate sources and the added incidence of the "street" availability of prescription drugs easily leads to suspicion that "controlled legalization" would very quickly get out of control.

Another aspect of the argument for legalization is that if we eliminated the criminal element from the drug trade, we would eliminate the most severe drug-related problems in our society. I would suggest that some of the most serious problems caused by drugs are not only apparent in the life of the abuser or the crimes the addict commits, but also in the lives of those directly affected by the addict. If the truism that each alcoholic/addict directly affects at least four or five other people is accurate, then any spread in the availability and use of currently illegal substances could bring about consequences our society cannot afford to ignore.

"Our society, however, like the addicts we fear and pity, still seeks a quick fix."

The use of drugs by those who are unable to participate in the "American dream," who use alcohol or drugs to medicate away their anger and frustration, will not be decreased by this legalization. If anything, the removal of criminal sanctions and the increased availability would probably result in a sharp increase in addiction to a wide variety of drugs. The personal tragedies already seen in treatment centers, doctors' offices, clergy studies and city morgues would multiply. The potential loss of a generation of inner-city youth would become a harsh reality.

There is no single solution to our drug crisis. Our society, however, like the addicts we fear and pity, still seeks a quick fix. Solutions will be found in ongoing efforts on several fronts. The cost of criminal enforcement is high; the cost of increased treatment resources and prevention is high as well. I suspect however that the cost of the "modest proposal" of legalization would be many times higher. And I think we should stop measuring the cost in dollars alone.

Since the end of the Second World War we have justified the expenditure of countless billions to defend our nation from outside enemies. Whether or not this policy made sense in the past, it is clear we no longer need to continue this expense. If we wish to prevent the destruction of our nation from the forces which have already exhibited the ability to "bury" us, we might well consider directing these defense dollars to the war on drugs, a war that must be fought on every front—criminal justice, health care, community organization and education.

We must rethink other national priorities as well. We must be willing to see the connection between the cutbacks in social services over the last 10 years, the decline in availability of affordable housing, a minimum wage that has not kept up with inflation, the subtle and not-so-subtle effects of racism and other forms of discrimination, and the rise in alcohol and drug addiction and crimes connected with this rise. We must admit that the bankers who look the other way while large cash transactions take place, the luxury auto dealers, realtors and jewelers who willingly sell their most expensive wares to youth who pay with a large pile of $100 bills, are as much a part of the drug trade as the kids selling a few pieces of crack.

As a nation we must see that the drug problem is not confined to a few notorious street corners in urban areas. We must admit that the problem will not go away even if we deputize half of our citizens and empower them to arrest the other half. We can turn every unused military base into a prison camp; we can give up our constitutionally guaranteed rights that guard our privacy and protect us from unreasonable surveillance, search and seizure; we can accept the most draconian tactic our fear and loathing of drugs and addicts will allow, or we can look at the whole range of societal problems that create the environment where the drug trade and drug addiction flourish.

Legalization Not the Answer

None of this, however, should lead us to the conclusion that since the law enforcement model has not worked, legalization is the only answer.

The resources currently being dedicated to fighting the war on drugs are inadequate. Budgetary fictions that allow for the dedication of a few new dollars and the renaming of other funds already marked for anti-drug efforts will not do. The use of confiscated money solely for criminal justice agencies is imprudent. The largest portion of this money should be returned to the very communities from which it came. It is money that would have otherwise been spent on food, housing, health care and education if people had not been living under the power of the demon addiction.

> ## "The weapons that we need to win this war are education for prevention and education for decent employment."

The war on drugs will not be won by making drugs more available. The war will not be won by passing stronger laws. The weapons that we need to win this war are education for prevention and education for decent employment. We need to increase resources for the treatment of drug addiction and treatment of poverty and hopelessness. We must ensure that the rights of all our citizens to adequate employment, housing, education and health care are finally met.

We can enter the 21st century with a commitment to serve the needs of all this nation's people. Or we can continue our useless efforts to fight against drugs, or dream up new and equally futile schemes and finally see our society destroyed not by external enemies but by our own lack of compassion for each other.

The choices concerning the fight against drugs made by federal, state and local governments are important for our present and future. They will determine the kind of society we will pass on to our children. The church must continue in its long-standing role as an advocate for those our society would render powerless and voiceless. We must not succumb to fear. We must not retreat to the safety of believing that the drug problem is unrelated to the larger unresolved issues of racism, classism and nationalism. We must instead continue to point out these connections to our members and to those who formulate government policy.

The powers and principalities that enslave God's children have not gone away or changed—they have merely adopted new tactics. The community of faith must meet these new tactics with the ageless message of life, truth and liberation which took flesh in Jesus of Nazareth.

Legalizing Drugs Will Worsen America's Drug Crisis

William Bennett

About the Author: *William Bennett is the former director of the Office of National Drug Control Policy. He is now a senior editor for* National Review, *a conservative, weekly newsmagazine.*

Since I took command of the war on drugs, I have learned from former Secretary of State George Shultz that our concept of fighting drugs is "flawed." The only thing to do, he says, is to "make it possible for addicts to buy drugs at some regulated place." Conservative commentator William F. Buckley, Jr., suggests I should be "fatalistic" about the flood of cocaine from South America and simply "let it in." Syndicated columnist Mike Royko contends it would be easier to sweep junkies out of the gutters "than to fight a hopeless war" against the narcotics that send them there. Labeling our efforts "bankrupt," federal judge Robert W. Sweet opts for legalization, saying, "If our society can learn to stop using butter, it should be able to cut down on cocaine."

Flawed, fatalistic, hopeless, bankrupt! I never realized surrender was so fashionable until I assumed this post.

Though most Americans are overwhelmingly determined to go toe-to-toe with the foreign drug lords and neighborhood pushers, a small minority believe that enforcing drug laws imposes greater costs on society than do drugs themselves. Like addicts seeking immediate eu-

phoria, the legalizers want peace at any price, even though it means the inevitable proliferation of a practice that degrades, impoverishes and kills.

I am acutely aware of the burdens drug enforcement places upon us. It consumes economic resources we would like to use elsewhere. It is sometimes frustrating, thankless and often dangerous. But the consequences of *not* enforcing drug laws would be far more costly. Those consequences involve the intrinsically destructive nature of drugs and the toll they exact from our society in hundreds of thousands of lost and broken lives . . . human potential never realized . . . ime stolen from families and jobs . . . precious spiritual and economic resources squandered.

That is precisely why virtually every civilized society has found it necessary to exert some form of control over mind-altering substances and why this war is so important. Americans feel up to their hips in drugs now. They would be up to their necks under legalization.

"When drugs are more widely available, addiction skyrockets."

Even limited experiments in drug legalization have shown that when drugs are more widely available, addiction skyrockets. In 1975 Italy liberalized its drug law and now has one of the highest heroin-related death rates in Western Europe. In Alaska, where marijuana was decriminalized in 1975, the easy atmosphere has increased usage of the drug, particularly among children. Nor does it stop there. Some Alaskan schoolchildren now tout "coca puffs," marijuana cigarettes laced with cocaine.

Many legalizers concede that drug legalization might increase use, but they shrug off the matter. "It may well be that there would be more addicts, and I would regret that result," says Nobel laureate economist Milton Friedman. The late Harvard Medical School psychiatry professor Norman Zinberg, a longtime proponent of "responsible" drug use, admitted that "use of now illicit drugs would certainly increase. Also, casualties probably would increase."

In fact, Dr. Herbert D. Kleber of Yale University, my deputy in charge of demand reduction, predicts legalization might cause "a five-to-six-fold increase" in cocaine use. But legalizers regard this as a necessary price for the "benefits" of legalization. What benefits?

Reduced Profits

1. *Legalization will take the profit out of drugs.* The result supposedly will be the end of criminal drug pushers and the big foreign drug wholesalers, who will turn to other enterprises because nobody will need to make furtive and dangerous trips to his local pusher.

But what, exactly, would the brave new world of legalized drugs look like? Buckley stresses that "adults get to buy the stuff at carefully regulated stores." (Would you want one in *your* neighborhood?) Others, like Friedman, suggest we sell the drugs at "ordinary retail outlets."

Former City University of New York sociologist Georgette Bennett assures us that "brand-name competition will be prohibited" and that strict quality control and proper labeling will be overseen by the Food and Drug Administration. In a touching egalitarian note, she adds that "free drugs will be provided at government clinics" for addicts too poor to buy them.

Almost all the legalizers point out that the price of drugs will fall, even though the drugs will be heavily taxed. Buckley, for example, argues that somehow federal drugstores will keep the price "low enough to discourage a black market but high enough to accumulate a surplus to be used for drug education."

Supposedly, drug sales will generate huge amounts of revenue, which will then be used to tell the public not to use drugs and to treat those who don't listen.

In reality, this tax would only allow government to *share* the drug profits now garnered by criminals. Legalizers would have to tax drugs heavily in order to pay for drug education and treatment programs. Criminals could undercut the official price and still make huge profits. What alternative would the government have? Cut the price until it was within the lunch-money budget of the average sixth-grade student?

2. *Legalization will eliminate the black market.* Wrong. And not just because the regulated prices could be undercut. Many legalizers admit that drugs such as crack or PCP are simply too dangerous to allow the shelter of the law. Thus criminals will provide what the government will not. "As long as drugs that people very much want remain illegal, a black market will exist," says legalization advocate David Boaz of the libertarian Cato Institute.

Look at crack. In powdered form, cocaine was an expensive indulgence. But street chemists found that a better and far less expensive—and far more dangerous—high could be achieved by mixing cocaine with baking soda and heating it. Crack was born, and "cheap" coke invaded low-income communities with furious speed.

"Legalization will give us the worst of both worlds; millions of *new* drug users *and* a thriving black market."

An ounce of powdered cocaine might sell on the street for $1200. That same ounce can produce 370 vials of crack at $10 each. Ten bucks seems like a cheap hit, but crack's intense ten- to 15-minute high is followed by an unbearable depression. The user wants more crack, thus starting a rapid and costly descent into addiction.

If government drugstores do not stock crack, addicts will find it in the clandestine market or simply bake it themselves from their legally purchased cocaine.

Currently crack is being laced with insecticides and animal tranquilizers to heighten its effect. Emergency rooms are now warned to expect victims of "sandwiches" and "moon rocks," life-threatening smokable mixtures of heroin and crack. Unless the government is prepared to sell these deadly variations of dangerous drugs, it will perpetuate a criminal black market by default.

"The simple fact is that drug use is wrong."

And what about children and teenagers? They would obviously be barred from drug purchases, just as they are prohibited from buying beer and liquor. But pushers will continue to cater to these young customers with the old, favorite come-ons—a couple of free fixes to get them hooked. And what good will anti-drug education be when these youngsters observe their older brothers and sisters, parents and friends lighting up and shooting up with government permission?

Legalization will give us the worst of both worlds: millions of *new* drug users *and* a thriving criminal black market.

3. Legalization will dramatically reduce crime. "It is the high price of drugs that leads addicts to robbery, murder and other crimes," says Ira Glasser, executive director of the American Civil Liberties Union. A study by the Cato Institute concludes: "Most, if not all, 'drug-related murders' are the result of drug prohibition."

But researchers tell us that many drug-related felonies are committed by people involved in crime *before* they started taking drugs. The drugs, so routinely available in criminal circles, make the criminals more violent and unpredictable.

Certainly there are some kill-for-a-fix crimes, but does any rational person believe that a cut-rate price for drugs at a government outlet will stop such psychopathic behavior? The fact is that under the influence of drugs, normal people do not act normally, and abnormal people behave in chilling and horrible ways. DEA [Drug Enforcement Administration] agents told me about a teenage addict in Manhattan who was smoking crack when he sexually abused and caused permanent internal injuries to his one-month-old daughter.

Children are among the most frequent victims of violent, drug-related crimes that have nothing to do with the cost of acquiring the drugs. In Philadelphia in 1987 more than half the child-abuse fatalities involved at least one parent who was a heavy drug user. Seventy-three percent of the child-abuse deaths in New York City in 1987 involved parental drug use.

In my travels to the ramparts of the drug war, I have seen nothing to support the legalizers' argument that lower drug prices would reduce crime. Virtually everywhere I have gone, police and DEA agents have told me that crime rates are highest where crack is cheapest.

4. Drug use should be legal since users only harm themselves. Those who believe this should stand beside the medical examiner as he counts the 36 bullet wounds in the shattered corpse of a three-year-old who happened to get in the way of his mother's drug-crazed boyfriend. They should visit the babies abandoned by cocaine-addicted mothers—infants who already carry the ravages of addiction in their own tiny bodies. They should console the devastated relatives of the nun who worked in a homeless shelter and was stabbed to death by a crack addict enraged that she would not stake him to a fix.

Irresponsible Behavior

Do drug addicts only harm themselves? Here is a former cocaine addict describing the compulsion that quickly draws even the most "responsible" user into irresponsible behavior: "Everything is about getting high, and any means necessary to get there becomes rational. If it means stealing something from somebody close to you, lying to your family, borrowing money from people you know you can't pay back, writing checks you know you can't cover, you do all those things—things that are totally against everything you have ever believed in."

Society pays for this behavior, and not just in bigger insurance premiums, losses from accidents and poor job performance. We pay in the loss of a priceless social currency as families are destroyed, trust between friends is betrayed and promising careers are never fulfilled. I cannot imagine sanctioning behavior that would increase that toll.

I find no merit in the legalizers' case. The simple fact is that drug use is wrong. And the moral argument, in the end, is the most compelling argument. A citizen in a drug-induced haze, whether on his backyard deck or on a mattress in a ghetto crack house, is not what the founding fathers meant by the "pursuit of happiness." Despite the legalizers' argument that drug use is a matter of "personal freedom," our nation's notion of liberty is rooted in the ideal of a self-reliant citizenry. Helpless wrecks in treatment centers, men chained by their noses to cocaine—these people are slaves.

Imagine if, in the darkest days of 1940, Winston Churchill had rallied the West by saying, "This war looks hopeless, and besides, it will cost too much. Hitler can't be *that* bad. Let's surrender and see what happens." That is essentially what we hear from the legalizers.

Fighting Back

This war *can* be won. I am heartened by indications that education and public revulsion are having an effect on drug use. The National Institute on Drug Abuse's latest survey of current users shows a 37 percent *decrease* in drug consumption since 1985. Cocaine is down 50 percent; marijuana use among young people is at its lowest rate since 1972. In my travels I've been encouraged by signs that Americans are fighting back.

I am under no illusion that such developments, however hopeful, mean the war is over. We need to involve more citizens in the fight, increase pressure on drug criminals and build on anti-drug programs that have proved to work.

Legalizing Drugs Would Harm the Poor and Minorities

Michael Parenti

About the Author: *Michael Parenti is an author whose works include* The Sword and the Dollar: Imperialism, Revolution, and the Arms Race.

A number of people are talking about legalizing the sale of narcotics. Supposedly, such a measure would take the criminals out of the supply system, the profits out of drug pushing, and the romance out of drug consumption. Certainly, for the pitiful addict who needs both an immediate fix and a gradual rehabilitation, drug consumption should be decriminalized under a controlled distribution. But across-the-board legalization fails to get at the real problem, which is not the *unlawful* consumption of narcotics but consumption itself.

It is argued that legalization would take the profits out of drug sales. But when did legalization ever take the profits out of anything? Tobacco and alcohol—to mention two legalized narcotics—are the source of multi-billion-dollar profits. The methadone program, a legalized alternative to heroin, brings in handsome profits for methadone producers while turning heroin addicts into methadone addicts.

In any case, the major problem is not the profits made by suppliers but the damage done to drug abusers and others in our communities. When something is made legal, it becomes more accessible, and when it is more accessible it is consumed more. All we would accomplish by le-

galizing drugs is to change the suppliers and increase the number of potential consumers. In fact, legalization sometimes does not even eliminate the old suppliers; it does not always take the criminals out of distribution. New York state's legalized lottery has not done away with the numbers racket or other forms of illegal gambling. The availability of methadone has not eliminated heroin. A controlled drug distribution system would not eliminate opportunities for unlawful distribution to new markets or to those who remain outside the programs for whatever reasons.

Finally, let's put to rest the myths about Prohibition, often cited by the advocates of legalization. Even with all the moonshine, bathtub gin, and bootleg whiskey imbibed, alcohol consumption was actually less during the Prohibition era than before or afterwards. After repeal, the incidence of alcohol-related diseases went up as consumption went up. Our two most dangerous and thoroughly legalized narcotics, alcohol and tobacco, available just about everywhere, respectively kill 30 and 60 times more people than does drug abuse. What does this say for legalization?

"We also need to smash the international drug trafficking itself."

Supply creates demand. When the British introduced great quantities of opium into China, it was not in response to popular demand on the part of the Chinese. For the British, it was a devilishly convenient way of creating a new market and turning a good profit on something produced in one colony (India) while propagating quiescence among the potentially explosive population of another colony (China). The Opium Wars were an attempt by the Chinese to resist British importation of a substance that was turning large numbers of Chinese into dopeheads. Somehow the Chinese knew that to "just say no" was not enough. So they attacked the British

Michael Parenti, "Saying 'No' to Legalized Drugs," *Political Affairs*, November 1989. Reprinted with permission.

pushers, the big suppliers who were bringing the stuff in and creating a demand.

What are we to do? To be sure, we need public education campaigns and rehabilitation centers and massive job and housing programs and other social services for those sectors of the population that are potentially most vulnerable to narcotics infestation. But we also need to smash the international drug traffic itself. We need to attack the suppliers, with the severest sanctions reserved for the most important drug merchants. The prime targets should be not the neighborhood pushers but the major suppliers. This is said to be a near impossible task. But a wholesale international war on major traffickers has never really been tried—except in China, Cuba, Indochina, and a few other places where revolutionary communist forces took state power. A war on drugs would not be impossible if we really made it our policy and enlisted the efforts of other nations like Pakistan, Thailand, Colombia, Peru, and Bolivia, getting them to be as tough on the drug traffickers as they are on their own peasants, students, and workers who struggle for social justice.

CIA Involvement

The CIA [Central Intelligence Agency] knows where the harvesting is done in Latin America and Asia. It knows the routes used by major suppliers like the Afghan "freedom fighters." For years the CIA knew about the large cocaine-smuggling operation between Argentina and the United States and the locations of the narcotics processing factories in Sicily, run by the Inzerillo and Spatola families and their connection to the Gambino family in New York. The CIA even knows what freighters shipped the stuff from Sicily to what ports in the Dominican Republic, and what airstrips in Central America are used and where they land in the United States, and what banks at home and abroad launder the billions of dollars. The CIA—and now the congressional investigation committee headed by [Massachusetts] Senator John Kerry—knows the names of the top officials and senior military of-

ficers in Ecuador, Venezuela, Colombia, Costa Rica, Guatemala, El Salvador, and elsewhere who pocket large sums to look the other way, or who, in some cases, are directly involved in the trade. . . .

On its own, the CIA could not move against the international drug traffic, even if it were so inclined. It would need a command from the White House. But no such policy ever came down from a Reagan—or Bush—administration that preferred to deal with drugs the way it dealt with other problems, skimming over the reality and relying on slick publicity hypes to maintain appearances.

You don't have to be a conspiracy theorist to wonder what kind of game right-wing policymakers are playing with the drug traffic. In this context I am intrigued by conservative news columnists who rail against the corrosion of American values and the destruction of the fabric of our society, yet seem oddly languid about narcotics. I don't blame them, either. If I were a right-winger I would have other things to worry about—the explosive potential of the black and Latino urban poor, for instance. I would be grateful that the urban uprisings of the '60s have not been repeated, despite the cruel cuts in human services. I would be delighted that the young men on the streets are not talking revolution, as did their counterparts of an earlier generation who joined the Young Lords and the Black Panthers. And I might not feel upset that it is because they are too busy shooting themselves up with needles and each other with guns.

African-American, Latino, and other community leaders have little patience with talk about legalization of drugs. They want an end to the flood of narcotics coming into their neighborhoods and they want the government to do something about it at both the international and the local level. But it appears that the government has another agenda. Drugs are an important instrument of repression and social control. The British imperialists knew this and, I suspect, so do our conservative pundits, the CIA, and the White House.

Chapter 3:
Is the U.S. War Against International Drug Trafficking Effective?

Preface

The U.S. Customs Service estimates that, in 1990 alone, nearly eight hundred tons of cocaine entered the U.S. from South American nations such as Colombia, Bolivia, and Peru. Mexico is the source of much of America's imported marijuana and some of its heroin. Most of America's heroin, hashish, and opium comes from Myanmar, Laos, Thailand, Afghanistan, Iran, Pakistan, Lebanon, and Syria. U.S. efforts to stop the flow of these illegal drugs are intensifying as ever greater amounts of drugs from these longtime sources continue to enter the United States.

The two primary goals of America's international drug trafficking policy are reducing the production of illegal drugs in foreign countries and stopping drug traffickers from smuggling them into the U.S. This policy, like most U.S. drug policies, began in the early 1970s as part of the Nixon administration's drug control efforts. During Nixon's term of office, the Coast Guard, the Customs Service, and the Drug Enforcement Administration (DEA) began vigorously intercepting drugs coming into the United States.

To assist these agencies in stopping the flow of drugs, the government passed a variety of laws that permitted enforcement agencies to search private property more freely, extradite foreign nationals to the U.S. for trial, and seize the assets of wealthy drug traffickers. New laws also increased prison penalties for drug possession.

A virtual army of personnel enforce these laws. They shut down secret warehouses where drugs are kept and laboratories where drugs are manufactured, trace drug money as it is being "laundered" or sent through banks and businesses to conceal its origins, intercept drug shipments, and build conspiracy cases against organized crime figures involved in drug trafficking. The Reagan and Bush administrations enhanced the power of the drug interdiction agencies by drafting the military to aid drug trafficking eradication efforts. For example, military intelligence personnel spy on drug traffickers, and other military personnel train the drug enforcement agents in survival techniques and the use of weapons. The military loans drug enforcement agencies assault helicopters and sophisticated radar planes and shares information gained from National Aeronautics and Space Administration satellites.

In addition to its efforts at preventing drugs from entering the country, the U.S. attempts to discourage foreign countries from producing drugs. By working closely with the governments of drug-producing countries, the U.S. hopes to aid in curtailing the activities of the powerful trafficking organizations known as drug cartels. Efforts to thwart the cartels include U.S. participation in raids in the major drug-producing countries, the spraying of herbicides designed to destroy coca plants and opium poppies, and the provision of badly needed economic aid to drug-producing nations. This aid, in the form of trade agreements, loans, and military equipment, is used to encourage these countries to comply with their own drug trafficking laws. Fear of the cartels' violence also motivates these foreign governments to cooperate with U.S. anti-drug measures. Other methods include negotiating the extradition of known foreign drug traffickers to the U.S. to stand trial for breaking American drug laws.

National Security

Those who support the government's efforts against international drug trafficking argue that the methods described above are necessary not only to reduce drug trafficking, but also to protect national security. The violence the drug cartels perpetrate against legitimate governments in drug-producing countries poses a significant threat to both U.S. and global security, experts maintain. In Colombia, for example, the cartels retaliated against government pressure to reduce drug trafficking by assassinating members of the judiciary as well as presidential candidates who had opposed the cartels' drug operations. Narcoterrorists, the more violent cartel members, have planted bombs on airplanes and in public places to frighten the government into cooperating with the cartels. The cartels have even attempted to elect some of their members to the Colombian government in order to con-

tinue their business without governmental interference. Had they succeeded, the U.S. would have lost important influence in Colombia and in the region. The cartels' violent retaliations could also have extended into the United States and threatened U.S. government officials.

Critics of U.S. policy charge that the government is using the drug war in foreign countries to increase America's control over impoverished, left-leaning Asian and Latin American countries. These critics contend that manipulating these small countries into alliance with the U.S. is the real goal of the drug war. According to peace activist and magazine editor Peter Drucker, "The Bush Administration . . . is making the expansion of the drug trade an excuse for more U.S. intervention."

Other critics of the government's international drug policies support its motives but believe its methods are hopelessly ineffective. These critics blame governmental bureaucracy, arguing that competition between the Customs Service and the DEA for government and media recognition and praise, combined with poorly planned operations, have decreased the drug war's effectiveness in seizing major shipments of drugs and arresting key figures in the international drug trade. These critics, among them former DEA agent-turned-author Michael Levine, charge that key members of the government's drug war are more interested in personal glory and media attention than in reducing the supply of drugs. Levine writes that the war on drugs is "the biggest, costliest, and most dangerous failure of American policy since Vietnam."

The articles in the following chapter debate the effectiveness of the government's drug trafficking policies and the effect of these policies on international affairs.

Is the U.S. War Against International Drug Trafficking Effective?

Yes: U.S. Campaigns Against Drug Trafficking Are Necessary

An International Campaign Against Drug Trafficking Is Necessary
Drug Trafficking Is a Global Crisis
International Cooperation Can Fight the Drug Trade
U.S. Campaigns Against Cocaine Producers Are Necessary
The U.S. Needs an International Drug Trafficking Policy

An International Campaign Against Drug Trafficking Is Necessary

James A. Baker III

About the Author: *James A. Baker III is the U.S. secretary of state. Baker made the following statement before the United Nations General Assembly Special Session on Narcotics in New York City on February 20, 1990.*

These are promising times for the world community. From South Africa to Eastern Europe, from the democratic movements in Asia to the new generation of democratic leaders in Latin America, we hear the stirring cry of freedom. People of faith, conviction, and courage are struggling and prevailing against difficult odds.

The old world of dogmatic dictatorships is on its way out. Tragic throwbacks to repression only serve to remind us that the new world of secure, prosperous, and just democracies has not yet arrived. And it will not come automatically. We all must work to bring it into being and ensure that it will last.

Global war brought [the United Nations] into existence in 1945. And it was with solemn determination that the UN founders pledged, in the opening words of our Charter, ". . . to save succeeding generations from the scourge of war. . . ."

Especially now, at this promising time, it is critical for the nations of the world to recall the fundamental aims that unite us. For if we fail to support the goals of the UN Charter—peace, human dignity, justice, respect for sovereign

James A. Baker III, "Narcotics: Threat to Global Security," *Department of State Dispatch*, September 3, 1990. Public Domain.

rights and international law, concern for the well-being of all the world's peoples— if we fail to do our utmost to accomplish these aims, then we could end up living in a future that resembles our troubled past.

Even as we work together to eliminate war and conflict, there are other troubles that will not wait and that are bringing untold sorrow to mankind. Even as we heed the cry of freedom and democracy, we must not fail to hear another cry. This cry is not the affirmation of freedom but its negation, not the uplifting of democracy but its degradation. It is the call of the drug addict.

"Drugs pose a serious threat to global security."

That cry concerns all of us, and it is urgent. We hear it close to home—to my home, to your home, and to the homes of our neighbors in the world community. None of us—not one nation—remains untouched. None of us—not one—is safe from the danger of drugs.

Drugs pose a serious threat to global security. We are here at this special session because we recognize this bitter truth. We fully recognize the growing importance of combatting drugs. I particularly wish to thank the governments that have played leading roles in preparing the agenda before us.

I would now like to review for you the comprehensive approach my government is taking to help rid my country and the world of illicit drugs.

First, I will describe America's national drug strategy, which centers on the need to reduce the use of drugs at home.

Second, I want to share with you the results of the summit in Cartagena, where President Bush and the leaders of Colombia, Bolivia, and Peru formed the world's first anti-drug cartel.

Finally, I will offer my government's thoughts on how the United Nations can best assist in the global fight against narcotics.

First is our national drug strategy. The American people consider drugs the number one problem facing the United States. And winning the war against drugs is a top priority for President Bush and, therefore, a top foreign priority for me. The Bureau for International Narcotics Matters at the Department of State, ably led by Assistant Secretary [Melvyn] Levitsky, has done a first-rate job of ensuring that narcotics control issues are fully integrated into our diplomatic efforts.

Our drug control strategy calls for an attack on the drug problem in all its aspects—consumption, trafficking, illicit production, treatment, and rehabilitation. My government is placing greater emphasis than ever before on preventive education programs, treatment, and rehabilitation. We aim to stop the trafficking in all illicit drugs, not just cocaine. Heroin, marijuana, and the so-called designer drugs are also major threats. And we are attacking the problems of domestic cultivation and trafficking.

"Narcotics are a deadly threat to all nations that are exposed to them."

This kind of comprehensive approach calls for increased resources. Since the Bush Administration took office, the domestic anti-drug budget has increased 67% to $7.6 billion. And our international anti-drug budget, including border and off-shore interdiction efforts, has increased 73% to $3.1 billion.

We fully realize that attacking the problem of domestic consumption is our most critical challenge. As long as the demand for drugs by Americans remains voracious, our nation faces an endless, uphill struggle to halt supply. We are making progress. Domestic drug use dropped 37% from 1985 to 1988, and cocaine use was cut in half over the same period. But we have a long way to go.

We are determined that drug users in the United States face the hard facts: Their behavior is not just a personal indulgence. American users act as paymasters to organized murderers. Profits from every kilo of cocaine bought in the streets of America buy the bullets which rob democracies of their dignity and freedom. American users aid and abet the drug cartels which in turn foment and exploit regional and global instabilities. When Americans feed their habits and enrich the cartels, it's like they're giving succor to terrorists. American users are accessories to criminals who poison children. Their habits also contribute to the murder of the land. Coca farmers have destroyed acres of forest lands; traffickers have dumped millions of gallons of precursor chemicals into rivers.

I regret to say that narcotics has become a big business, a very big business in my country. In fall 1989 in Los Angeles, agents seized 22 tons of warehoused cocaine. If all the kilo packages we seized were stacked, one on top of the other, the pile would be a mile and a half high—that's a mountain of misery half the height of the tallest mountain in the continental United States. It was estimated that the street value of the seized cocaine exceeds the individual gross national products of well over 100 of the nations represented in this chamber today. And this was just one warehouse. Imagine the veritable Mt. Everests of misery we haven't found!

Thus, consumption and supply, dependency and exploitation, greed and violence become a vicious circle—in truth, like a dragon chasing its own barbed tail. That circle of misery and death must be broken. America is helping to break it—both at home and with our partners abroad.

Partners in the Drug War

This brings me to my second topic: [the] summit in Colombia. As you know, President Bush and I traveled to Cartagena where we met with our counterparts from Colombia, Bolivia, and Peru. In Cartagena, the summit partners pledged to attack the merchants of drugs and death from every angle—production, distribution, finance, and use. President Bush was unequivocal in his commitment to reduce demand for drugs in the United States. We agreed that it was pointless to apportion the blame between producer nations and consumer nations—narcotics are a deadly threat to all nations that are exposed to them. We and our summit colleagues are determined to break the back of crack and put the illicit cartels out of business.

By going to Cartagena, the President demonstrated our country's absolute determination to fight the drug war for however long it takes. We have assured our partners that we will not fail to support them in the drug fight.

As part of our support, from FY [fiscal year] 1989 to FY 1991, the United States will increase sevenfold our international drug budget for Colombia, Bolivia, and Peru. Our total economic assistance will more than double to those Andean nations [in 1991] as they undertake tough counternarcotics programs and apply sound economic policies.

Colombia's Courage

It is fitting that the summit was held in Colombia. We applaud Colombia's courageous decision to seize and destroy labs, arrest and prosecute narcotics offenders, extradite traffickers and money launderers, and challenge the cocaine empire.

No nation has so bravely confronted the drug lords or made greater sacrifices. No nation here can remain indifferent to Colombia's fate. The scale of drug-related violence in Colombia is horrific, even to those among us who have experienced firsthand the violence that has been so sadly a part of our turbulent century.

In one short and brutal decade in Colombia, the Medellin and Cali traffickers have killed over 1,000 public officials, 12 Supreme Court justices, over two dozen journalists, and more than 200 judges and judicial personnel, not to mention the scores of men, women, and children who happened to be going about their daily lives in the wrong place at the wrong time. And no amount of laundering can wash the blood off money stained by drugs. The so-called kings of cocaine are criminals—criminals of uncommon power and uncommon brutality.

Time and again, President Barco has put his own life on the line to free his nation from the deadly grip of the drug cartels. Together with President Barco, Presidents Bush, Garcia, and Paz all recognize their responsibility to take the lead in combating cocaine, our common enemy. Together at Cartagena, we reaffirmed the need for development, trade, and investment to strengthen growth-oriented economic policies in order to offset the economic costs of counternarcotics programs. We agreed to work in concert to heighten public awareness of the debilitating effects that drug production, trafficking, and abuse have on our countries. We agreed to provide economic assistance to help strengthen the legitimate economies of the Andean nations. And we agreed to strengthen the law enforcement capabilities of our countries to bring traffickers to justice. President Bush told his Andean colleagues that he would raise these issues with the G-7 (the major industrialized democracies) at the Houston summit and with other developed countries as well. The United States seeks to improve and strengthen narcotics consultation and cooperation with other developed countries to bolster international support of producer-country counternarcotics efforts.

> ## "There is no country . . . so proud or so great as to be able to rid itself of drugs without the help of other nations."

Finally, we and our Andean colleagues agreed to urge all countries to ratify, as soon as possible, the UN Convention Against Illicit Traffic in Narcotic Drugs and Psychotrophic Substances. When ratified, the 1988 convention will foster worldwide cooperation in such areas as money laundering, asset seizure, precursor chemical control, extradition, investigation, intelligence gathering, and information sharing. I am pleased to report that President Bush signed the instrument of ratification for the United States on February 13, 1990. We deposited the signed instrument of ratification with the United Nations.

Ratification by all countries will help us in regional efforts to combat cocaine and also increase worldwide cooperation against illicit drugs of all kinds.

By fostering worldwide cooperation, the United Nations plays a crucial role. It is imperative that we make maximum use of the UN instruments and the UN system as a whole to buttress our efforts at the national and regional levels.

There is no country here so proud or so great as to be able to rid itself of drugs without the help of other nations. Nor is there any country here so small that it cannot support in some way this important international effort. Together we can work more effectively than in isolation. We can accomplish more in concert than at odds with one another. This special session affords to us all, the community of nations, an opportunity to work together decisively against drugs.

We must seize this opportunity now. For if we let it pass, our inaction will condemn more children to suffering and want, more families to destruction, more governments to the assaults of drug cartels. And more of the threads that hold together the very fabric of civilized society will unravel.

That is why the President and I are convinced of the timeliness and efficacy of this special session. We have the opportunity to set an action-oriented course for the UN system.

The Global Program of Action

It is my government's hope that adoption of the Global Program of Action, and the related Political Declaration, will take us considerably closer to ridding the international community of the drug scourge—provided, of course, that the program commits us to concrete activities, that it is fully implemented by the UN agencies of the system, and that it is backed by complementary efforts at the national and regional levels. Certainly we the member governments cannot ask the United Nations to do things that we will not do at home. Nor can we ask the United Nations to undertake ambitious programs without financial backing and a strong infrastructure with which to carry them out. We must order our priorities in such a way as to accomplish our aims within the framework of a unitary approach to the entire UN system and through zero real program growth in budgets.

"Freedom and democracy are in the ascendancy, yet they face formidable odds. . . . Drugs are among their mortal enemies."

The Global Program of Action will reinforce the solid foundation which we have built already; by this I mean the two established international drug control treaties now in effect and the new convention against illicit trafficking which I mentioned earlier. In addition, we have other mandates such as those contained in the comprehensive multi-disciplinary outline from the 1987 International Drug Conference and UN General Assembly Resolution 44/141, adopted in December 1989. All of these documents give us the legal and program basis as well as the clear authority with which to proceed. So let us use these tools effectively before we endeavor to write new treaties. We want to strengthen our systemwide efforts and ensure maximum cooperation, coordination, and efficiency in the conduct of all UN programs.

To be sure, there is a good case for improving and reinforcing our multilateral infrastructure. We agree that member countries should allocate more resources to UN anti-drug efforts in order to complement domestic counternarcotics efforts. We are more committed than ever to working with other governments, so that the UN system may be a stronger, more responsive partner in the drug fight. With the help of the Secretary General and all member states, the President and I are hopeful that the Global Program of Action will energize a dynamic drug control effort of worldwide scope.

In our global war against drugs, we regard as natural allies all nations sharing the resolve to resist this scourge. Traditional friends and traditional adversaries alike must pool their efforts. Indeed, many of us already have joined forces, despite political and economic differences. Together we will combat the multinational drug empires on every front. Together we will hold to account any government that grants safe havens to drug profiteers, that actively permits the laundering of money, that turns a blind and uncaring eye to drug abuse and drug trafficking. We will give no quarter.

I began these remarks by saying that we are living in promising times. Freedom and democracy are in the ascendancy, yet they face formidable odds. Undoubtedly drugs are among their mortal enemies, for freedom and democracy are universal ideals that speak to the dignity of every individual. And if these ideals are to be realized, every individual must make a contribution to his or her society and to the world community. An individual caught in the grip of drugs becomes a slave—no longer a free or a responsible person. And the same thing can happen to entire nations.

But such tragedies do not have to happen—not to our citizens, not to our countries, not to the world community. It's up to us—each of us, all of us together. A great deal is at stake.

We know that we cannot cleanse the world of drugs in one generation. Yet I believe I am justified in ending on an optimistic note. More than ever before, nations all over the world are working together on the global drug problem. The United Nations has greatly helped to bring this about.

"We must . . . rid God's good earth of the evil scourge of drugs."

From the Soviet Union to Jamaica, from Spain to Malaysia, nations are joining forces in the fight against narcotics. We, the peoples of the world, must keep up the fight—in the deep jungles and mountain valleys where coca and poppies are grown, in the urban jungles ruled by corruption and cruelty, in shadowy backrooms where drug-stained money is laundered, and in the dark recesses of the soul—there perhaps most of all.

Now, today, for the sake of our children and our grandchildren, we must do all that is humanly possible to rid God's good earth of the evil scourge of drugs.

Drug Trafficking Is a Global Crisis

Mary Ellen Sullivan

About the Author: *Mary Ellen Sullivan writes for* Current Health 2, *a monthly magazine on health issues published for high-school students.*

The lure of drugs is strong. For dealers, money motivates. For users, the desire for pleasure or escape usually prompts the entry into drugs. The quest to repeat the experience drives addiction.

Unwittingly, each user fuels an international drug economy that is built on violence, greed, and a callous disregard for human life.

The drug business is an ugly one, full of exploitation, wrecked health, and wasted lives. It also is a big business, the biggest in the world, with an annual volume exceeding $300 billion (some estimates go as high as $500 billion). But it is a big business that law enforcement agencies, national governments, and many small but powerful local initiatives are working to destroy. What are the chances of their doing this in the '90s?

There are more than 40 million illegal drug users throughout the world—more than half of them in the United States alone. In fact, the United States is the single biggest market for the illegal drug trade.

Once thought of as merely a health or a social problem for drug users and their families, drug abuse in the United States during the last five to 10 years has created a set of problems so destructive and far-reaching that solving them has

become one of our country's top priorities. Why? Consider:

• Chief Justice William Rehnquist of the U.S. Supreme Court reports that the number of drug-related cases in the federal courts rose 85 percent between 1986 and 1990.

• The U.S. Department of Justice says that half of all men arrested for serious crimes are drug users.

• Between 1986 and 1988, there was an 1,100 percent increase in the number of semi-automatic weapons (the weapons favored by drug dealers and also the weapons involved in several mass murders at school playgrounds in recent years).

• In urban areas, entire neighborhoods are taken over by drug gangs making them unsafe for residents. Also, in these neighborhoods innocent children are often killed in the crossfire of warring drug gangs.

• The spread of the deadly disease AIDS currently is highest among intravenous drug users. . . .

• Approximately one in 10 babies in the United States is born with illegal substances in his or her system.

"Drugs have become a global issue."

Although the United States' drug problem right now seems uncontrollable, we're not the only ones with problems. Drugs have become a global issue. Use has dramatically increased in Europe and even in such previously untouched areas as the Soviet Union. Violence is a way of life—and a fact of life—for the international drug traffickers, where informants are routinely tortured and killed, and opponents are murdered by hired killers for as little as $10. And some Third-World countries' entire economy is based on the illegal drug trade.

Take, for instance, Colombia. . . . Cocaine is this country's major export, bringing in more than $4 billion a year and supplying about 80 percent of the world's cocaine. Entire villages in the Andes mountains depend on the coca leaf crop, from which cocaine is extracted, for their existence, not to mention the cities that have come alive from the conspicuous spending of the high-level drug traffickers. Medellin, the home of the country's biggest drug cartels, or organizations, has million-dollar high-rise apartments equipped with huge satellite dishes for picking up American TV shows, expensive clothing and jewelry stores, imported cars, and other luxuries. Accompanying this opulence, however, is a staggering level of violence: Medellin has the highest murder rate of any city in the world not at war.

In addition, in many Latin American and Caribbean countries, the drug organizations have corruption on their side. With the drug traffickers' policy called "plomo o plata" (which literally means lead or silver, or a bullet or a bribe), they have managed to buy off and scare people ranging from local police officers to a country's highest leaders. In Colombia, this policy reigns supreme: In August, 1989, a leading presidential candidate and anti-drug campaigner was shot down at an open-air political rally. More than 50 judges and two cabinet members were assassinated between 1988 and 1990 after trying to crack down on the drug cartels. Making law enforcement even more difficult is the fact that in Colombia and neighboring countries, some elected officials are known drug dealers.

Asian Heroin

In Burma, the Southeast Asian country that is the world's largest producer of heroin, the drug warlords have private armies to protect their businesses. There are no restrictions for crossing the border into neighboring Thailand. And the laws are such that dealers can only be arrested if they have possession of the drug—and they make it a policy never to touch it.

Clearly, the drug problem is complex and destructive. Here's a closer look at this world issue.

Supply and demand. That's what rules the drug trade. It's classic Keynesian economics.

Says a writer in the Spanish news magazine *Cambio 16*, "On the day that a pound of bananas is worth more than a pound of cocaine, there will be no more South American coca farmers."

And, conversely, the day Americans stop craving drugs, the world supply will shrink.

"The day Americans stop craving drugs, the world supply will shrink."

Marijuana, cocaine, and heroin are the drugs with the highest demand worldwide. In the United States, there are 18 million marijuana and hashish users, 700,000 heroin addicts, and an estimated 7 million who regularly use cocaine.

Mexico actually supplies more drugs to the United States than any other country, growing its own marijuana and heroin and serving as an entry point for Colombian cocaine.

Colombia, Peru, and Bolivia produce almost all of the world's cocaine. The coca plant thrives in the mild, high-altitude climate of the Andes mountains.

Most of the heroin that reaches the United States comes from the opium grown in the poppy fields of what's called the "golden triangle," where Burma, Laos, and Thailand converge. Iran, Pakistan, and Afghanistan also ship this drug to our country.

The majority of illegal drugs slip into our country through southern Florida and across the Mexican border—drop-shipped onto high-speed boats, packed into private planes, hidden in imported goods, and concealed on bodies. Customs officials say they've seized drugs in the most improbable places: in coffins, in flower shipments, in diapers, and in beer cans. They've reported heroin-laced shampoo and dog collars containing cocaine.

Once it gets here, the attraction of the drug world is particularly strong for inner-city kids who can make $200 to $3,000 a day selling crack. Some children start as early as 8 or 9 years old as lookouts for drug dealers, warning them when police enter the neighborhood. Lookouts make about $100 a day. In a few years they can graduate to "runners," transporting drugs from the makeshift factories where drugs are processed to the dealers. Their salaries also graduate—to about $300 a day.

By the time they are teenagers, they can become "king of the street" or dealers. An aggressive crack dealer can rake in more than $15,000 a week. That's more than half a million dollars a year. This money buys them the status symbols that make them neighborhood heroes—Mercedes Benzes, BMWs, Rolex watches, gold chains, designer clothes.

"Our war on drugs is being fought in skirmishes, using guerrilla tactics."

It's no different for the South American peasant. The $1,000 offered by traffickers for every 2.5 acres to plant coca, whose leaf cocaine is made from, often means the difference between eating and starving. Nor is it different for the local *poseros*, or processors, who grind the coca leaf into paste. They fare even better: It's not unusual to see color televisions in their shacks and four-wheel drive vehicles in their dirt driveways. And so it goes all the way up the ladder. The people who chemically process the coca paste, turning it into the powder form it is sold in, make even more. Pilots can earn $5,000 a kilo to transport the drug out of the country. And, of course, the leaders of the cartels are millionaires. *Fortune* magazine estimates Pablo Escobar, one of Colombia's biggest drug barons, is a billionaire.

Big bucks are in the heroin trade, too. Opium from Burma costing $170 can be turned into $2 million on the streets of New York or Europe with minimal processing.

In the fight against the drug trade, the United States is making a full-blown assault. FBI [Federal Bureau of Investigation]. DEA [Drug Enforcement Administration]. CIA [Central Intelligence Agency]. Coast Guard. Customs agents. Local police. Schools. Hospitals. The legal system. Congress. Everyone's getting involved. The federal government budgeted $6 billion for 1989.

"Drug Czar" William Bennett wants more. "The bill will be big," he says, "but the bill for not doing something will be bigger: $150 billion to $200 billion."

It seems, however, whatever the United States spends is never enough. The federal government's dollars seem like pennies compared with the millions the drug dealers have to spend. Often they have faster boats, more powerful weapons, and a cold-blooded lack of hesitation in killing anyone who stands in their way.

In addition, our overloaded legal system has difficulty handling the number of cases it has. In some cities, only a small percentage of adults arrested on drug charges actually serve time. Cases where the drug offender is a minor—as is true with the majority of crack offenders—mostly go through the juvenile court system. This involves a series of court supervisions, probations, and foster homes for first-time offenders. Sometimes it takes as many as seven or eight arrests before a juvenile dealer is jailed.

Making Progress

But the United States is making progress. Each year surpasses the last in the number of drug seizures, drug busts, drug-related arrests. In Washington, D.C., between 1983 and 1987, drug arrests increased by 45 percent, drug prosecutions by more than 500 percent, and drug convictions by more than 700 percent. One of Colombia's most powerful drug kingpins is currently serving a life sentence in a Florida prison. But our war on drugs is being fought in skirmishes, using guerrilla tactics, under cover of night. It is a war where the enemy is everywhere—and hard to find. Right now we're winning many battles but still losing the war.

International Cooperation Can Fight the Drug Trade

The U.S. Office of National Drug Control Policy

About the Author: *The U.S. Office of National Drug Control Policy is the headquarters for the U.S. war on drugs.* The National Drug Control Strategy *is an official statement of the federal government's aims, goals, and priorities in the worldwide war against drug trafficking.*

In September 1989, the *National Drug Control Strategy* established an international strategy designed to disrupt and dismantle the multinational criminal organizations that support the production, processing, transportation, and distribution of drugs to the United States and to other nations. The chief emphasis of that strategy is to attack the international drug trade by focusing on efforts aimed at the points of greatest value to the drug trafficking organizations and networks.

It is clear that the United States cannot assume the burden of combatting drugs by itself. A cornerstone of our international drug control strategy, therefore, is to work with and motivate other countries—those that are involved in production, transit or consumption, as well as those that have little or no drug problem as yet—to engage their own resources and efforts to defeat the drug trade. Only through a broad, cooperative international effort can we achieve the objectives of reducing the foreign supply of drugs while working with other countries to dismantle

From "International Initiatives," *National Drug Control Strategy* by the U.S. Office of National Drug Control Policy. Public Domain.

their own illicit drug operations, reduce the demand for drugs, and combat the worldwide drug trade.

A major component of our international efforts is a strategy aimed at supporting the principal cocaine source countries—Colombia, Peru, and Bolivia—in their efforts to control and defeat the drug trade. U.S. strategy is to work with the host governments to disrupt and destroy the growing, processing, and transportation of coca and coca products within these source countries, with the long-term goal of effecting a major reduction in the supply of cocaine from these countries to the United States, while also working to reduce the demand for drugs by users in the United States.

> **"Only through a broad, cooperative international effort can we . . . combat the worldwide drug trade."**

The national strategy seeks to attain three near-term goals. The first of these is to strengthen the political will and institutional capability of Colombia, Peru, and Bolivia, to enable them to take the needed steps to disrupt the activities of, and ultimately dismantle, the cocaine trafficking organizations. This involves supporting the commitment of the three host governments' political leadership against narcotics trafficking, by providing enhanced security training and equipment, and military assistance. The strategy also incorporates expanded economic assistance, beginning in Fiscal Year 1991 and conditioned on the drug control performance and the existence of sound economic policies of the host countries, to offset some of the economic dislocations associated with successful drug suppression efforts. It also includes assisting these countries to strengthen their ability to prosecute, extradite, and punish narcotics traffickers, illicit arms traffickers and drug money launderers, through the application of resources needed to reorganize and strengthen the laws and legal institutions now in place. Finally, it involves supporting the resolve of judges and other individuals within the legal system to prosecute and sentence traffickers.

"Heroin currently ranks second to cocaine as the greatest foreign drug threat to the United States."

The second short-term goal is to increase the effectiveness of law enforcement and military activities of the three countries against the cocaine trade. This involves assisting them in isolating key coca growing areas through measures aimed at controlling road, river, and air access, and controlling their national airspace by providing real-time air targeting data through appropriate channels while helping them to develop a rapid response capability against air trafficking threats. Attacking the cocaine trade involves blocking shipments of key precursor chemicals, by controlling their importation and distribution, and interdicting the movement of chemicals already within the region; destroying existing laboratories and processing centers; and controlling the importation and distribution of illicit munitions. And it means carrying out eradication programs on a case-by-case basis, with a view to their effect on total country production and their costs and benefits when compared to other drug control programs in the same country or areas. The likely political consequences of proposed eradication programs will be carefully weighed before such operations are pursued. As drug suppression efforts succeed, our strategy calls for U.S. economic assistance to help provide legal, self-sustaining, income-earning alternatives to growers and workers. Such assistance will be applied in coca producing areas and in contiguous regions which have been the source of permanent and seasonal migration to the coca-producing zones.

The third near-term goal is to inflict significant damage to the trafficking organizations which operate within the three countries, by working with the countries concerned to disrupt or dismantle trafficking operations and elements of greatest value. This involves focusing on trafficking leaders and their key lieutenants, to incapacitate them through arrests, prosecution, and incarceration; impeding the transfer of drug-generated funds; and seizing the assets of traffickers within the United States and in other countries where they operate. . . .

While heroin currently ranks second to cocaine as the greatest foreign drug threat to the United States, it is the primary drug of use in Europe and Asia. Although there is no firm estimate of heroin availability or use in the United States, the drug is known to have found new markets through combination with other drugs, and smokeable varieties of heroin. The high volume of opium production, as well as heroin's great profitability and addictive properties, add urgency to cooperative efforts to suppress the international trade in heroin.

Yet heroin may prove even more difficult to control than cocaine, because much of the world's opium and heroin is produced in countries such as Afghanistan, Burma (Myanmar), Laos, and Iran, where U.S. government and Western influence is greatly limited, and political unrest makes it difficult for these countries to exercise control over production areas. Moreover, opium and heroin production, distribution, and consumption patterns show an alarming persistence and resistance to control, as evidenced by the fact that poppy cultivation has moved across the Mexican border into Guatemala, while Pakistan, Iran, and Thailand have become net *importers* of the drug to satisfy their burgeoning addict populations.

Future Strategies

The Administration has accordingly undertaken a government-wide study of the threat which will form the basis for our future strategies. All major aspects of heroin suppression will be examined.

Following the pattern of our overall international strategy, our goals include strengthening the political will and institutional capability of cooperating opium- and heroin-producing countries to combat their drug trade; increasing the effectiveness of host country law enforcement and military organizations to detect, monitor, and apprehend traffickers and seize major shipments; and inflicting significant damage on the trafficking organizations that operate within the source countries and distribution areas. . . .

The increasingly global nature of the heroin threat will require greater participation both by other developed countries and by the producer and trafficker countries. We expect to work closely with members of the European Community, Canada, Japan, and Australia, as well as the Soviet Union, to develop effective approaches to opium-producing countries where the United States has limited access, and to share the burden of controlling the growth and production of opium and heroin.

"Mexico cultivates sufficient *cannabis* to satisfy an estimated 25 percent of the U.S. marijuana demand."

Increased emphasis will be given to strengthening joint measures, financial control mechanisms, and conspiracy laws to target money launderers, and to detect, seize and confiscate traffickers' assets. Attention will be given to the role of the United Nations and regional organizations in international heroin suppression. In addition, emphasis will be given to the ratification by other countries of the U.N. (Vienna) Convention, which calls for the criminalization of the production, cultivation, transportation and trafficking of heroin, as well as other drugs, and calls for the criminalization of money laundering, illegal arms and chemical precursor trafficking. We will encourage regional organizations to

assume greater responsibility for playing an active role in this process. Finally, since a key to successful narcotics control is public awareness in producer, trafficking, and consumer countries, we will improve U.S. international and regional diplomacy and public awareness programs, focusing on all aspects of the opium and heroin problem as it affects consumers and producers alike.

Marijuana Control

Foreign marijuana control remains an important element of our international strategy. U.S. domestic marijuana control efforts support our foreign initiatives in this area because of the health threat posed by marijuana use, because international agreements obligate us to domestic control programs, and because the vigorous pursuit of our own marijuana reduction programs supports our efforts to convince other countries to engage in strong marijuana control programs of their own. As the Drug Enforcement Administration and other Federal agencies intensify their efforts to eradicate domestically produced marijuana, therefore, we will continue to pursue *cannabis* eradication programs with other producing countries. At the same time, U.S. funding of foreign marijuana control programs will be weighed against the use of the same funds for programs to control other foreign drugs that have greater potential for damage. In certain countries where narcotics control programs are directed against the production and trafficking of coca or opium *and* marijuana, resources and priority attention will be given to efforts which can have the greatest impact in reducing the supply of the most dangerous illegal drugs entering the United States.

Drug transit countries present an array of problems and opportunities significantly different from countries that produce illegal drugs. On the one hand, drug trafficking and use have taken a serious toll within a number of these countries, which are therefore willing to work closely with the United States and other nations to the degree that their concerns about national sovereignty and their own resources permit. On the other hand, many transit countries have permissive drug laws and lax financial regulation; underfunded law enforcement, investigatory, prosecutory, and judicial systems; and undeveloped law enforcement intelligence capabilities. Several produce drugs, have their own powerful domestic drug trafficking groups, are used as transshipment areas by multinational drug organizations. Transit areas of special concern include Mexico, Central America, and the Caribbean.

Mexico is a principal source for drugs entering the United States, both as a producer of marijuana and opium, and as a major transit country for cocaine. Mexico cultivates sufficient *cannabis* to satisfy an estimated 25 percent of the U.S. marijuana demand, accounts for a significant amount of the heroin supplied to the U.S. market, and is a transshipment area for at least half of the cocaine that enters the United States. Since the inauguration of the Salinas Administration in 1988, the Mexican Government has embarked on a vigorous effort to diminish the supply of drugs to and within Mexico, and their transit to the United States. Several major Mexican figures connected to Colombian trafficking organizations have been arrested and their organizations have been disrupted. Mexico has also ratified the 1988 U.N. [United Nations] Convention and has negotiated numerous bilateral anti-drug agreements with other countries.

"The formation of a Western Hemisphere multinational counternarcotics force has been suggested."

To reduce the flow of drugs from Mexico and to disrupt Mexican, Colombian, and other narcotics trafficking organizations, the Administration will continue to develop cooperative actions related both to drug supply reduction within and through Mexico, and drug demand reduc-

tion within Mexico. In cooperation with the Office of National Drug Control Policy and other concerned departments, the Department of State will be responsible for coordinating all U.S. plans and programs supporting U.S.-Mexican anti-drug efforts. In the area of law enforcement, the United States will pursue cooperative initiatives to identify and dismantle trafficking organizations, to improve tactical information sharing with appropriate Mexican Government authorities, and to help in the development of Mexico's interdiction programs aimed at smuggler aircraft crossing Mexican airspace or landing in Mexico. Eradication will be supported in conjunction with interdiction efforts, where it is effective and can contribute to a net reduction of Mexican drug crop production. . . .

Central America and the Caribbean

Central America has gained in importance as a transit area for cocaine shipments to the United States. One country, Guatemala, now produces a significant quantity of opium. The Department of State, working with other Federal agencies, will increase U.S. and joint U.S.-host country intelligence efforts to identify and track drug traffickers by air and land through Central America to Mexico, by expediting the installation of the Joint Information Collection Center (JICC) system.

The broad objectives of U.S. drug control strategy in the Caribbean are to deny safe havens to drug traffickers, and to prevent drug production, storage, and transit operations, and drug-related activities such as money laundering. Much has been done to deter traffickers' free use of Caribbean airspace and waters through the application of U.S. interdiction programs, but special attention will also be given to initiatives focused on the Caribbean countries and their territorial waters and airspace. With respect to these initiatives, the Administration will seek ways to improve local intelligence and law enforcement capabilities, strengthen Caribbean banking laws and financial regulations, and increase national criminal asset seizures. It will also seek to improve access to the territorial waters and airspace of producer and transit countries. In the area of law enforcement information sharing, the Administration will work cooperatively to strengthen the current JICC system and assist Caribbean countries to establish appropriate new JICCs that can become the basis for a broad network of linked centers for the exchange of drug law enforcement intelligence and tactical data throughout the region. The Office of National Drug Control Policy, through the Supply Reduction Working Group, will develop and coordinate U.S. initiatives to enable Federal agencies to disseminate tactical air data to countries identified as primary originators or receivers of drug trafficking flights.

The formation of a Western Hemisphere multinational counternarcotics force has been suggested as a means to broaden international drug control efforts while overcoming national sovereignty concerns by requiring that such a force be utilized only upon the invitation of a host government. At the request of the United States and other countries, the United Nations . . . included the concept of a multinational counternarcotics force among the range of issues [considered at] the February 1990 General Assembly special session on narcotics control issues. The concept has been the focus of considerable attention, but no Western Hemisphere country has yet expressed a willingness to permit a multinational group of foreign troops to conduct drug-control operations within its borders. . . .

The United Nations

The United Nations Convention Against Illicit Narcotic Drugs and Psychotropic Substances has been signed by more than 80 countries. At the Administration's urging, the U.S. Senate gave its advice and consent to the Convention on November 22, 1989. The ratification of the Convention by other signatory states will continue to be a priority issue in U.S. bilateral relations.

The Administration will give priority to the development of bilateral or multilateral law en-

forcement cooperation with consumer, producer, and transit countries. The six Mutual Legal Assistance Treaties—MLATs—that were approved by the Senate on October 24, 1989, should facilitate the transfer of law enforcement information, and help develop evidence for investigative and prosecutorial purposes in the United States and abroad. The Administration will seek the conclusion of additional MLATs.

"The governments of major drug producing and drug transit countries should be held accountable."

The September 1989 National Drug Control Strategy stressed the need to continue to assist countries through existing international and regional organizations, including the United Nations. The Administration will support multinational initiatives that hold significant promise of increasing the international commitment to drug control.

Since the announcement of the September 1989 National Drug Control Strategy, the Administration has undertaken a major initiative through the Department of State to engage the support of consumer countries in harmonizing our efforts to control the production and trafficking of drugs worldwide. We have proposed to Canada, the major countries of Western Europe, Japan, and Australia, the formation of a consultative mechanism to enhance international assistance to producer countries aimed at increasing the effectiveness of international drug control actions, and we will pursue this initiative in the months ahead. We will emphasize the importance of specific international actions to support broad anti-drug initiatives at major multinational meetings . . . and within these fora seek cooperative ways to contain world drug supply and demand. . . .

The Administration will ensure the coordination of overseas law enforcement activities in a manner that does not place undue restraints on contacts or intelligence collection. U.S. Ambassadors and principal officers will continue to provide overall guidance and oversight of foreign country narcotics programs as an undelegable responsibility. They will ensure the coordination of all agency activities personally. In major drug source and transit countries, the Ambassador may elect to establish a fully dedicated Narcotics Control Coordinator who will support the efforts of the Deputy Chief of Mission to oversee all U.S. narcotics control activities within the host country.

Several U.S. law enforcement agencies have jurisdictional responsibilities in foreign drug-related law enforcement matters, as well as an interest in drug-related intelligence collection. These include the Treasury Department, which has responsibility for money laundering control programs abroad, the U.S. Customs Service, which has established programs to counter all smuggling, including the smuggling of drugs, and the U.S. Coast Guard. Also involved is the FBI [Federal Bureau of Investigation], which has a mandate to collect evidence to support drug investigations under stipulated circumstances, such as in Italy and Canada. Apart from such limited circumstances, all drug law enforcement operations will continue to be conducted under the auspices of the Drug Enforcement Administration, and the DEA will coordinate drug law-enforcement intelligence collection overseas on behalf of the United States Government. . . .

"The flow of money does not recognize national boundaries."

Continuing existing policy and practice, the activities of U.S. military units in an anti-drug role abroad, including Defense Department anti-drug activities in support of U.S. Ambassadors or principal officers, and support of host country military forces in an anti-drug role, will be coordinated with the Department of State

and other Federal agencies, and with the appropriate theater Commander-in-Chief.

The statutory certification requirement, which establishes a direct relationship between United States assistance to major illicit drug producing and transit countries and their positive performance on drug control, remains an important element of U.S. international drug control strategy. As the 1989 *National Drug Control Strategy* noted, the governments of major drug producing and drug transit countries should be held accountable for their performance on drug control. In bilateral relations with such countries, therefore, the United States will continue to emphasize the requirement for cooperation with U.S. drug control efforts and for effective independent actions to suppress the drug trade. . . .

International Information Initiatives

In concert with our other international policies and programs to attack the drug problem, an active public information campaign will provide vital information to foreign publics, leaders, and government officials to build support for United States and host country actions to combat drug production, trafficking, and consumption.

The United States Information Agency, with policy guidance developed by the Department of State and supported by other Federal agencies, will lead our coordinated international information efforts. These initiatives will focus on providing information to foreign audiences about the threat posed by the drug trade to national security, economic welfare, and the environment, and educating them about the consequences of illicit drug use. Our international information programs will also describe our own domestic drug problem, and our progress in fighting it.

As the September 1989 *National Drug Control Strategy* stated, programs directed at reducing drug consumption abroad will be emphasized. These programs will be aimed at drug-producing, transit, and consumer countries, as well as countries that currently have little or no drug problem, to strengthen their resolve and ability to resist the expansion of drug use or trafficking within their own national borders. . . .

Money Laundering

The flow of money does not recognize national boundaries. As we tighten our own regulations and enforcement procedures to prevent money launderers from using the U.S. financial system, they will turn increasingly to foreign banks and transfer mechanisms to disguise the source of their funds and convert them to legitimate use. The Administration's money laundering strategy seeks to attain three primary goals: the prosecution and incarceration of money launderers and the leaders and members of drug trafficking organizations; the freezing, seizure, or confiscation of criminally derived assets; and the deterrence of individuals or institutions from cooperating with money launderers or their clients through the enforcement of existing laws and regulations, the enactment or strengthening of laws and regulations where needed, and the certainty of sanctions in the event of noncompliance.

"In our bilateral relations, we will urge the enactment and enforcement of national laws similar to our own."

To this end, the Administration has created a multi-agency policy review mechanism—a Drug-Related Financial Crimes Policy Group termed a "Financial Targeting Group" in the September 1989 *Strategy* —chaired by the Deputy Director for Supply Reduction of the Office of National Drug Control Policy. The Drug-Related Financial Crimes Policy Group (DFCPG) will review and recommend strategies to combat money laundering and to establish and maintain strong cooperative relationships at the Federal and State levels. It will also work to strengthen State money-laundering laws and the States' regulation and monitoring of non-bank financial institutions which are licensed by State and local governments. The DFCPG will oversee and coordinate Federal government policy related to financial regulation and intelligence; international financial programs; the interdiction and seizure of illicit currency and monetary instruments; procedures and issues involving the identification, tracing, freezing, seizure, and confiscation of criminally derived assets; and other U.S. actions designed to counter drug money laundering, both domestically and internationally. . . .

The Department of the Treasury's Financial Crimes Enforcement Network (FINCEN), which is overseen by a board chaired by the Department of the Treasury with the participation of the Justice Department and other agencies, will analyze Treasury Department financial reporting information, as well as other information and intelligence provided by participating agencies, and disseminate its analytical product. Treasury will also develop a mechanism that will allow for information-sharing relationships with foreign financial information services to specifically address the financial flow of illicit proceeds, permitting financial intelligence to be passed between U.S. and foreign law enforcement entities. Needed financial information will be made available to domestic and cooperating foreign regulatory and law enforcement authorities, where appropriate, for their use in money laundering and related investigations. Such dissemination will be subject to strict safeguards to ensure the proper use of such financial information and protect the privacy of those conducting legitimate transactions.

Countering Money Laundering

The Administration will intensify contacts with the financial and non-financial industry communities in the United States and abroad to urge their active support for measures to counter money laundering. It will formally request that banks, other financial institutions, and retail businesses report suspicious cash transactions at all levels. The Department of the Treasury will develop, with private sector industries, data recording equipment and procedures to record, correlate, and alert Federal authorities to large cash deposits at and below regulated thresholds on a real-time basis. Special attention will be given to the feasibility of regulations and means to record wire transfers.

The Administration will emphasize bilateral and multilateral cooperative approaches with foreign governments to prevent the use of the financial system for money laundering. We will pursue, through the Department of State, the conclusion of bilateral and multilateral cooperation agreements, including the ratification of the U.N. Convention, which support measures to facilitate the identification, tracing, freezing, seizure, and confiscation of criminal proceeds, and which support the enactment of laws which criminalize money laundering. In bilateral relations, we will negotiate with a number of countries pursuant to Section 4702 of the Anti-Drug Abuse Act of 1988 (the Kerry Amendment) to ensure that their banks and non-bank financial institutions maintain adequate records of financial transactions, and that they share financial information with the United States. We will also work with other countries toward the goal of sharing seized assets with producer or transit countries that develop information leading to such seizures.

The Chemical Diversion and Trafficking Act is the foundation of United States efforts to reduce the production and illicit transfer of essential precursor chemicals. The Act and regulations promulgated pursuant to it impose stringent domestic controls on the export of chemicals used in the illicit production of cocaine, by identifying drug chemical purchasers in the cocaine producing countries and stopping shipments to bogus or uncooperative purchasers. These controls will be enforced by the Drug Enforcement Administration and the U.S. Customs Service. . . .

National Laws

In our bilateral relations, we will urge the enactment and enforcement of national laws similar to our own and seek the establishment of investigative and monitoring programs in other countries. Special emphasis will be given to encouraging European efforts to stop the flow of essential and precursor chemicals to drug producing countries.

U.S. Campaigns Against Cocaine Producers Are Necessary

Melvyn Levitsky

About the Author: *Melvyn Levitsky is assistant secretary for international narcotics matters. The following is a statement by Levitsky before the Subcommittee on Western Hemisphere Affairs of the House Foreign Affairs Committee, Washington, D.C., June 20, 1990.*

I welcome the opportunity today to discuss the President's Andean strategy and outline our policy goals and objectives in this area. Cocaine control is our number one priority and our main focus has been, and will continue to be, the Andes.

The President's historic meeting in Cartagena, Colombia, in February 1990 signaled a new era in narcotics cooperation with our Andean partners. No longer is the drug issue simply a law enforcement problem. We are working with Colombia, Bolivia, and Peru to explore ways to strengthen law enforcement, military, intelligence, and economic cooperation, including opportunities for expanded trade and investment in order to attack the drug trade in a comprehensive way. The President's Andean strategy seeks to bolster these countries' capabilities on all fronts. The programs we have are cooperative programs. We cannot do the job without a strong effort from the Andean countries, the countries that surround the Andean region, and the transit countries through which cocaine passes.

Melvyn Levitsky, "The Andean Strategy to Control Cocaine," United States Department of State Bureau of Public Affairs, July 1990. Public Domain.

The Andean strategy is a multifaceted approach to the complex problem of cocaine production and trafficking. Of course, the main front in this war is here at home. But as we work to diminish our own demand for and consumption of drugs, we must also work hard to reduce the international supply; otherwise, it will be more difficult to sustain effective domestic programs in law enforcement, education, prevention, and treatment.

In 1989, the administration completed a comprehensive plan to work with the three Andean governments to disrupt and destroy the growing, processing, and transportation of coca and coca products within the source countries in order to reduce the supply of cocaine entering the United States. In September 1989, the President's National Drug Control Strategy directed that a 5-year, $2.2 billion counter-narcotics effort begin in FY [fiscal year] 1990 to augment law enforcement, military, and economic resources in Colombia, Bolivia, and Peru. After careful negotiations between the United States and each of the individual cooperating governments, implementation plans have been prepared to ensure effective use of the assistance.

> ## "Cocaine control is our number one priority and our main focus . . . [is] the Andes."

The administration's $2.2 billion plan provides a cooperative approach for working with the three major Andean governments to disrupt and destroy the growing, processing, and transportation of coca and coca products within the source countries in order to reduce the supply of cocaine from these countries to the United States. Congress has authorized and appropriated funds for the first year of this plan. For FY 1990, approximately $230 million in economic, military, and law enforcement assistance is being offered to the three Andean countries for counter-narcotics-related initiatives. In 1991, we are asking for $423 million, including narcotics-related economic assistance.

The Andean strategy has three major objectives.

First, through concerted action and bilateral assistance, it is our goal to strengthen the political will and institutional capability of the three Andean governments to enable them to confront the Andean cocaine trade. With new governments in Colombia and Peru, it will be essential for the US Government to help them address the full range of their drug-related problems.

Second, we will work with the Andean governments to increase the effectiveness of the intelligence, military, and law enforcement activities against the cocaine trade in the three source countries, particularly by providing air mobility for both military and police forces and making sure they are well equipped and trained and that they cooperate in an integrated strategy. It has become clear that the Andean countries cannot conduct effective anti-narcotics operations without the involvement of their armed forces; this is especially true where the traffickers and insurgents have joined forces, as in Peru. Specific objectives include efforts to isolate key coca-growing areas, block the shipment of precursor chemicals, identify and destroy existing labs and processing centers, control key air corridors, and reduce net production of coca through aerial application of herbicides when it is effective to do so.

Significant Damage

Our third goal is to inflict significant damage on the trafficking organizations which operate within the three source countries by working with host governments to dismantle operations and elements of greatest value to the trafficking organizations. By strengthening ties between police and military units and creating major violator task forces to identify key organizations, the bilateral assistance will enable host government forces to target the leaders of the major cocaine trafficking organizations, impede the transfer of

drug-generated funds, and seize their assets within the United States and in those foreign nations in which they operate. Intelligence is a critical component of this strategy. We have worked closely with the intelligence community and law enforcement agencies to focus intelligence collection on these targets. In short, we have developed a strategy that is coherent, focused, and determined.

"The financial resources of the narcotics traffickers . . . permit [them] to challenge or defy . . . local governments."

A major tenet of this strategy is the incorporation of expanded economic assistance beginning in FY 1991 and directed toward offsetting the negative economic dislocations we know will occur. This assistance will, in turn, strengthen the political commitment of the three Andean nations to carry out an effective counter-narcotics program. US economic assistance is, in general terms, linked to counter-narcotics performance and to follow-through with economic policy reform. In harmony with the views of the three Andean governments, our direct economic assistance and other initiatives support economic alternatives for those directly involved in the cultivation of and trade in coca. Examples of such assistance include crop substitution and other economic alternative activities, drug awareness, administration of justice, balance of payments, and export promotion. The assistance reflects our conclusion, incorporated in the Declaration of Cartagena, that a comprehensive, intensified counter-narcotics strategy must include understandings regarding economic cooperation, alternative development, and encouragement of trade and investment. As vigorous host government programs against the drug trade and economic policy reform initiatives become more effective, our economic assistance will increase in the outyears (1991-94) of the Andean strategy. We are not seeking to impose law enforcement, security, or economic assistance on these countries. These are programs that require cooperation and mutual agreement. Our intensive dialogue with the Andeans is refining a common understanding of what is needed and what is possible on both sides.

Let me deal directly with concerns which have been raised regarding the role of the Andean militaries in the drug war and potential human rights abuses. There is no reason to expect that US military aid will undermine democracy or civilian rule in the Andes. On the contrary, I believe it will help to strengthen both democracy and the international struggle against illegal narcotics for the following reasons:

• US security assistance will be negotiated with and delivered through the civilian governments;

• An impoverished, poorly trained and equipped military, unable to feed its troops, is far more susceptible to corruption and human rights abuses; and

• The military is far more likely to take a constructive approach if actively engaged in the drug war as opposed to being left to criticize civilian efforts from the sidelines. The involvement of the military, as in our own country, can bring a significant resource in the war against drugs if properly coordinated and directed by civilian authorities.

Misconceptions

I would also like to set out a number of points that address misconceptions that have grown up in recent months about the so-called militarization of the US counter-narcotics effort. Like many slogans, the use of emotionally charged and sometimes politically motivated words like "militarization" is a gross oversimplification that does not do justice to the effort either to understand or deal with the complex problems of international narcotics.

In the first place, the level of our security assistance is only a part of our total effort. Of some $129 million in counter-narcotics funds re-quested for Peru in FY 1991, for example, only about $40 million is for military assistance, and much of that is for maintenance support and infrastructure improvement. Nor do we contemplate large levels of US military presence in the Andes. We have never maintained such a presence, and our strategy includes as one of our tenets the determination not to Americanize the effort to work with local governments.

Second, our decision to encourage greater participation of the local militaries in the counter-narcotics efforts parallels the evolution of our own policy that projects a greater role for the Department of Defense in the war on drugs in the United States. Indeed, the militaries in the Andean states are an important component of the governments and their involvement is a sign of greater overall national commitment in dealing with the problem.

"Guerrilla organizations are becoming involved in narcotics trafficking."

Third, while we believe the militaries of the Andean states need to play a more constructive role, we never have nor will force military assistance on these countries. Nor is the assistance we are providing of a nature to create large, new forces in the region. We are developing the specialized skills and units required to conduct or support meaningful counter-narcotics operations, not creating major combat units. We should remember the immense size of the countries we are dealing with and that the narcotics processing facilities and growing areas are spread over large areas, often in remote locations. Narcotics law enforcement units are neither equipped nor trained to address the increasingly paramilitary nature of the problem. Further, as the case of Bolivian military support for counter-narcotics operations demonstrates, military support in some cases can be an effective way to avoid duplicating a parallel military capability within police narcotics enforcement agencies.

The financial resources of the narcotics traffickers, such as those in Colombia, enable them to hire private armies and terrorists on a national and international scale. Their ability to buy manpower and equipment surpasses the police capability and, in some cases, calls into question even the military's ability to respond effectively. These capabilities permit the narco-traffickers to challenge or defy the sovereignty of local governments in a way unprecedented in our experience.

US counter-narcotics policy, therefore, should not be characterized as a "militarized" effort, but rather one that seeks to provide legitimate governments with the tools and assistance to help defend their political sovereignty.

Drugs and Insurgency

But the problem does not end there. There is now a further complicating factor, and that is the degree to which so-called guerrilla organizations are becoming involved in narcotics trafficking, either in providing protection in return for profit or in engaging in the production and sale of coca.

The effort of the United States to help these countries deal with "narco-insurgents" has raised the specter of counterinsurgency—specifically, whether the United States should engage in supporting Andean militaries, some with past records of human rights abuses, in waging a struggle against insurgent groups which are clearly involved in many aspects of narcotics trafficking. We cannot gloss over past abuses in some countries. We do not support these and never will. But neither should we succumb to the romantic notion of downtrodden peasant masses protesting in arms against social injustice, nor depict organizations like the Sendero Luminoso (Shining Path) of Peru or the FARC (*Fuerzas Armadas Revolucionarias de Colombia*— Armed Revolutionary Forces of Colombia) in Colombia as champions of human rights. Moreover, these groups are now becoming narcotics traffickers themselves, profiting from the environment of drugs and using drug monies to finance further violence.

"We are beginning to see that our efforts are having an impact in the Andes, and on the streets of the United States."

In such groups, we are dealing with professional organizations of tight-knit cadres whose human rights abuses, indiscriminate bombings of civilian targets, use of torture, terrorism on a national scale, and barbaric brutality are plainly part of the public record in Colombia and Peru. While the US attitude toward these problems is well known, the United States has not provided significant financial assistance to any of the Andean nations to deal with these specific problems. We are focusing our effort on counter-narcotics, not on counterinsurgency, but we cannot lose sight of the fact that it is the insurgents who have become involved in narcotics and, along with the traffickers, created a militarized situation.

Let me also point out the following. At this point, we have not concluded a security assistance agreement with the government of Peru. We have done some advance planning and held discussions with officials of the government, but no programs of assistance can go forward without such an agreement. While it is our belief that the narcotics situation in the upper Huallaga Valley cannot be dealt with effectively without the involvement of the Peruvian military, this is a Peruvian government decision. And, of course, it will be a decision as to whether the counter-narcotics performance of the Peruvian institutions involved in the struggle will justify the provision of economic assistance. Our request for economic assistance for Peru in 1991 is based on the assumption of effective counter-narcotics performance.

Our counter-narcotics work in Bolivia does

not create a significant military capability; it, too, focuses on improving the military's ability to support counter-narcotics efforts. This includes improvements in riverine programs by the Andean navies to interdict the flow of precursor chemicals and drugs on Bolivia's waterways.

The involvement of the Colombian military in supporting counter-narcotics law enforcement operations over the past 2 years proves the effectiveness of this approach. Recently, the Colombian military, using equipment supplied by the United States, with the police seized over 18 tons of cocaine in one transportation complex deep in the Colombian jungle.

It is basic to our policy that human rights remain under continuous review to determine whether government policies justify, reinforce, or call into doubt our continued assistance relationship. State Department human rights reports on Colombia and Peru have been candid in their criticisms and, in fact, received praise from human rights groups. We will work with the Andean militaries to eliminate human rights abuses as they increase their involvement in antinarcotics operations. Our training, in fact, will emphasize human rights and civic action.

Involvement of US military personnel and organizations is clearly defined, limited, and subject to continuing review. The US military role is to provide support and development of host country capabilities. It will provide training and operational support, materiel, advice, and technological and maintenance support to cooperating nations' counter-narcotics organizations. Defense personnel will not participate in actual field operations.

Contrary to some media reports, the levels of counter-narcotics-based economic assistance planned for in the president's Andean strategy outweigh the levels of military assistance being offered. Over the 5 years that the strategy covers, from FY 1990 to 1994, economic assistance will total over $1.1 billion, versus approximately $676 million in security assistance. Moreover, this does not include other economic assistance such as food aid and trade preferences for the Andean region. . . .

Optimism for the Future

In closing, I would like to take this opportunity to say that I believe that we and the Andean governments will have many opportunities for progress as we work together to attack all aspects of the cocaine trade. We are optimistic. The price of coca leaf is down in Peru and Bolivia. As a result, in Bolivia voluntary eradication of coca is up—1990 has already surpassed 1989's total—and increasing numbers of growers are moving out of the illegal industry. DEA [Drug Enforcement Administration] laboratory analysis indicates that purity levels of cocaine at both the wholesale and retail levels are down and prices have increased at the wholesale level in many areas throughout the nation. Cartagena ended the argument over who is to blame for the drug crisis; we now have a consensus on the nature of the problems we face and a solidifying common front against the drug trade.

"We now have . . . a solidifying common front against the drug trade."

Success will not happen overnight, but we are beginning to see that our efforts are having an impact in the Andes, and on the streets of the United States. Provided we are prepared to sustain our activities and not allow our thinking to be clouded by false analogies and oversimplifications, I believe we will continue to make progress toward a goal the American people have made clear that they support.

The U.S. Needs an International Drug Trafficking Policy

Scott B. MacDonald

About the Author: *Scott B. MacDonald has written many articles on Latin America and has published several books on the topic, including* Mountain High, White Avalanche, *from which this viewpoint is taken.*

The cocaine trade is a major security and health problem for the majority of governments and peoples in the Americas. The Andean *narcotraficantes* have a long reach, with political and military clout in their homelands and increasing influence through their extensive trade routes to North America and Europe. As demonstrated in the case of Panama, the avalanche has done damage elsewhere. And beyond Panama, there is evidence of alternative routes through Central America, Mexico, and the Caribbean. In early 1988, a grand jury in Miami indicted Haitian Colonel Jean-Claude Paul on drug charges, with the evidence strongly pointing to the cocaine trade from the Andean countries as a rising problem. Moreover, the June 1988 coup that ousted civilian Haitian president Leslie Manigat from office was allegedly over Colonel Paul's continued visibility in the government and U.S. pressure to have him removed. Given that the Andean avalanche is pouring down the Andes into Brazil, Paraguay, and Argentina, the cocaine trade has taken on hemispheric dimensions. What should be done? . . .

Cocaine is not the only item on the menu of

Excerpted from *Mountain High, White Avalanche: Cocaine and Power in the Andean States and Panama* by Scott B. MacDonald with one-time reprint permission from the Center for Strategic and International Studies, Washington, D.C.

illicit drug consumption in North America, nor are the Andean countries the sole source of narcotics. Opium, hashish, and heroin come into the United States from Asia's Golden Triangle and the Golden Crescent. Their flow is not only south to north, but east to west and west to east. Therefore, a drug czar will need a foreign policy; without it, other policy initiatives are doomed to failure.

The foreign policy has three dimensions:
- a broad, global perception of the problem and international cooperation in attacking it.
- specific policies for certain areas—for example, for the Golden Triangle or the Andean countries.
- a long-standing commitment to pursue those policies that survive election-time promises.

The Andean nations of Bolivia, Chile, Colombia, Ecuador, and Peru have reached a crossroads in their history. They are locked in a struggle with the power of cocaine that is accompanied by a high government mortality rate. The U.S. public is, sadly, not getting this message. The U.S. government, the Congress, and the U.S. public should carefully examine the trade in cocaine, the influence of the *narcotraficantes*, the links with radical, leftist guerrilla forces, and the difficulty of maintaining a democratic political system (or moving in that direction) under these pressures and those imposed by the debt crisis.

"The cocaine trade is a major security and health problem for the majority of governments and peoples in the Americas."

The U.S. policy on drugs suffers a lack of coordination that . . . is growing. And there is an overconcentration on Central America. Although the struggles of El Salvador, Nicaragua, and Guatemala should not be dismissed as insignificant, their relative importance in comparison to what is happening and can happen in the

Andean states is vastly overblown.

Consider a statistical comparison of Central America and the Andean States. Central America, including Belize and Panama, has a population of about 23.4 million, while the Andean states have 95.4 million. Colombia alone has 29.19 million people compared with the two countries U.S. Latin policy is primarily concerned with—Nicaragua (3.38 million) and El Salvador (4.91 million). The Andean states, in general, have more diversified economies and are larger in sheer size than their Central American counterparts. This size difference is reflected in the 1987 nominal GDP [gross domestic product] of Costa Rica ($4.4 billion) and Venezuela ($42.3 billion).

Andean Trade

The Andean states carry on far more significant trade with the United States. U.S. trade with Costa Rica, Panama, and Guatemala roughly equaled a little over a billion dollars each in 1986 and 1987. El Salvador's trade with the United States was a little under $1 billion. In comparison, U.S.-Colombian trade was worth $3.3 billion in 1986, with U.S. exports accounting for $1.45 billion. Venezuela's trade with the United States was $7.4 billion, with U.S. exports to that Andean country reaching $3.6 billion. A rough estimate, based on World Bank figures, puts Central America's trade relationship at a value of $4 billion annually compared with $16 billion for the Andean states.

Total external debt for Central America totals $16 billion. The possible impact of El Salvador's refuting its external debt of $1.6 billion would hardly cause a ripple. U.S. banks already have sizable reserves set aside on Nicaragua's $5 billion debt. If Colombia were torn apart by intense internal violence and the economy were disrupted to the point that it was unable to make its repayments, a rescheduling for the $18 billion would be of considerable concern to Western financial sectors. The size of the Andean economies and the growing sophistication of trade issues, more in the case of Venezuela than

the others, demand a more coherent response and greater attention from the United States.

The cocaine trade is one of the major threats confronting the Western Hemisphere in the late twentieth century. In its wake have come rising addiction, societal disruption, and an increase in criminal and political violence. In such cases as Bolivia and Colombia, the cocaine trade has even challenged the existence of the state and its ability to govern. Because the Andean states are at the core of this issue, ought they not logically assume a higher profile in U.S. policy-making? It is crucial to realize that the political turmoil in Central America is not disrupting U.S. society, but the cocaine trade is a major societal problem. In a sense, all the hoopla over Central America has had little real effect on the lives of most U.S. citizens, but cocaine from the Andean states has brought a problem home to North America.

In the past, U.S. policy toward the Andean states has had low priority. Latin America traditionally lags behind relations with Western Europe, Japan, the Soviet Union, and China. Moreover, U.S. Latin policy usually emphasizes Cuba and other areas of possible "communist" infiltration. Grenada in the Caribbean and Nicaragua and El Salvador in Central America became important only when the left threatened either to come into power or actually came into power. Although the cocaine trade has elements of the East-West struggle in it, it does not neatly fit the traditional leftist-threat scenario. . . .

"The Andean nations . . . are locked in a struggle with the power of cocaine."

An Andean policy is decidedly needed, and there are a few broader policy options that would reinforce movement in that direction.

It is worthwhile to consider certain suggestions made by the Organization of American States Conference on the Traffic in Narcotics.

These soft options underline community participation and include the following:

- establishment of an inter-American clearinghouse through which a steady flow of information, experiences, ideas, and programs could be exchanged.
- promotion of community-level organizations in every major district of every city, town, and village of the Americas to mobilize schools, churches, neighborhoods, medical centers, and social clubs in joining the fight against drug use.
- improvement of statistical and epidemiological information on drug use, especially on the patterns of consumption. These data are pressing because of the scarcity of data on drug administration, dosage, and frequency of use. Both for prevention and treatment, an enhancement of such knowledge in the inter-American community would greatly facilitate effective action.

"Cocaine from the Andean states has brought a problem home to North America."

There has already been some movement along these lines because joint effort with Latin and Caribbean governments against *narcotraficantes* is a core policy objective. Enforcement has benefited from a greater sharing of intelligence, joint maneuvers in drug-producing regions, and an upgrading of extradition treaties between nations. Colombia, Brazil, and Peru have already coordinated antidrug campaigns in their shared border regions, and meetings have been held between the respective drug-enforcement police of those countries. The United States has actively conducted missions with Bolivia, Mexico, the Bahamas, and Jamaica.

The Organization of American States also supports a strengthening of enforcement measures, including:

- more frequent regional and interregional training seminars and workshops for drug law enforcement personnel.
- more rapid, secure, and direct means of communication.
- stronger bilateral agreements between states with common problems arising from the illicit traffic.

Joint Efforts

U.S. support of joint efforts is also important, especially given the greater U.S. enforcement resources. U.S. support for antinarcotics forces in the Americas remains highly important. Although it is important to observe the line between actual U.S. troop involvement in armed clashes with Latin and Caribbean *narcotraficantes* and providing logistical support to local enforcement in Bolivia, the U.S. military can play a positive role, but only at the invitation of another country. Washington should provide Latin and Caribbean governments with the technical means of improving their strategic reach. Renssalaer W. Lee III has noted that "Latin governments still will need better weapons, transport, communications systems, and support services."

The development of greater regional cooperation against the drug trade hinges largely upon relations between the United States and its Latin American neighbors. There has traditionally been a love-hate relationship between the Northern and Southern hemispheres, which has, more than once, led to mutual suspicion and hostility. The Latin American drug trade calls for both North and South Americans to rise above the various periods of estrangement and to work together in a mature relationship. The equation is simple: the drug trade negatively affects all nations in the Americas. Ought not the problem be brought under control by all (or most) of those same nations?

There is a need for innovative measures that are mutually reinforcing and that integrate the other issues and problems that confront Latin American and Caribbean economic development and legal trade. Lee noted:

The United States has to integrate narcotics control with its other hemispheric priorities. Tradeoffs may be unavoidable, at least in the short term. The experiences of Colombia and Bolivia suggest that antidrug measures may harm a country financially by driving dollars from the banking system, thus reducing the value of the local currency and worsening debt problems.

Although the idea of a Common Market of the Americas remains distant, measures must be taken to strengthen legal economies by pushing back the forces of protectionism and gradually advancing toward greater free trade. Protectionism in itself is a dangerous force, but in the drug trade, it negatively reinforces the movement from legal products to illicit products. The subsidization of and ongoing cuts in the U.S. sugar quota system in the 1980s, for example, have been key forces in pushing Belizean and Jamaican cultivators out of sugar and into marijuana cultivation. In Bolivia the near bankruptcy of the economy from a downturn in tin prices (as a result of worldwide tin subsidies and the development of chemical substitutes) led local *campesinos* to turn to coca production. Although economic development (or the lack of it) is often overlooked as a core element of the Andean cocaine trade, it is a significant factor in making the illegal narcotics trade tempting.

Drug and Debt Issues

One possible option not yet attempted is to combine debt and drug issues in an antinarcotics campaign. The Latin debt crisis cannot be blamed as the cause of the drug trade in the Americas, but it is part of the problem. Austerity programs often deplete law enforcement budgets, reduce already low salaries, and drive down the nation's standard of living. These conditions, in turn, create a lack of resources for launching and sustaining effective antinarcotics campaigns and thus open the door to official corruption.

Difficult economic conditions also enhance the attractiveness of the drug trade. In many countries where unemployment in the legal economy is high, the cultivation, refining, and export of cocaine, marijuana, heroin, and synthetic drugs provide a livelihood. Legitimate economic enterprises, seeded with narcomoney, also provide employment and income. At the lower economic level, most individuals involved in the drug industry seek economic survival. At higher levels, greed is clearly the motive.

"An Andean policy is decidedly needed."

There have been a number of instances in which Latin *narcotraficantes* have offered to repay the country's external debt in return for amnesty (for example, in Peru and Bolivia). As of mid-1988 there have been no takers, at least publicly, among the governments in Latin America and the Caribbean. The offer, however, is tempting. In return for a pardon, one of the most significant obstacles to national development could be removed. What has made governments balk has been international reaction and the possible long-term impact of officially acknowledging the power of the *narcotraficantes*. With freedom to move in society, would they seek to mobilize their wealth and influence to affect the formal political system in presidential races? What would happen to a nation with a *narcotraficante* elected as chief executive? Nations with *narcotraficantes* in positions of authority . . . have found the situation difficult.

An option that counteracts the siren-like allure of using narcomoney to repay external obligations is to adopt a program that links debt reduction and narcotics enforcement. Countries that pursue antidrug campaigns can have the U.S. government purchase portions of their debt on the secondary market and give it to them as a form of antinarcotics assistance. If the United States wanted to assist Mexico with its antidrug program, for example, $10 million of Mexican debt could be bought on the secondary market, where the value of that country's debt has an actual worth of under 50 cents for each dollar at face value. Officially, $20 million of Mexican debt paper would be given to the Mexican government, which could then put that capital to use inside the country. As a result, Mexico's official debt would be reduced by $20 million, and the United States would have helped a friendly government combat its drug problem. Moreover, the U.S. financial system would be strengthened by encouraging a healthier Mexico capable of repaying its debt to the U.S. banks.

"Greater regional cooperation against the drug trade hinges largely upon relations between the United States and its Latin American neighbors."

The packaging of a debt-reduction, antinarcotics program would have other important benefits. For many countries, an additional item on the new debt-reduction menu would help them make advances in the overall economy and, it is hoped, improve the standard of living. Improved living conditions, fiscally stronger states, and improved enforcement agencies with greater reach would provide a stronger bulwark against the spread of the drug-insurgency nexus and narcoterrorism.

Especially important under this approach is investment in rural modernization. Rural modernization in this sense has been defined by Kempe Hope:

The cardinal aim of rural development is viewed not simply as agricultural and economic growth in the narrow sense, but as balanced social and economic development, including the generation of new employment; the equitable distribution of income; widespread improvement in health, nutrition, and housing; greatly broadened opportunities for all individuals to realize their full potential through education; and a strong voice for all rural people in shaping the decisions and actions that affect their lives.

In the remote country areas where the drug insurgency nexus has developed, the preconditions for such development must be eradicated. This can be done through either direct financial assistance or, as suggested here, by debt-equity swaps linked to antinarcotics programs.

The cocaine trade affects all nations in the Western Hemisphere, reaching into each society and influencing, in some fashion, its political and economic climate. The Andean states and Panama have reached a historical crossroads where they will either move forward or sink backward into a malaise of narcopolitics and narcodevelopment. The cocaine trade has also made the region more important to a still unaware United States. It remains a potential avalanche threatening to inundate the nations below with a white flood of cocaine. Unless a more coherent U.S. policy gives the Andean states a higher priority, the tremors are already developing that will trigger that avalanche.

Is the U.S. War Against International Drug Trafficking Effective?

No: U.S. Campaigns Against Drug Trafficking Should Be Stopped

The U.S. International Drug War Threatens All Nations
International Cooperation Cannot Fight the Drug Trade
The U.S. Campaign Against Cocaine Producers Is a Fraud
The U.S. International Campaign Against Drug Trafficking Is Ineffective

The U.S. International Drug War Threatens All Nations

Diana Reynolds

About the Author: *Diana Reynolds is an assistant professor of political science at Bradford College, Bradford, Massachusetts, and a research associate at the Edward R. Murrow Center of the Fletcher School of Law and Diplomacy at Tufts University in Medford, Massachusetts.*

In its July 7, 1990, issue, *Newsweek* revealed that the United States is planning a hemispheric drug raid which would use the armies of three South American nations to strike a decisive blow against the cocaine cartels in the region. Quoting briefing papers obtained from the U.S. Southern Command military headquarters in Panama, *Newsweek* reported that the attack will be coordinated by the Southern Command's General Maxwell Thurman—or "Mad Max," as he was called after his overkill tactics in the invasion of Panama, in which he deployed 24,000 U.S. troops to capture General Manuel Noriega—and will use the armies of Colombia, Bolivia, and Peru.

All the logistics, planning, training, and support for the operation would be provided by the U.S. military. A Defense Department analyst familiar with Southcom's activities told *Newsweek,* "We wouldn't pull the trigger, but we'd point the gun." Thurman is also prepared to send in U.S. commandos for a simultaneous regional attack

Excerpted from "The Golden Lie" by Diana Reynolds. This article first appeared in the September/October 1990 issue of *The Humanist* and is reprinted by permission.

on the cartel's entire support structure.

Politicians in Washington claim that they are reluctant to accept Southcom's radical scenario, but it may be too late. At 3:00 AM on the final day of its 100th session, Congress passed, without scrutiny or debate, perhaps the most draconian piece of legislation in this nation's history: the Anti-Drug Abuse Act of 1988. The act not only gives the military a berth wide enough to accommodate Mad Max's Ramboesque foreign adventure but reverses the 1975 congressional prohibition on training the police forces of brutally repressive regimes. On the domestic front, the act constitutes the wholesale suspension of civil liberties whenever drugs are involved. Under this legislation, those "suspected" of using or selling drugs—or associating with those who do—are subject to evictions, raids, curfews, random searches, drug testing, summary forfeitures of property, denial of federal benefits and drivers' licenses, and military occupation of their neighborhoods and towns. Title IV of the act, section 4205, entitled "Military Assistance for Anti-Narcotics Efforts," authorizes U.S. military assistance to friendly governments for the purpose of controlling illicit narcotics production and trafficking. Combined with the War Powers Act of 1974, which gives the U.S. president blanket authority to commit U.S. troops to combat for up to 90 days, the act is a clear green light for the hemispheric raid.

> ## "The Drug War [has produced] . . . a dangerous wartime mentality which says that 'anything goes' in the pursuit of victory."

After six years of government-inspired hysteria, Americans have become thoroughly convinced that this nation faces a drug epidemic of crisis proportions. Consequently, the Drug War has become a God-and-country national security issue with widespread public support. So much so that within the body politic there is a danger-ous wartime mentality which says that "anything goes" in the pursuit of victory. . . .

In fact, the Drug War is now our most effec-tive golden lie. A *golden lie* is a strategic political tool, first articulated by Plato in *The Republic*. As Plato saw it, any government seeking political stability needed a basic myth—or mass delu-sion—to unify its population and mobilize sup-port for its policies. Historically, governments have been able to win the support of large num-bers of their citizens for policies that were based upon such mass delusions as the belief in witches, national or ethnic superiority, or nonex-istent internal and external enemies.

America's Golden Lie

America's golden lie during the four decades after World War II was the carefully nurtured public perception of an evil expansionist, mono-lithic, Soviet-led, communist world empire. . . .

However, in the mid-1980s, the foundations of anti-communism began to crumble as Soviet President Mikhail Gorbachev initiated pere-stroika, glasnost, peace overtures to the United States, military withdrawal from Afghanistan, and a loosening of the Soviet political vise on Central and Eastern Europe. In 1988, President Ronald Reagan, the anti-communist's anti-com-munist, officially declared the age of the "evil empire" over. Indeed, by 1990, communism had all but collapsed in Eastern Europe. The Warsaw Pact was defunct, and Gorbachev himself had declared the Soviet Union "a second-rate power."

Just as the myth of the evil Soviet empire was dissolving, however, another, more powerful one was created to take its place: the evil narcotics empire. Between 1982 and 1987, as the Reagan administration orchestrated a massive income transfer from America's poorest 20 percent to its 200,000 richest families—cutting loose the thin safety net of social services which kept the un-derclass barely afloat and withdrawing govern-ment investment in education and job train-ing—a bipartisan effort was whipping public

opinion into a frenzy over America's "drug cri-sis." . . .

The facts about drug use during this period, however, clearly show that only about 1 percent of the American population, mostly the rural and inner-city poor, were experiencing a drug "crisis." Sara Diamond, author of *Spiritual War-fare*, in a new study, "Manufacturing Consent for the War on Drugs," points out that—with the ex-ception of 1986, when crack cocaine entered the market, causing addiction and emergency room admission rates to escalate—there was no na-tionwide drug epidemic in the 1980s. Diamond adds that the data available from the National Institute for Drug Abuse's statistical series shows that cocaine- and heroin-related emergency room admissions declined steadily from 1985 to 1988.

"The United States is not expe-riencing a drug-related crime wave."

Al Giordano, in examining the NIDA data, supports Diamond's contentions. NIDA con-ducts household surveys every few years and high-school and young adult drug-use surveys on an annual basis. The NIDA data show that there were about 500,000 cocaine addicts or heavy users in the United States during the 1980s. While occasional cocaine use by high-school seniors increased sharply from 1975 to 1979, it was nearly level from 1980 to 1986. In the general population, the estimated number of those who have used cocaine at least once in a 30-day period decreased from 5.8 million in 1986 to 2.9 million in 1988. A 1988 NIDA survey showed that cocaine use among all age groups decreased by 25 percent over that year. Gior-dano concludes from his analysis:

> There is a serious crack problem among in-ner city and rural poor. It is in the underclass for whom life is miserable. . . . Fifty percent don't finish high school, job opportunities are

limited and people wonder why they are attracted to crack.

And yet, the new golden lie has redefined the social problem of drug abuse during the 1980s as a matter of national security. The punitive nature of the Drug War focuses attention on the alleged weakness and pathology of the individual drug user while diverting attention from the pathological social and economic environments created by government policies.

Contrary to conventional wisdom, the United States is not experiencing a drug-related crime wave. Government surveys show that, between 1970 and 1987, burglary rates fell 27 percent, robbery rates 21 percent, and murders 13 percent. Yet the fastest-growing portions of federal, state, and local budgets are for prisons. Over one million Americans are currently incarcerated—a higher percentage of the population than any other nation in the world, authoritarian or democratic. Since 1972, the proportion of Americans in prison has increased over 200 percent; there was a 14.6 percent increase in the first six months of 1989 alone....

Although President Bush, Secretary of State James Baker, and Drug Czar William Bennett extol the virtues of their anti-drug tactics as good for democracy, human liberty, and individual freedom, others—including civil libertarians, federal judges, and city mayors, conservative and liberal alike—disagree. As conservative economist Milton Friedman wrote in an impassioned open letter to Bennett in *The Wall Street Journal*, "The very measures you favor are a major source of the evils you deplore."...

"The supplying of repression in Latin America can be justified under the rubric of fighting narco-traffickers."

The deafening silence over Southcom's plan for a hemispheric assault indicates that further U.S. intervention and the supplying of repression in Latin America can be justified under the rubric of fighting narco-traffickers. It has become the perfect cover for counterinsurgency operations.

In late June 1990, Congress began investigating whether the Bush administration's plan to spend some $40 million training the Peruvian military to fight drug traffickers is really a plan to help that country combat leftist rebels. Senator John F. Kerry, whose Subcommittee on Narcotics, Terrorism, and International Operations is conducting the hearings, commented, "It is a backdoor slide into military involvement in another country."

A Paramilitary Campaign

At the same time, coincidentally, the Drug Enforcement Administration announced that it would end its role in a paramilitary campaign aimed at disrupting the flow of cocaine from the Andean countries. The DEA will begin a "phased withdrawal" of its agents in Peru and Bolivia, who have accompanied the police and military on raids against clandestine laboratories, airstrips, and other drug-trafficker hideouts as part of Operation Snowcap. Although the DEA claims that it will turn these operations over to the locals, it is more likely that a "private" American enterprise and the U.S. military will replace the DEA.

When questioned about the phenomenal increase in military aid given to Peru by the United States to fight the Drug War—from $2 million in 1989 to $46.9 million in 1990—one DEA official in Washington said, "We realize that adding a military color to it creates a perception of deja vu. When people see Huey helicopters and M-16s, there is a knee-jerk reaction that it looks like Vietnam." However, a U.S. military official was quoted in *Newsweek* as saying, "We're going back to what we know best, how to fight the commies." For its part, the Peruvian army is extremely eager to receive training and equipment for its war against the Shining Path guerrillas. The Peruvian army has little interest in fighting drugs, which brings at least $1 billion per year into the impoverished country. U.S. aid dovetails nicely with counterinsurgency needs.

The State Department, in an April 9, 1990, letter to Dante B. Fascell, chairman of the House Foreign Affairs Committee, stated that the anti-cocaine and anti-Shining Path missions are "inextricably intertwined." "It is inevitable that counternarcotics activities will at times require counterinsurgency efforts to regain government control over certain areas," wrote State Department Legislative Affairs Liaison Janet G. Mullions. Because of the sensitivity of foreign governments to an official American military presence, the State Department's Bureau of International Narcotics Matters has been coordinating the United States' foreign anti-drug intelligence, interdiction, and training programs since 1987. The INM has created a congressionally mandated "enterprise" that bears a striking similarity to the illegal contra "enterprise" contracted out of the State Department's Nicaraguan Humanitarian Assistance Office with the help of Oliver North at the National Security Council.

Although the INM is officially running American paramilitary operations against the drug industry, the work rules aren't clearly defined. Often, the retired U.S. Army Special Forces gunners who crouch at their door-mounted .60-caliber machine guns find themselves in combat situations. For example, U.S. pilots and gunners played a crucial role in a firefight with Shining Path rebels in May 1990 at a base in Santa Lucia, Peru. A number of the rebels were killed. . . .

Fact and Fantasy

The high level of American commitment to the "anything goes" strategy of the Drug War is based upon a narco-guerrilla thesis that is more fantasy than fact. Rensselaer Lee, in *The White Labyrinth*, his study of the politics of cocaine in Latin America and the United States, concludes that the interpretation of the narco-guerrilla connection depends less upon hard evidence and more upon the vagaries of politics and the motives of different institutional actors. In South America, the narco-guerrilla thesis serves a variety of political and institutional purposes: to discredit the left, to undermine any peace initiatives with the various guerrilla movements, to obscure the connection between cocaine traffickers and groups such as the military, and to extract more foreign aid from the United States.

Lee points out that, while cocaine traffickers and guerrillas often occupy the same areas, and while there are some linkages, there is no formal alliance between them. They are usually competitors and sometimes mortal enemies. Narcotics traffickers often clash with guerrillas over territorial control, relations with the coca-growing peasants, and distribution of economic benefits from the drug trade. While some insurgent groups finance their activities in part by taxing the cocaine industry, their financial nexus is in the upstream phase of the industry (cultivation and low-level processing) rather than the more lucrative downstream phase (refining and exporting). . . .

"There is strong historical precedent for the United States using the cover of anti-narcotics programs abroad."

The Peruvian army is an ally of the coca growers and traffickers; as an army officer told Lee, "We have to have popular support to fight terrorism. We have to be a friend to the population. You can't do that by eradicating coca."

While they maintain friendly relations with the coca growers and narco-traffickers, the Peruvian army and police are not friends of the Peruvian population at large, as a senior official at the U.S. embassy in Lima told *Newsweek* in May 1990:

This country has wholesale violation of human rights with disappearances, torture, summary executions and a demonstrated unwillingness or inability to police their own operations. And the situation isn't improving; it's getting worse.

The same can be said of Colombia, in line for $76.2 million of U.S. military aid for fighting the Drug War in 1990. A 1988 Amnesty International report, "Colombia: A Human Rights Emergency," identifies a deliberate policy of terror and political murder carried out by the armed forces. In 1988 alone, 1,000 political killings were attributed to the army death squads. . . .

The Dirty War

Often the military authorities actively collaborate in the "dirty war" waged in Colombia by drug dealers against leftist politicians and union leaders, which has claimed over 4,000 lives [from 1987 to 1990]. Americas Watch reports that the Colombian cocaine cartels financed, trained, and directed the paramilitary death squads that committed most of Colombia's political killings and massacres. The drug cartels provide schools for the training of assassins, finance contract killings, and provide refuge for the assassins on remote farms and ranches.

There is a pathetic irony in the tenfold increase in U.S. military aid—from $5.8 million in fiscal year 1989 to $53 million in fiscal year 1990—to fight the Drug War in Bolivia. It is highly probable that American foreign aid helped transform that country into the globe's second-largest cocaine producer. Hugo Banzer—military dictator of Bolivia from 1971 to 1979, who still controls 12 of the 17 government ministries, including interior and the army—was responsible for the development of the Bolivian cocaine industry, which today provides the impoverished nation with 300,000 jobs and accounts for half of its foreign earnings.

In the first ten months after Banzer's *coup d'etat*, Bolivia received $32 million in American economic aid—$25.3 million more than the *total* aid it had received from the United States between 1942 and 1970. U.S. military aid requests for Bolivia in 1973 and 1974 were three times greater than any sum given to a Latin American nation at that time. U.S. Defense Secretary Melvin Laird, explaining the massive increase

before the House Foreign Appropriations Committee for fiscal year 1973, claimed that the aid was to be used in combatting domestic insurgency. . . .

In 1975, when Bolivia's main revenue-producing commodities, tin and cotton, were falling on hard times, the country engaged in a massive agricultural transformation from cotton to coca. A 1979 DEA report estimated that the land used for cocaine production had tripled over a three-year period (the time it takes for a coca plant to mature) between 1975 and 1979. When Banzer first took power, Bolivia produced 3,000 metric tons of coca; by 1978, the output rose to 60,000 metric tons; and by 1982, it was 80,000 metric tons. . . .

"American aid helped transform . . . [Bolivia] into the globe's second-largest cocaine producer."

There is strong historical precedent for the United States using the cover of anti-narcotics programs abroad to aid authoritarian governments in "dirty wars" or campaigns of terror against their own populations. Michael T. Klare and Cynthia Aronson, in their seminal study *Supplying Repression*, document this activity during the last half of the 1970s. A congressional investigation found that the United States was making repressive regimes even more repressive through the Office of Public Safety, which trained and supplied weapons to brutal local police forces and death squads. Consequently, in December 1973, Congress voted to dismantle the OPS and to prohibit the U.S. government from entering into any new police programs abroad. On July 1, 1975, when section 660 of the Foreign Assistance Act of 1974 took effect, it became illegal to use U.S. foreign aid "to provide training or advice, or provide any financial support for police, prisons, or other law enforcement forces for any foreign government."

Nevertheless, despite the passage of section 660 and the dissolution of the OPS, the U.S. government continued to support the police forces of repressive foreign regimes by shifting such aid to other agencies. Through the State Department's International Narcotics Control Program (INC) and the Justice Department's DEA, Washington continued to provide equipment, training, and advisory support to many of the same police units and continued to aid a wide range of politically motivated internal security and intelligence operations in countries receiving assistance.

Overseas Narcotics Advisers

In 1974, the year after Congress terminated the OPS, funding for anti-drug programs jumped over 600 percent. By 1978, all of the INC personnel in Latin America were former "public safety advisers" brought in from the OPS. The Government Accounting Office, noting the continuity between the OPS and the INC, stated, "Overseas narcotics advisers perform essentially the same functions that public safety advisers used to perform." Between 1973 and 1981, the INC awarded $240 million to the law enforcement agencies of a number of corrupt and brutal regimes, including Argentina, the Philippines, and Pakistan. By 1980, over 90 percent of INC funds went to Mexico, Bolivia, Colombia, Peru, Ecuador, Thailand, and Burma—all with regimes heavily implicated in international narcotics trafficking.

With the Anti-Drug Act of 1988—its reversal of section 660 of the Foreign Assistance Act of 1974, its authorization of military assistance to friendly governments to fight narcotics trafficking, and its suspension of the Bill of Rights whenever drugs are suspected at home—what had to be done covertly in the past can now be accomplished overtly, with the enthusiastic support of the American public. The new golden lie has unified public opinion, mobilized support for the draconian provisions of the Anti-Drug Act of 1988, and legitimized American participation in "dirty wars" abroad and at home.

International Cooperation Cannot Fight the Drug Trade

M. Cherif Bassiouni

About the Author: *M. Cherif Bassiouni is a law professor at De Paul University College of Law in Chicago, Illinois; the president of the International Association of Penal Law; and president of the International Institute of Higher Studies in Criminal Sciences.*

Drug-related problems have reached a perceived crisis level in many consuming countries, particularly in the United States and other Western European societies. The real crisis is a result of crimes committed in connection with drug trafficking and by those engaged in the drug business, as well as by users and abusers who commit crimes to support their drug needs. Producing countries have also started to appreciate the extent of social, economic and political problems resulting from cultivation, production and consumption of drugs. Transit countries and countries used for recycling of drug proceeds are also experiencing problems similar to those of producing countries.

As a result, the multi-faceted and worldwide effects of drugs on the social, economic and political well-being and stability of a number of countries have reached a level of unprecedented international concern. The 1990 Special Session of the General Assembly on Drugs has evidenced that concern.

International and national efforts in confronting this new phenomenon, however, lag far behind the multi-faceted problems created by interdependent cycles of production and consumption, including intermediate stages of distribution, transportation and recycling of funds, in addition to secondary and tertiary consequences in social, health, political and economic spheres.

"So long as there is demand, there will be supply."

Unfortunately, international and national responses aimed at complete control of cultivation, production, traffic, use and abuse of drugs have so far failed. Consuming societies cannot control consumption, and producing states cannot control production. The essential reason is that so long as there is demand, there will be supply and, *mutatis mutandis*, so long as there is supply, it will generate demand. Furthermore, it should also be recognized that supply will always find its way to demand. There are indeed too many transit routes in the world to effectively intercept the movement of drugs from producing to consuming countries.

The cumulative impact of these and other factors affecting the international community's ability to effectively control drugs requires a new, critical appraisal of the international system of drug control and its predication on certain assumptions concerning the ability of national systems of control to effectively fulfill their expected goals.

International efforts at controlling drugs began in 1912 when it appeared that an estimated ten million Chinese had become opium addicts. The world community at that time sought to control the spread of opium addiction making its way to the United States and Western Europe. Since then, thirteen international instruments have been developed culminating with the 1988 Convention Against Illicit Traffic in Narcotic Drugs and Psychotropic Substances which was signed by eighty-nine states and ratified by four states [as of January 15, 1990].

The evolutionary process of international legislation has therefore been consistent. At first, it dealt with opium because of its perceived dangers in the Western societies of the United States and Europe. Gradually, however, the range of concerns encompassed other types of naturally based drugs such as the coca derivatives and various types of *cannabis sativa* (marijuana, hashish, quat and Indian hemp).

Until 1971, the thrust of international controls was by the consuming countries of the West over the producing ones of the Third World. This occurred because consuming countries experienced social problems as a result of consumption, whereas the producing Third World countries had no such social problems. The latter derived economic benefits from the cultivation and traffic of naturally produced drugs. But the consuming countries' rationale was that ultimately the problems of drug consumption would spread to the producing countries. They argued that economic dependence on drug-related profits would create economic, social and political problems for producing countries. Thus, international cooperation was deemed indispensable for the world community as a whole. These arguments are as valid today as they were fifty years ago.

"There are indeed too many transit routes in the world to effectively intercept the movement of drugs."

Notwithstanding these predictions, consuming countries of the West have failed to provide the necessary assistance for economic development to Third World producing countries, and production of drugs has continued to increase. Gradually the consuming countries used treaties to place expanded international controls on the producing countries. At first, efforts were aimed at curtailing and later eliminating the cultivation of natural drugs. As a result, the producing countries had to bear additional costs in law enforcement and divert vital resources to carry out these obligations.

The 1961 Single Convention on Narcotic Drugs is today the most universally accepted Convention in the field of drug control. It is, after the United Nations Charter and the four Geneva Conventions of August 12, 1949, the multilateral treaty with the largest number of State-Parties.

However, by 1970 it was obvious that the 1961 Single Convention needed to be strengthened in order to make it more effective. By 1970, the process began by which the 1961 Single Convention would be amended, ultimately culminating in the 1972 Protocol Amending the 1961 Single Convention.

Chemical and Pharmaceutical Drugs

During that same period, the international community came to the realization that some specific controls over chemical and pharmaceutical drugs should also be established. While efforts to amend the 1961 Single Convention to strengthen it were ongoing, a parallel effort was undertaken to develop another convention which ultimately became the 1971 Convention on Psychotropic Substances. These two efforts which should have logically been integrated into a single convention proceeded along separate paths.

The international community at that time was divided between consuming and producing countries of natural drugs and of chemical and pharmaceutical ones. However, that division did not represent identical parties. With respect to the natural drugs, most of the producing countries, as stated above, were and still are Third World developing countries, while the consuming ones were, and still are, the industrialized Western countries. With respect to the chemical and pharmaceutical drugs, however, the producing countries were, and still are, mostly the Western industrialized countries (as well as other industrialized countries of Eastern Europe, but they were less active on the international marketing arena) while the consuming countries include the Third World developing countries. In short, the main consumption of natural drugs was in the industrialized West, while consumption of chemical and pharmaceutical drugs included the developing countries.

"International structures established to control drugs are . . . without any effective enforcement powers."

While the developed countries of the West desired to impose strong controls over the cultivation, production and traffic of natural drugs originating in the developing countries, they were unwilling to impose the same types of controls over their own chemical and pharmaceutical industries. Because of that imbalance, the obligations of consuming and producing countries (which are largely derived from their relative power positions and their social and economic condition) affected the 1972 Amending Protocol to the 1961 Single Convention on Narcotic Drugs by producing a much stronger system of control than the one established by the 1971 Convention on Psychotropic Substances.

The imbalance that exists between these two systems of control has not yet been redressed. One of the reasons for this situation is that throughout the world a pattern of behavior in chemical drug consumption has become part of daily life. The widespread habituation to the taking of drugs from benign aspirin, cold tablets or vitamins, has generated a culture of pill-taking, which made it much easier and more acceptable to take other types of pills, even though they produce harmful effects. The taking of one pill as opposed to another may be a question of slight difference. This situation made social and legal controls of psychotropic substances more difficult than the control of natural drugs. The type of social and legal controls that derive from

a generally unacceptable pattern of behavior involving injecting heroin or snorting cocaine is obviously easier than that of controlling the taking of pills whose apparent use is generally accepted behavior if for no other reason than the difference in the color or shape of the pill is not a significantly distinguishing factor to make it socially reprehensible.

The differences in patterns of socially acceptable, as opposed to socially unacceptable behavior, as well as what may merge into legitimacy and what may readily appear to be outside social legitimacy, tend to make the disparity in the international perception of the dangers of drugs, as well as the ensuing control mechanism, less readily observable. As a result, what we see is a strong imbalance in the attempt to control the natural drugs in contrast to the chemical and pharmaceutical ones.

Alternative Approaches

It must also be pointed out that the originators of the international narcotics control system were not promoting the complete control of the drugs by eliminating the cultivation of what are called "illicit drugs." Because the international system still recognizes the legitimacy and legal validity of the cultivation of drugs, they are deemed licit if cultivated under the monopoly or control of a state. The international narcotics control system, as well as the system of national control, is one that grants a monopoly of cultivation and processing of natural drugs to the states. The reason is due to the medical purposes of such natural drugs, as in the case of morphine. However, it nonetheless appears incongruous to have a co-existence of a licit system of cultivation and processing under the monopoly of a given state, as well as a licit system for trafficking by the state and by chemical and pharmaceutical companies through the dispensing of drugs for valid medical and therapeutic purposes, while at the same time deeming illicit the production and traffic of these substances when they are not under the control of the state and outside state regulation for use. While there is no doubt that a valid distinction exists between what is licit for medical purposes and what is not, it is essentially a qualitative and judgmental distinction. This does not have the same social and socio-psychological impact as banning the cultivation of all drugs because they are *malum in se* [inherently evil].

"There is no adequate way of . . . assessing both the supply and the consumption of drugs throughout the world."

An alternative to the existing scheme can easily be conceived whereby all natural drugs—the opium poppy, the coca bush, the *cannabis sativa*—could be banned throughout the world and their eradication collectively decreed by the world community; and in order to provide for morphine and other drugs which derive from the opiates, the United Nations could assign the task of limited cultivation of such a crop to a given country for the benefit of all other countries.

In short, an opium poppy farm could be established in a given country under international control and would probably require no more than a thousand hectares to satisfy the world's medical needs. Such cultivation could easily be internationally controlled and there would not be the problem of having different countries grow these crops under local controls to produce that which is ostensibly for their pharmaceutical needs. Experience has clearly indicated that in almost every country where licit cultivation exists there is a portion of it that goes into illicit traffic. There is also no reason why, on such a simple subject, the world community could not agree to abolish cultivation everywhere in the world in order to concentrate it in a single plot of land and develop a worldwide consortium. The costs of such licit cultivation would certainly be low. And there would be no genuine economic interest on the part of different countries—interested in purchasing their needs for legitimate pharmaceutical production—to claim that such a monopoly concentration of the cultivation in one country would affect them detrimentally. The cultivation of a single hectare of the opium poppy would cost approximately $500 to $800 per crop. Even if we assume an inflated cost of $1000 per hectare, the production of 1000 hectares would only be $1 million per year. If the total needs of the world community in producing morphine based drugs is a total cost of $1 million for the poppy, there is simply no legitimate economic reason to prevent it.

That such an idea has not taken root, even though it has been suggested, at least by this writer since 1971, is evidence that an international control effort does not necessarily evidence the will of states to fully cooperate at all levels.

The International Control Structure

The international narcotics control system, as stated above, is predicated on a licit system of cultivation and production and only those activities which exceed the licit quota system become illicit. Under such a system states may produce based on their estimated needs, and could export the surplus to other states based on an import/export certification system. But, in the final analysis, such a system would depend almost entirely on voluntary international cooperation. Without direct international controls it rests only on the ability of those international organizations that supervise such a system to denounce a potential violator to the world community.

In addition to the above, the international narcotics control system is predicated on an indirect control system, by which states undertake certain international obligations arising out of treaty obligations and then assume the task of carrying them out through their national legal system in reliance upon their national implementation measures.

In a sense it is almost incongruous to think that an international system, which presumably would operate at the top of the pyramid in the structure of states, ultimately winds up distributing enforcement powers to the bottom of the pyramid, namely to the participating states. Under the present system, international structures established to control drugs are designed only as administrative support, funding or monitoring organizations, without any effective enforcement powers.

The United Nations

1. The United Nations Commission on Narcotic Drugs, was established in 1946 by the Economic and Social Council as the policy-making body of the United Nations system with respect to drug matters. Its membership consists of forty members elected by the Economic and Social Council and it reviews the overall global drug situation and prepares policies, as well as sponsoring international conventions.

2. The United Nations Division of Narcotic Drugs essentially serves as the administrative body, the secretariat and executive arm of the Commission on Narcotic Drugs. It assists members in the implementation of the various drug Conventions and provides services and facilities to the Commission on Narcotic Drugs. It publishes annual and analytical reports, as well as various national reports required by international treaties, and deals with coordinating the work of the United Nations and World Health Organization, as well as various governments.

3. The International Narcotics Control Board (INCB) was established under the provision of the 1961 Single Convention on Narcotic Drugs. It was established to limit the cultivation, production, manufacture and use of drugs to the adequate amounts required for medical and scientific purposes. In short, it is the body that establishes the quotas for countries, based on their estimates of need for the chemical and scientific licit purposes. The Board consists of thirteen members elected from the State-Parties. These members serve ostensibly in their personal capacity, but in reality they are genuine government representatives. The INCB works closely with the Commission on Narcotic Drugs and cooperates with other bodies, such as the World Health Organization and the United Nations Fund for Drug Abuse Control. But it must be clearly understood that such cooperative undertakings are purely dependent upon the will of the Board. What is particularly interesting is that this Board is created by treaty and operates with total and complete independence from the Commission on Narcotic Drugs.

4. The United Nations Fund for Drug Abuse Control (UNFDAC) is the only multilateral body which was created to provide technical assistance as well as funding relating to crop substitution. In recent times, it has evolved from that narrow role of being a funding agency to one that provides technical assistance for all forms of drug abuse and illicit trafficking, including the field of law enforcement. It was created in 1971 by the Secretary-General and was established as a multilateral body to which a number of countries voluntarily contribute. Because contributions to UNFDAC are voluntary, the projects it undertakes are dependent upon such voluntary contributions of those different countries. UNFDAC operates subject to the control of the Secretary-General of the United Nations, but it does not have any obligation to either work or, in fact, cooperate or correlate its activities with the other bodies mentioned above, just as these other bodies have no obligation towards each other.

"If supply cannot be controlled . . . how can it be expected that international and national controls can be effective?"

In addition to these four main bodies, we find that there are several other agencies within the United Nations that deal with drugs. The World Health Organization is mandated under the 1971 Convention on Psychotropic Substances to provide advice on the chemical and pharmaceutical substances that would fall in the four schedules of drugs established under the terms of the Convention. The Crime Prevention and Criminal Justice Branch of the United Nations also deals with the crime-related aspects of drugs. The Center for Human Rights has certain administrative tasks with respect to human rights dimensions related to drugs. In that respect, two other United Nations bodies also are directly involved, namely The Commission on Human Rights and the Subcommittee on the Prevention of Discrimination and Protection of Minorities because of their mandate in human rights-related aspects of drug use and abuse. In addition, all the United Nations bodies involved in the area of human rights deal also with criminal justice and law enforcement insofar as there are human rights issues. This, of course, extends to illicit trafficking in drugs.

One must marvel at the reasons why the international community would create such a diversity of organizations, each working under different bureaucratic headings at the international level, with separate functions. Little wonder that efforts at controlling both the licit and illicit cultivation, traffic, distribution and use of drugs has not been successful. This raises the question of whether the international community is genuinely interested in the control of the cultivation, manufacture and distribution of illicit drugs, or whether it is merely seeking to express its disapproval of these activities, but unwilling or unable to undertake the necessary steps to make that concern effective.

It is clear to anyone interested in the subject that there is no adequate way of quantitatively and qualitatively assessing both the supply and the consumption of drugs throughout the world. With respect to supply, the assessment is based on an extrapolation of figures predicated on the amount of drugs seized and a very loose correlation between the number of arrests and seizures of drugs in different countries and the estimated linkage between these arrests on the one hand and supply and consumption on the other. The supply side of drugs has been consistently increasing over the past fifty years and there is no way to assess how much more it can increase or where such increase will come from.

The Consumption Side

The problem of assessment is the same on the consumption side. In the United States, for example, the estimates of occasional cocaine users fluctuates between the figure of under 800,000 up to the figure of 5,000,000. The fluctuation in numbers between the users of marijuana range from 1,000,000 to 5,000,000. The estimated number of heroin users fluctuates from 300,000 to 800,000. The same uncertainty exists in most countries where the estimated number of users, depending upon the type of drugs, varies enormously. There is also a large discrepancy between the estimates of occasional users of the

cannabis sativa derivative and those of cocaine and coca bush product derivatives.

It is therefore astonishing that the assumptions derived from both the supply and the consumption of drugs are predicated on figures which are so tenuous and uncertain. Surely, if the total number of heroin addicts in the United States was 300,000 and the total number of cocaine users was less than 800,000, the dimension of the problem would be much different than if the higher of the estimated figures were to be taken into account. The same is true for many countries where certainty as to the number of regular users and occasional users is almost totally absent.

> # "An example of the international community's inability . . . to effectively cooperate is in the area of financial controls."

What is probably worse in terms of assumptions is the fact that no estimates exist as to the potential capabilities in various parts of the world for additional supply. This might be because few governments are willing to admit the fact that capacity for supply cannot be controlled, let alone eliminated. There is a limitless capacity of supply. Thus, for example, if it is believed that the eradication of the coca bush in Bolivia, Colombia and Peru would eliminate the problem of cocaine supply, one would have to realize that this conclusion is entirely wrong because similar geographic and weather conditions may exist, not only in the Andes, but also in the Amazon area of Brazil, in the Indian subcontinent, in the Philippines and in Indonesia. The fact is that coca is already cultivated in all these areas.

These considerations must also be viewed in light of potential expansion of cultivation and increased production in presently producing and consuming countries. An enormous potential for increased cultivation and production in many states not presently producing also exists. Furthermore, increased use and abuse in producing and consuming countries and further potential increase of use and abuse in almost all countries of the world, is a realistic hypothesis that must be taken into consideration when assessing the extent of the problem.

The spread of cultivation in consuming countries to meet the needs of the demand is already well established. Marijuana, for example, is now extensively produced in the United States and, according to some estimates, domestic production is now fulfilling 25% of the needs of U.S. consumption.

If supply cannot be controlled, because there will always be a potential for supply somewhere, how can it be expected that international and national controls can be effective? The assumptions made by both international and national policymakers are predicated on two erroneous factual assumptions of production and consumption and of supply and demand. Without adequate knowledge of these figures, it is quite logical to conclude that the consequences derived from any assumed figures will lead to erroneous outcomes.

Drug Money

The supply side of drugs is essentially a worldwide business enterprise which the United Nations estimates to be "a $500 billion per year business." Those who engage in it do so for profit and no other reason, save possibly for some ideologically motivated group seeking to finance its illegal activities from such revenue sources. . . .

An example of the international community's inability or unwillingness to effectively cooperate is in the area of financial controls. Financial controls over the entry into the financial circuit of drug proceeds has proven almost impossible, notwithstanding some occasional successes. The bank secrecy laws of so many countries make the tracing of drug proceeds more difficult. To sort out the white, black and gray money that flows

through the financial system is next to impossible. Money, as the saying goes, has no odor and thus cannot be closely detected once it enters into the legitimate financial pipeline. Thereafter the investments made with such proceeds are even harder to retrace. The conclusion is that in the absence of a worldwide uniform system of financial control of all funds entering the legitimate financial pipeline, no effective controls can be expected even though some countries, like Switzerland, have made progress in curbing bank secrecy laws. This situation leaves the profit incentive in drugs significantly unaffected by occasional seizures of drug proceeds. . . .

"Production of drugs in developing countries can be measured in direct relationship to the world economy."

In addition to the above, one must also consider the weaknesses of the various national law enforcement and criminal justice systems. Within each state there are administrative divisions and bureaucracies which frequently operate in sealed compartments, and at times even compete with each other, resulting in the weakening of the national enforcement systems. The administration of criminal justice in every country does not operate as a single cohesive system. All criminal justice systems have at least four subsystems: law enforcement, prosecution, judiciary and corrections. Each one of these is frequently divided into further smaller and sometimes competing units. The levels of integration and cooperation between the sub-systems and units of the criminal justice system are usually limited, and as stated above, they also suffer from the syndromes of competition. These organizational difficulties are also at times aggravated by internal political considerations, personal jealousies, animosities and ambitions, which at times seem to supersede institutional and national interests. The drug business, however, no matter how segmented it may be, does not have to operate under such constraints. The national criminal justice systems are presumed to work as a barrier to criminal activity. When it comes to the drug business, however, that system resembles a net whose webs are large enough to allow the fish to swim through it uncaught and unscathed.

The free enterprise type of activity that characterizes the drug business is also free of the bureaucracies that hamstring national and international agencies seeking to control the problem. Thus, while states rigidly observe the confines of their territorial jurisdiction, those in the drug business do not, and that permits them to exploit to their benefit the jurisdictional and operational gaps in interstate cooperation. . . .

On the economic plane, certain developing societies whose economies depend on the financial flow of drug-related resources find their economies gradually crippled as their dependency on drug income increases because their other productive means which are less profitable diminish. This is particularly true of agricultural societies, such as Bolivia and Peru, for whose *campesinos* the growing of the coca bush is more profitable and less painstaking than, for example, growing coffee or raising livestock. Such a choice is, however, also dictated by the lack of developmental capabilities and weaknesses in the infrastructure of these countries. This situation is a vicious cycle: the production of drugs flourishes in underdeveloped economies, while also preventing development—one problem feeding upon the other.

Drug Income

The same phenomenon also extends to developing transit states where the income from handling the flow of drugs and recycling its proceeds provides easy and quick profits which detrimentally affect the stability of their economic system. Thus, the economic viability of such states, and hence the social, economic and political stability, are imperiled.

Surprisingly, however, international and national efforts at curtailing supply and cutting off transit routes have not focused on the rather obvious need to offer economic development assistance in a significant and comprehensive manner to these developing countries. Production of drugs in developing countries can be measured in direct relationship to the world economy and consequently to the specific national economies of those producing countries. The foreign debt of such developing-producing countries and the falling prices of commodities are directly linked to the economic dependency of these countries on income generated by drug production. . . .

"The overall approach to international control of drugs is woefully deficient."

It is unequivocally established that the problems of crime related to drugs derive from the fact that drugs are illicit. As a result, the arguments made by the proponents of decriminalization cannot be taken lightly. This is particularly so because it is easily demonstrable that the political will of states in creating an effective and integrated international control scheme for the complete eradication and control of drug cultivation and traffic does not exist, nor is it demonstrated by the actions of governments up to now. Similarly, the divisions between various international organs, as well as the lack of direct enforcement powers given to them, and the lack of a truly integrated international legal control and implementation system, once again demonstrates the lack of will of states to effectively control that phenomenon.

It is also well established that the national systems of criminal justice have not been able to develop the types of mechanisms for bilateral and multilateral cooperation in such a way as to render their international cooperation effective. Internally, the national systems of criminal justice, subject to their traditional divisions of law enforcement, prosecution, judiciary and corrections, with all the sub-systems or sub-administrative and bureaucratic divisions that exist between them render these systems ineffective at controlling the problem of drugs at the national levels, let alone of being effective in controlling the problem at the international level. . . .

There are a number of international modalities which have been relied upon in all aspects of international cooperation in crime-related matters. They are:

1. extradition;
2. judicial assistance and cooperation in the area of securing tangible and intangible evidence;
3. transfer of criminal proceedings;
4. transfer of prisoners; and
5. recognition of foreign penal judgments.

It is interesting that so far these various mechanisms of international cooperation have remained at a very primitive level. Only three countries have enacted integrated national legislation on interstate penal cooperation: Germany, Switzerland and Austria.

These integrated national approaches provide more flexibility than is available in countries that use these modalities in an uncoordinated and disparate fashion. . . .

"Production of drugs increased more significantly than the number of offenders and users."

At a different level, it must be noted that there are no new international or regional organizations that have been created to operate in the field of international cooperation in penal matters, though international cooperation has indeed increased. However, specific undertakings are yet to be developed. For example, there could be regional informational clearinghouses for law enforcement cooperation and sharing of data and information about international, regional and even local organizations engaging in drug-related crime. At present there is no central data-base or central office to provide technical assistance to one another. . . . Once again, it is important to question the will of governments to make more effective international cooperation. . . .

More Seizures

Over the years, international, regional and national efforts have only resulted in more seizures of drugs, more arrests of drug offenders, more arrests of drug users, more costs in law enforcement, and significant burdens on the criminal justice systems. Worse yet is the added human and social costs, particularly the increased levels and incidences of violence and victimization. Yet production of drugs increased more significantly than the number of offenders and users. The bottom-line remains negative, and that negative balance also is on the increase. Some see the ultimate conclusion of this process as the decriminalization of the use of hard drugs, much like the de facto decriminalization via nonenforcement of marijuana usage in the United States and many Western European societies. Some countries, like the Netherlands, have embarked on that course of conduct for over a decade. Others, like Switzerland and Germany, have allowed certain areas of some cities to be free from law enforcement activities. In Zurich's main park there is even free distribution of needles to heroin addicts as a way of reducing AIDS and other health hazards, while in Frankfurt an area of the city operates free of police interference with the sale and use of drugs.

The overall approach to international control of drugs is woefully deficient as is the national control in most legal systems of the world. It is unlikely that the present trend of existing controls will succeed. Whether or not the world community can think of a more integrated and effective international system that would provide greater opportunities for the control of supply and demand, as well as for an effective system of suppression of traffic, is very much in doubt. To suppress any form of trafficking, one must assume the ability to control both supply and demand or to control either supply or demand or, at least, to be able to disrupt major trafficking networks. None of these exist. So how could there be a continued criminalization if neither supply nor demand nor suppression of trafficking can be effectively achieved?

My own conclusion is that the world community is at this point interested in making an apparent "good faith" effort. But, after a period of time, *de facto* decriminalization is likely to occur.

Social Costs

The schemes and scenarios for decriminalization are supported by an objectively defensible cost-benefit analysis of the costs of drug control versus results obtained. Some of the research also attempts to quantify the human and social costs and hypothesize as to what would occur in the event of decriminalization. The outcome is clearly unfavorable to the existence of a controlled approach. However, no one can assess the human and intangible social costs resulting from decriminalization. For others, the effort at controlling the harmful effect of drugs should not be abandoned before genuine and effective integrated international and national efforts are undertaken. They too are correct because such efforts have never been undertaken, even though they are the common subject of political pronouncements.

The prospects for effective international controls are so remote, however, that one can only agree with the principle of control with the knowledge that its effective implementation is unlikely, and one must consider other alternatives. Neither control of supply or demand, or both, will ever eliminate a problem which, by its very nature, cannot be totally eradicated—history teaches us that much. The goal therefore has to be to control or limit the harmful consequences. But levels of social tolerance are subjective and depend within each society on different factors, particularly psychological perceptions based on value judgments, which will also vary in time. A new approach must be found, if for no other reason than it may be dictated by the exigencies of objective (and quantified subjective) cost-benefit analysis. The search may well be for a new balance between advocates of total criminalization and those of total decriminalization. But in the final analysis, any new approach will have to depend on the willingness of all states to cooperate effectively at many levels. Whether it is possible to have faith in this prospect will depend on the degree of one's optimism about a process which has for so long failed to attain its avowed goals.

The experience of the 1960's in Western industrialized societies with respect to marijuana is indicative. While I do not think that legalization of the use of drugs will occur in the next quarter century, I would venture to guess that decriminalization will nonetheless occur in a *de facto* sense. This has been the experience with marijuana. It seems possible that the same will occur with respect to the use of cocaine and heroin and heroin-related products. . . .

"The experience of the 1960's in Western industrialized societies with respect to marijuana is indicative."

There is no doubt that an integrated series of strategies operating at different levels can be developed nationally and internationally to cumulatively achieve a reduction of the levels of harms of this problem in order to render it more manageable and more tolerable by the states directly affected and by the world community as a whole. Most observers of this phenomenon, however, would agree that these results are not likely to occur. The only hope would seem to be a natural process of use reduction that could occur as a result of greater worldwide awareness of the dangers and harmful effects of drugs. Where governments have failed, perhaps the good judgment of peoples all over the world can partially succeed.

The U.S. Campaign Against Cocaine Producers Is a Fraud

Peter Drucker

About the Author: *Peter Drucker is program staff-person for National Mobilization for Survival, a network of peace and social-justice groups based in New York City. He is also an editor of* Against the Current, *a bimonthly socialist magazine.*

In the 20th century, U.S. counterinsurgency wars fought against revolutionary movements have created ideal conditions for the spread of drug cultivation, trade and use. . . .

In the 1980s and 1990s, U.S.-funded wars in Central America and the South American Andes have been breeding grounds for the cocaine trade. Latin American debt, which reached $368 billion by 1985, has encouraged production of this uniquely profitable export. Cocaine and its cheap derivative crack have replaced heroin as the most feared drugs in the United States. Crack-related violence has become common in many neighborhoods. U.S. allies in armies, governments, death squads, the underworld, respectable banks and corporations have been among the beneficiaries.

[U.S.] intervention did not create drug use. But each successive intervention has contributed to increasing drug problems in the United States. Today 25 million people in the U.S. are estimated to spend $50 billion each year on drugs. With 5% of the world's population, the U.S. consumes about half the hard drugs on the world market—although more than fifty other countries are involved in drug production, processing, distribution or money laundering.

Yet the Bush administration, disoriented by cuts in Soviet military spending and deprived of anti-communism as an effective ideological prop for Third World intervention, is making the expansion of the drug trade an excuse for more U.S. intervention. Invading Panama, sending warships to Colombia and training troops in Peru have all been justified as part of a "war on drugs."

"Intervention abroad in the name of fighting drugs helps fuel the drug trade."

In fact, the U.S. government's war on drugs has not interfered with the accelerating growth of the drug trade. Cocaine imports were about 24 tons a year when Reagan chose Bush to head the war on drugs in 1981; imports rose to 85 tons by 1984 and over 200 tons by 1988, despite drug war programs costing $10 billion. Andean land planted in coca increased by 250%. The purity of cocaine sold on the street rose from 12% to 80%. A kilogram of cocaine in Miami fell from $60,000 to $11,000, close to an all-time low.

Bush's drug war is an abject failure. Bush himself, as CIA [Central Intelligence Agency] head and policymaker during several years when CIA involvement in the drug trade continued unabated, has personally helped to ensure that failure. Other government officials who plan and direct the drug war probably believe in it, but their policies are not stopping the drug trade and cannot stop the drug trade. On the contrary, intervention abroad in the name of fighting drugs helps fuel the drug trade. The more carefully one looks at each part of the world where the United States has intervened, the more striking the link between intervention and drug trade expansion becomes.

Coca, the plant from which cocaine and crack are made, is native to the Andean mountains.

Adapted from "Drug Wars and the Empire" by Peter Drucker. Reprinted with permission of National Mobilization for Survival, Inc., 45 John St., Suite 811, New York, NY 10038, (212) 385-2222.

People have been growing and chewing coca leaves there for thousands of years. The plant has been central to Quechua and Aymara native cultures as a food, a medicine, a symbol used for sealing contracts, an element in religious rituals and a means of social bonding as well as a drug. Today 25,000 Peruvian peasants produce coca legally under contract from the National Coca Enterprise.

But Peru's and Bolivia's incorporation into the world market has transformed coca from part of native culture to an export crop. Cocaine and crack, the drugs made from coca and sold in the United States, have different physical effects, a different social meaning and very different consequences for Peruvian society.

About 50-75% of the coca used for the cocaine sold in the United States comes from Peru's Upper Huallaga Valley between the eastern Andes and the Amazon basin, where the peasants have higher incomes than anywhere else in Peru. Coca brings between $800 million and $1.2 billion each year into the Peruvian economy and about $600 million into the Bolivian economy. Even though 1989 coca prices were one-fifth of 1980 prices—and under 1% of the market value of cocaine—no other crop on the market yields more than a seventh of coca's earnings per hectare.

"U.S. government policy has contributed to turning Colombia into a virtual one-crop country."

About 300,000 Peruvians and a comparable number of Bolivians live off coca production. In a country like Peru, where a third of the population is unemployed, that means a lot. One foreigner has commented that banning the drug trade in Peru is like "asking a country that's fighting the Civil War and going through the Great Depression at the same time to suddenly take on Prohibition as well."

The U.S. began military operations in the An-des with Operation Blast Furnace in 1986, which brought Drug Enforcement Administration (DEA) agents, 160 U.S. military personnel and six UH-60 Blackhawk helicopters to the Chapare region of Bolivia. Although Blast Furnace barely made a dent in coca production, 1988's Operation Snowdrop in Peru was modeled on Blast Furnace in many ways: D.E.A. agents, UH-l Huey helicopters, Special Forces and Green Berets. Suspended in early 1989, Snowdrop resumed in September 1989 with the completion of a Vietnam-style forest fortress at Santa Lucia, complete with airstrip, two helicopter pads, trenches and housing for 200 troops.

Coca Production

Yet despite hundreds of millions of dollars, use of napalm and the dangerous herbicide "Spike," 8,000 deaths and eradication of thousands of hectares of coca fields, many experts say that total Peruvian land planted in coca has increased to as much as 200,000 hectares (from 7,000 in 1973). Many Peruvian and Bolivian commanders earn good money by simply doing nothing, for which drug merchants reward them. At the same time, coca production has spread over the border to Brazil, out of U.S. forces' reach.

The U.S. military presence in Peru and Bolivia, in part motivated as an anti-drug tactic, also has another function: as an attack on the Bolivian and Peruvian left. In Bolivia U.S. agents reportedly took part in June 1988 in a massacre at Villa Tunari, and attacked the town of Santa Ana in June 1989, killing five people. The Congress of Bolivian Peasant Unions and the Bolivian Central Workers Union have condemned U.S. intervention and repression. Tens of thousands have marched.

In Peru, U.S. forces have clashed with the Maoist guerrilla group Sendero Luminoso [Shining Path]. An intolerant and brutal organization, Sendero has been compared to Pol Pot's Khmer Rouge for the barbarity of its tactics. Peasants in the war zones live under a two-headed reign of terror, in which the army will torture, mutilate or kill them if they fail to support the army and Sendero will torture, mutilate or kill them if they fail to support Sendero. The Peruvian left fears and condemns Sendero, which systematically kills leftists whom it sees as rivals.

Sendero Protection

Yet Sendero is deeply entrenched in the Upper Huallaga Valley and controls 90% of the area, thanks in part to the U.S.-funded and directed drug war. Sendero protects the valley's peasants from drug traffickers and sets "fair" prices for their coca. It also protects them from the U.S. eradication campaign. At the same time, Sendero seems to have had some success in decreasing Peruvian peasants' dependence on coca. The United States rarely offers any alternative to coca: only 3.6% of the 1990 Andean drug war budget is earmarked for crop substitution. Sendero, while collecting $30-40 million a year from coca taxes and buying its guns from the traffickers, prohibits its members from using drugs and has apparently had some success in encouraging peasants to branch out into food crops.

The drug war has helped Sendero grow, which has in turn helped justify deeper U.S. involvement. In the spring of 1990 the Bush administration announced plans for a second fortress, this time not for the war against drugs but openly for the war against Sendero. Sendero says it has no alternative but to allow coca production while the war continues. U.S. intervention is ensuring that the war and drug trade both do continue. Although most of the coca that ends up as cocaine or crack is grown in Peru and Bolivia, very little of it is exported directly from Peru or Bolivia to the United States. In the drug trade as in the global economy generally, division of labor has become the rule. Just as General Motors makes more money now by having auto parts produced in one country and assembled in another, the drug industry has the coca that is grown and pounded into paste in Peru and Bolivia processed into cocaine in laboratories in Colombia.

Today about 80% of the illegal cocaine in the United States comes from Colombia, with Colombian cocaine sales in the United States estimated at $16 billion. A half-million Colombians work in the cocaine industry; hundreds of thousands more depend on it indirectly. Although most of the profits from Colombian cocaine sales stay in the United States, the $24 billion that Colombia earns from drug exports dwarf earnings from any of the country's legal products. As a result, those who dominate the drug trade dominate Colombia. U.S. government policy has contributed to turning Colombia into a virtual one-crop country. The results are short-term prosperity for many Colombians but devastating problems for the society as a whole.

"Bombing Colombia is no more effective in stopping the drug trade than bombing New York would be."

Colombia's development into a drug-centered economy was not inevitable. Its land is not well suited to coca growing. In the 1950s and 1960s it seemed on its way to becoming an industrialized society. Production of textiles, steel, cement and chemicals grew. But when the world economy entered its downturn in the 1970s, markets for Colombian manufactured goods shrank, its debt grew and poverty worsened. Washington has increased Colombian dependence on cocaine by imposing stiff tariffs on Colombian flower imports.

The consequences of cocaine have been worse for Colombian cities than U.S. cities, though the U.S. media rarely notices. Colombia has about half a million cocaine addicts. It also has more than its share of the violence that comes with the illegal trade. In the drug capital of Medellin there are often twenty murders a day, so that gunshot wounds are now the leading cause of death for people of all ages.

Much of the violence helps to prop up the rule of the cocaine oligarchy, which has much the same outlook and methods as landowning oligarchies in Central America. Unions and peasant organizations are anathema to the drug merchants. Drug lords finance death squads that killed 3,000 people in 1988, mostly organizers, leftists and human rights activists. The Patriotic Union alone, the largest group on the Colombian left, had 900 members killed in three years. Leaders of the M-19 group, which gave up guerrilla warfare in early 1990 to take part in elections, have also been killed. The military and police often work together with drug merchant-financed death squads.

Bush's answer has been more aid for the military and the police. The Bush administration sent $65 million in military aid to Colombia in late 1989, along with up to 100 U.S. military personnel, and asked for $90 million more in 1990. One Colombian politician (underestimating the brutality of Bush's domestic drug war) has said that the U.S. drug war means "educational videos in the United States, bombers for Colombia."

Yet bombing Colombia is no more effective in stopping the drug trade than bombing New York would be—actually less effective. The price of cocaine is much higher in New York than in Colombia, so that most of the profit from cocaine is added on in the United States. In the words of Colombian writer Gabriel Garcia Marquez, any military war on drugs in Colombia is bound to be "long, ruinous and without a future."

Cocaine, Contras, and Panama

U.S. policy has done more than contribute to economic conditions that increased South America's dependence on cocaine. U.S. government agencies have been trailblazers along the trade routes by which cocaine has reached the United States. Their motivation has been much the same as for the other big players in the drug trade: they wanted money.

The U.S. executive branch was set on funding counterrevolution in Central America at a time in the 1980s when the public was against it and Congress was at least temporarily bowing to public opinion. When the Reagan administration was unable to get legal funding for Nicaraguan contras, it turned to an easier source: drugs.

The Christic Institute estimated that at one time in the 1980s, the contras were smuggling a ton of cocaine a week into the United States. The White House staff made the smuggling possible. The notebooks of Reagan staffer Colonel Oliver North contain many references like this one (from July 12, 1985): "$14 million to finance [arms] came from drugs."

"Any real solution to the drug trade would have to focus on the demand for drugs in the United States."

Tolerance for drug dealing was not restricted to a few mavericks in the White House. It spread through every agency responsible for fighting drugs. The CIA put its connections and favorite small airlines—which hired Medellin cartel pilots at the dealers' disposal. According to the *Houston Post*, the CIA used Texas savings and loan institutions to launder drug money, contributing to several savings and loan failures. . . .

The U.S. government was not troubled by scruples about countries like Costa Rica that objected to having the drug trade in their territory. When Lewis Tambs arrived in Costa Rica as U.S. ambassador, he said that "he had really only one mission in Costa Rica, and that was to form a Nicaraguan resistance southern front." By July 1989 Costa Rican embarrassment over U.S. and contra drug dealing led President Oscar Arias to bar Tambs, North, Richard Secord, John Poindexter and former CIA station chief Joseph Fernandez from Costa Rican territory. In December 1989 the Costa Rican public prosecutor reported that contras involved in the drug trade targeted Eden Pastora for assassination, among other reasons because he refused to get involved in the drug trade.

Other Central American governments had fewer reservations. The Guatemalan military joined enthusiastically in the contra support operation. The White House ignored charges that the Honduran military had joined in the drug trade. Most helpful of all to the CIA and the contras was Panamanian dictator Colonel Manuel Antonio Noriega.

In 1976, two drug-enforcement officials recommended that Noriega be killed in order to stop his role in the drug trade. But Noriega, who had been on the CIA payroll since the late 1960s, was untouchable. CIA Director George Bush met with Noriega soon after the recommendation was made. The DEA sent him letters thanking him for his help in the drug war.

Meanwhile, his importance in the drug trade increased. In 1981 he made contact with heads of the Medellin cartel when he hosted talks between the drug-financed Colombian death squad Death to Kidnappers and the guerrilla group M-19.

"Nonintervention alone will not cut off the supply of drugs."

Noriega's usefulness to Colombian drug dealers and the U.S. government multiplied many times thanks to Oliver North, who used Noriega as a link between Colombian dealers and Nicaraguan contras. Having become the most powerful man in Panama in 1983, Noriega worked with North to make Panama a contra logistical and funding base. Arranging drug deals was one major way in which Noriega helped.

U.S. government support for Noriega did not end because of anything to do with drugs. The change came only in 1987 or 1988, apparently when his support for the contras waned. That his role in the drug trade provided the main U.S. pretext for the December 1989 invasion which overthrew him is supremely ironic. In fact, U.S. demands for restrictions on drug money laundering by the new Endara government were quietly dropped when it turned out that four of its top officials had interests in the banks.

Is There an Alternative?

Any real solution to the drug trade would have to focus on the demand for drugs in the United States, where users would have to be offered a chance at meaningful lives. But a comprehensive program for dealing with the drug trade would also have to include changes in U.S. foreign policy. U.S. intervention in the Third World has consistently brought the drug trade in its wake; any program to end the drug trade would have to include an end to U.S. support for . . . drug-dealing armies and police. On grounds of drug policy alone, there is a good case for abolition of the CIA, for years a hub of the global drug trade.

Nonintervention alone will not cut off the supply of drugs, however, as long as Latin America and other parts of the Third World are so dependent on the drug trade for hard currency and economic survival. A U.S. government that was fighting the drug trade effectively would cancel Latin American debts, begin aid programs that encourage Latin American agricultural self-sufficiency and give favorable treatment for Latin American exports to the United States, making crop substitution programs practical.

The right's answers to the drug crisis—repression and intervention—have been tried and failed. Our only hope is a program that deals with the crisis' underlying causes: racism and poverty at home, imperialism and poverty abroad.

The U.S. International Campaign Against Drug Trafficking Is Ineffective

Michael Levine

About the Author: *Michael Levine was an agent of the Drug Enforcement Administration (DEA). In his twenty-five years of service in the DEA, he served as a group supervisor and an international undercover agent. His book* Deep Cover, *excerpted here, is based on his experiences.*

This [viewpoint] is about the biggest, costliest, most dangerous failure of American policy since Vietnam—the war on drugs. As the availability of drugs in the U.S. increases to unprecedented levels, at the lowest prices in history, we are being bombarded with hype—from ex-President Reagan's "We've turned the corner in the war on drugs" and Attorney General Edwin Meese's promise that Operation Snowcap (our government's two-hundred-million-dollar-a-year main thrust in South America) would "cut the availability of cocaine in the U.S. by fifty percent," to the supposed Colombian murder contracts on our bureaucrats and politicians, to the endless seizures and arrests called "drug-war victories."

As I write this, President Bush and—the latest rabbit out of the political hat—the "drug czar" are playing the media for all it's worth to convince us of the effectiveness of the drug war. It would have been laughable—had people not been dying—that when the Colombian government defied the cocaine cartels and our govern-

ment rushed them a sixty-five-million-dollar "emergency package" of military equipment, it turned out to be all the wrong stuff. "The total package is more suitable for conventional warfare than the kind of struggle we are waging," said Major General Miguel Gómez-Padilla, the chief of the seventy-thousand-member Colombian national police force. Another Colombian official said that the aid will serve as a "symbolic show" of American support.

Can it really be the case that, after two decades of so-called drug war, our government did not know what equipment and aid Colombia really needed? Or was the sixty-five million in useless equipment nothing more than another public-relations hype aimed at American voters and taxpayers? *See! We are really fighting a war, America. We've got them on the run! Vote for us! Fund our programs!*

> ## "This . . . is about the biggest, costliest, most dangerous failure of American policy since Vietnam—the war on drugs."

Or is the truth that our leaders cannot, and do not really want to, win a *real* drug war? Is it that the secret agencies and interests that *really* pull the strings of foreign policy believe that our two hundred-billion-dollar-a-year drug habit is a *necessary* subsidy to keep the millions of poor in Third World countries from turning to communism? Has the choice of drugs over communism led our government to the halfhearted war on drugs and to the resulting cold sacrifice of the lives of those fighting that war?

Colonel Oliver North, for example, was given access to classified DEA [Drug Enforcement Administration] information involving the first undercover penetration of the infamous Medellín, Colombia, cocaine cartel by an informant, Barry Seal, because it was believed that the Colombians were bribing high-level members of the Sandinista government of Nicaragua. It would have been a great propaganda coup for North in his "divine" struggle against communism. Seal was clearly one of the most significant informants in DEA's history and the drug investigation one of the most important and far-reaching. When it turned out that the bribery information was not accurate, North decided that he wanted to use Seal to ferry money to the Contras. Finally, one of the DEA "suits" (law enforcement bureaucrats and administrative types) objected. "But that'll blow the [drug] case," he whined. When an angered North didn't get his way, he leaked the story to the press. Seal's cover was blown and he was murdered by the Colombians.

The drug case was over, a life was lost, and North—while his secretary and shredding-machine partner, Fawn Hall, snorted a couple of lines of coke herself—continued blissfully on his anticommunist mission from God. The war on drugs had been seriously damaged on the whim of a loose cannon in the basement of the Pentagon, yet not a word of complaint was heard from the suits, the other bureaucrats, or the politicians—the leaders of the drug war. In fact, the whole incident might have gone undiscovered were it not for the Iranscam Senate hearings.

An Inside Joke

If the war on drugs is our number-one priority, as our leaders never tire of telling us, why the hell was that boob given a key investigation to play with in the first place?

One of the favorite inside jokes of John Lawn (DEA administrator and chief narcotics enforcement officer in the U.S.) is to quote ex-President Reagan: "We've turned the corner in the war on drugs." It's a line that always gets a laugh among the suits. Well, the time has come for the American public to be let in on the joke.

I will offer evidence that the North incident was no fluke; that the drug war is sacrificed regularly in favor not only of the war against communism but of a multitude of other interests; and that alongside these interests, human life and the ravaging of our society have become an in-

side joke.

I compiled the evidence by turning my skill at undercover against those in control of our drug war—the suits. I documented every one of their misdeeds until I had enough evidence to make an accusation that would stand up in court. In fact, I would like the reader to think of himself or herself as a grand juror reading a criminal indictment.

"The drug war is sacrificed regularly in favor not only of the war against communism but of a multitude of other interests."

Chief among the accused are the suits—the leaders of this war. They are the ones you see on television, a badge hanging from their breast pockets, standing alongside the local bureaucrats and politicians, in front of tables piled with drugs, guns, and money, taking credit for another victory, another record drug bust, despite the fact that there are more drugs available at cheaper prices than ever before. They are the ones you saw looking appropriately somber at the funeral of an undercover officer killed trying to arrest a drug dealer for the sale of one gram of cocaine, while the traffickers smuggling tons are protected by our own government. *"His life was not given in vain,"* says the suit to the television camera, *ignoring the reality of the failure of the drug war.* They are the experts seen on the news programs and panel shows, who, despite the unchecked torrent of drugs into this country, self-righteously tell us, *"Law enforcement is doing its part."*

Supporters of the Drug War

The co-conspirators of the suits are the politicians and bureaucrats who support the drug war. *"What is needed is more funding for law enforcement, education, and rehabilitation,"* they bleat at anyone who will listen, knowing that even the most medically educated in our society—physicians—are among the biggest drug abusers, and that rehabilitation programs are about as effective as aspirin against syphilis in stopping our drug epidemic.

The suits, politicians, and bureaucrats are more the Enemy, in a real war on drugs, than any drug dealer who ever lived. It is their mistakes, false promises, and ineptitude that keep us on a path to more useless death and destruction. They—like the generals and the politicians of Vietnam—don't gamble with their own lives; they risk those of others. Their primary concerns are public image, their individual careers, and the funding of their election campaigns and bureaucracies. They are the ones who most fear the words of the frontline soldier.

A Battle with Drugs

*To my family and friends, I'm sorry. I just can't stand the drugs anymore . . .*wrote my brother David sometime during the early morning hours of February 27, 1977. According to his landlady he had been pacing the floor, playing his radio loud all night. She thought she had heard voices but could not be sure if it was the radio or David talking to himself. He must have suffered terribly during that long, lonely night. Not long before dawn he put a gun to his head and pulled the trigger, ending his life and his nineteen-year battle with heroin.

Our father had to wade across a floor covered with blood and brain matter that clung to his shoes to find the suicide note; my brother had left it in a bureau drawer. He must have changed his mind back and forth all night, sticking the letter in a drawer and taking it out, and finally when things seemed blackest and another delay more painful and frightening than the idea of death, he forgot the note and quickly pulled the trigger.

'Fuck life! Fuck the note! Fuck the world!' might have been the words of any of the thousands of druggies who have managed to touch my life. My brother's final act spoke them with great eloquence.

Until the note was found the Miami police

had listed the death as a possible homicide. 'You never can tell with these druggies,' said a detective, thinking he was talking to a DEA agent with nothing more than a professional interest in the case.

No, you never can tell with these druggies.

Foreign Devils

By the time my brother had killed himself our family had suffered with his addiction for nineteen years, twelve of which I had spent as an undercover federal agent. It was easy for me to believe the rhetoric of the suits and politicians, blaming our nightmare on some dark, money-hungry foreigners. I can now understand why we continue to vote for and fund the drug war. It is much easier to hate than to seek truth.

In 1978, the year that DEA transferred me to Buenos Aires, Argentina, I was full of hatred for the "foreign devils" responsible for my brother's death, and a one-hundred-percent believer in the war on drugs and my role in it. I was totally unprepared for the education in the real world of international politics and drug trafficking that I was about to receive.

> ## "I can now understand why we continue to vote for and fund the drug war. It is much easier to hate than to seek truth."

By late 1979, after a series of successful undercover adventures in Argentina, Uruguay, and Bolivia, I managed to penetrate the Roberto Suárez organization—the biggest cocaine-producing cartel in history. From the very beginning I found myself battling forces within my own agency who, for reasons I could not understand at the time, were opposed to the investigation. With the aid of a small group of dedicated undercover agents, I defied the DEA hierarchy and overcame a series of roadblocks to the investigation that put all our lives on the line, and succeeded in making the biggest drug case of that decade. Eight hundred fifty-four pounds of cocaine base were seized and two of the most powerful drug dealers in our history arrested after I paid them nine million dollars in a Miami bank vault. It was the first time that we had proof that drug traffickers were in control of a government. The case also resulted in astonishing indications that drug traffickers had already infiltrated the highest levels of other South American governments. It was called "the biggest sting operation in history" by the media; the only problem was that it was the American people who wound up getting stung.

Instead of our government pursuing the investigation and its implications with all its resources, strange things began to happen. All charges were dropped against one of the two defendants and the bail of the other was mysteriously lowered, after which he was allowed to leave the United States without the slightest hindrance by our government. The biggest sting operation in law-enforcement history was suddenly without any defendants, and no one in our government seemed to care. My belief in the drug war was, for the first time, shaken to its foundation. What happened next blasted it to kingdom come.

The Roberto Suárez organization began a revolution in Bolivia to oust the element in that government that had dared to cooperate with DEA in allowing my sting operation to happen—a revolution supported by our CIA. When the smoke cleared, thousands had been tortured and killed and the cocaine traffickers were in control of Bolivia.

CIA Involvement

At the time this was all incomprehensible to me. It just didn't make sense that the CIA would be aiding drug traffickers in the takeover of a government. I began to complain, first through government channels, and finally, when that got no results, with a letter to the media. Within months I was mysteriously put under a long and intensive internal-affairs investigation that touched every corner of my professional and personal life. At the same time, Roberto Suárez issued contracts for my murder throughout the Americas.

In January 1982 I was removed from my post in Argentina and transferred to DEA headquarters, where I found myself more threatened by the so-called good guys in this drug war than I'd ever been by the enemy. One of the suits at headquarters who had taken a liking to me had counseled, "A bureaucracy has a short memory. Keep your mouth shut and show them that you're not a threat, and you'll come out okay."

"I knew the truth—the war on drugs was a fraud and we were all being sacrificed for nothing."

I learned the lesson quickly. This was not a battle to be fought alone, and America of the late seventies and early eighties was just not threatened enough by drugs to really give a damn. The ruthless internal-affairs investigation and veiled threats had frightened the hell out of me. If I was to survive, I had to keep my mouth shut. Yet, being an undercover agent is far too murderous a life-style to live if you don't believe in what you are doing. It did not take much for me to convince myself that the Suárez case was a fluke. I would not allow myself to believe that the suits and politicians, as a matter of policy, would let Americans lose their lives in a war they did not want to win.

Just the same, being the professional investigator that I was, I had carefully documented everything that had happened, and dreamed wistfully of one day writing a book entitled *The Case That Might Have Won the Cocaine War.*

As it turned out, the suit was right. Before long, when it became apparent that the internal-affairs investigation would leave me unscathed, and that I no longer posed a threat, to the suits, of complaining outside DEA, my undercover talents were once again called upon. I was again deeply submerged in undercover work and too involved in my own survival to think of anything else. I managed to brainwash myself into again being a "believer" in the drug war, and above all, my role in it.

Mounting Evidence

During the next five years—when I wasn't working undercover on some of the most sensitive and far-reaching cases in the agency—I was assigned duties as special operations officer, South American division; desk coordinator, cocaine desk; supervisor, Vice President's South Florida Task Force; group supervisor, New York Drug Enforcement Task Force, and group supervisor, New York Field Division; inspector in place (inspecting and evaluating DEA's world-wide field operations); and finally, as an instructor in "Narcotics Undercover Tactics" and "Informant Handling."

It was a period of time during which I turned a blind eye to the mounting evidence of the truth about our war on drugs, when more narcotics cops and agents—street men, not suits, *never* suits—were killed and injured than ever before and I felt the hurt of all their losses as if they were mine. It was a time when my son, Keith, became a New York City patrolman and began regularly risking his life in one bizarre drug-related incident after another, and I began hating myself for my cowardice. I knew the truth—the war on drugs was a fraud and we were all being sacrificed for nothing.

Chapter 4:

How Has Drug Trafficking Affected the U.S.?

Preface

Drug trafficking is one of the world's most lucrative businesses, netting, according to Drug Enforcement Administration (DEA) estimates, between $100 billion and $180 billion every year. It is also one of America's most perplexing and intractable problems. Drug trafficking has increased America's crime rate, congested its criminal justice system, contributed to the decline of its inner cities, and corrupted its children. Although in the past two decades the U.S. has devoted billions of dollars, thousands of people, and millions of hours to stopping drug trafficking, this illicit industry and its accompanying problems have continued to expand.

In the 1980s and 1990s, drug trafficking and ancillary crime have increased at an alarming rate. The Federal Bureau of Investigations and the Drug Enforcement Administration report that the number of drug arrests rose from approximately 800,000 in 1985 to more than 1.3 million in 1989. Three-quarters of the arrests were for drug possession. The remaining 25 percent were for transporting and dealing drugs. According to a Cato Institute analyst, nearly 2,400 murders committed annually across the nation are connected to the drug trade. This number includes innocent victims in random shootings as well as carefully planned executions of police informers by drug traffickers. In New York, for example, the police department reported that 38 percent of the murders committed in 1987 were drug related. The same Cato Institute study reports at least 40 percent of the property crimes around the country are also related to drugs. This increase in crime has contributed to the sense of urgency surrounding the drug problem.

Drug crime has also greatly contributed to the congestion and, many critics say, the breakdown of the U.S. criminal justice system. Each year, police arrest more than one million people for drug offenses, and each year the number continues to grow. This number does not even include crimes such as robberies, prostitution, and murders that are directly related to drug use. The rising number of drug-related cases has affected the courts' ability to punish offenders appropriately. Mandatory sentencing guidelines passed by the state legislatures to keep drug offenders off the streets have contributed to the overcrowding of America's prisons. In response to this and to the overwhelming number of cases, some violent offenders are allowed to serve reduced sentences or even probation instead of serving jail time. These criminals then return to America's communities, perhaps to continue committing crimes.

The communities most affected by drug trafficking and ancillary crime are America's urban minority neighborhoods. Without question, the majority of drug trafficking occurs in crowded cities such as the south side of Chicago, East Los Angeles, and the Bronx in New York. Neighborhoods in these communities have become open-air drug markets where young gang members buy and sell drugs on nearly every street corner. Often these young people are members of large gangs like the infamous Los Angeles-based Crips. These violent gangs control much of the nation's drug flow. They are also responsible for much of the violent crime associated with the drug trade.

Drug dealers take control of these neighborhoods through intimidation and violence. Other residents are afraid of being robbed for drug money, accidentally murdered in a gang shootout or drive-by shooting, or intentionally murdered for saying the wrong thing to the wrong person. In some neighborhoods, children are permitted to go outside only during the few hours the drug dealers and their customers sleep. Parents fear their children may be robbed, murdered, or persuaded to join one of the drug-dealing gangs. Gang graffiti covers the walls and boards cover the windows of the abandoned houses and businesses in these communities. Many businesses and families have fled the inner city to safer places. The media often portray these besieged and decaying neighborhoods as war zones. Many experts would say the media portrayals are not far from the truth.

Tragic Effects

Perhaps the most tragic effect of drug trafficking on these poor neighborhoods is that drug dealers routinely recruit young children. Seduced by the flashy wealth of the dealers, children join the gangs and then act as lookouts and couriers. By their mid-teens, many of these children have become dealers themselves. When asked why they are in such a destructive and violent business, they uniformly reply that working in the drug industry pays better than the few minimum-wage jobs available. Benjamin Hooks, executive director for the National Association for the Advancement of Colored People, states, "Drugs are doing to us what the Ku Klux Klan could never do—destroy[ing] our families."

While politicians debate solutions to the drug problem, drug trafficking and violence continue. The articles in the following chapter detail the effects drug trafficking has had on the United States.

Drug Trafficking Has Increased Organized Crime

Edwin J. Delattre

About the Author: *Edwin J. Delattre is the Olin Scholar in applied ethics and a professor of education at Boston University in Massachusetts. His latest book is* Character and Cops: Ethics in Policing.

Persistent application of RICO (the Racketeer Influenced and Corrupt Organizations Statute) is unraveling the criminal empire of La Cosa Nostra in the United States. Yet today, an array of nontraditional organizations distinct from La Cosa Nostra is involved in unprecedented levels of organized crime, ranging from highly sophisticated narcotics trafficking and money laundering to targeted and shockingly indiscriminate street violence. We are being diverted from combating the pernicious activities of these groups by a misguided debate over the legalization of drugs.

These new crime groups now generate immense criminal profits in the United States. Some of them—white-supremacist outlaw motorcycle gangs, black street gangs originally mainly in Los Angeles (now also in Chicago and New York), and Hispanic gangs—are largely home-grown. Others, including Asian organized crime, Colombian drug trafficking organizations, and Jamaican posses, spring from foreign-based criminal organizations. Newly powerful organized crime now constitutes an enormous, malevolent presence in America.

Criminal organizations perpetrate many kinds of crimes: narcotics trafficking, money laundering, smuggling weapons and aliens, contract murder, kidnapping, counterfeiting identification documents, burglary, robbery, auto theft, gambling, loan sharking, extortion, arson, medical insurance and welfare fraud, bank fraud, prostitution, pornography, infiltrating private industry, and corrupting public institutions. Their drug-related activity poses a serious threat, not only to the adult population who use drugs, but also to children involved as their agents.

Four white-supremacist outlaw motorcycle gangs—the Hell's Angels from California, the Outlaws from Illinois, the Pagans from Maryland, and the Bandidos from Texas—have approximately 152 chapters throughout the United States and parts of Canada. Their 3,000 members, plus many more thousands of associate members, traffic in amphetamines ("speed") and weapons; they also specialize in contract murder, arson, extortion, and prostitution. They can be expected to play a major part in the new methamphetamine ("ice") traffic in the United States.

They use gang-associated women—whom they treat as property—to infiltrate telephone companies, government offices, and police departments. The gangs fortify their facilities with electronic surveillance equipment and heavy weaponry, and they routinely conceal poisonous snakes where police would search in any raid.

"[Criminal organizations'] drug-related activity poses a serious threat."

The "big four," however, do not begin to tell the story of organized crime by outlaw motorcycle gangs in America. There are over 500 other known motorcycle gangs in the United States that engage in similar criminal activities, many of which have been associated with La Cosa Nostra.

At least five distinct Asian cartels traffic in drugs in the United States, fueling the belief among some law enforcement officials that

Asian-organized crime could become America's most intractable crime problem. As many as 50 Chinese triads (political and criminal organizations dating from the seventeenth century identifying themselves by a triangular emblem) have organized criminal tongs and street gangs such as the Ping On, United Bamboo, and Ghost Shadows in American cities. Gangs based in Hong Kong and Taiwan (the Big Circle Gang, for one) also operate in the United States. These Chinese criminal organizations traffic primarily in heroin, and they run large gambling, extortion, and prostitution rackets. Some of them exercise great power over the Chinese entertainment industry in the United States.

"Asian organized crime could become America's most intractable crime problem."

By 1984, the President's Commission on Organized Crime had gathered evidence of Chinese group criminal activity in 26 cities from every major region of the United States. It also heard testimony describing the savagery of the triads, whose heroin smuggling tactics have been known to include murdering babies, storing drugs inside the corpses, and having women carry them across national borders pretending to nurse them.

Japan's Yakuza crime syndicate is well-anchored here as well, with heavy involvement in smuggling weapons to Japan, narcotics, gambling, management of foreign criminal investments in American corporations, and control of the North American Japanese tourist industry. Through the purchase of American businesses and real estate, the Yakuza launders huge sums of money. Yakuza members are described by Japanese law enforcement officials as "Boryokudan," or violent ones.

With a worldwide roster of over 100,000 members, the Yakuza resembles La Cosa Nostra in its structure. Its power in the United States may

grow as ice is pushed into the drug subculture. Ice, a Japanese product, was legal in Japan until 1952 and is still the drug of choice for many Japanese users. There are now 130,000 ice addicts in South Korea, and the drug has already hit Hawaii very hard. It became available on the streets in both California and New York City in 1989.

Ethnic Viet Ching (Chinese-Vietnamese) and Vietnamese criminal gangs have made their way into the United States since the collapse of South Vietnam. Noted particularly for property crimes and exceptional levels of violence in all their criminal activities, Vietnamese gangs operate in as many as 13 states coast to coast and are unusually mobile. One ranking police official told the Commission on Organized Crime that Vietnamese criminal organizations threaten to "make the Mafia look like a fraternity of wimps."

But Asian organized crime is not unique in its range of activities or in the routine acts of savagery by which it terrorizes victims and prospective witnesses in criminal prosecutions and eliminates criminal competition.

Colombian Cartels

The most grievous of all the organized crime developments in the 1980s relate directly to cocaine traffic. It is the demand in the United States for cocaine and for its even more dangerous derivative, "crack," that has emboldened the Colombian cartels and their drug-trafficking subsidiaries in the United States, the Jamaican posses, and the Los Angeles-based drug-dealing street gangs—the Crips and the Bloods. Federal authorities estimate that $87 billion in cocaine profits were laundered in 1988, compared to $34 billion in marijuana and $10 billion in heroin.

Colombian drug traffickers control cocaine production and wholesaling worldwide. The Medellin and Cali cartels dominate, and through a wholesale marketing and smuggling network that employs thousands of people, they distribute roughly 80 percent of the cocaine consumed in the United States including that which is converted to crack. No American city, suburb, or rural area is beyond their reach.

The wealth and power of the cartels has enabled them to cause governmental instability and terrorize entire populations. They can corrupt morally weak public servants anywhere in the world. In the United States, the Colombian traffickers employ Cuban Mariel-boat-lift criminals and Colombians illegally here for extortion and murder.

So sophisticated are the cartels that logistics involved in shipment and distribution of drugs, accounting, and movement of money are all managed with state-of-the-art technology. Cartel money laundering seems to be expanding in the United States to include more extensive real estate holdings, the construction of shopping malls and banks, and control of large import-export firms under covert Colombian ownership.

But technological and management sophistication is no guarantor of civility. The cartels are implicated in close to 1,000 murders in Colombia alone, including the killing of at least 596 national police officers. Even their tactics of bribery are extortionate: they offer "gold or lead"—"Take the money or make your wife a widow." Colombian traffickers in the United States not only murder anyone they can reach who opposes or betrays them, they also murder entire families as a message to employees and competitors alike, and they maintain a code of silence by the threat of reprisal against family members still in Colombia.

Jamaican Posses

Jamaican posses may be the greatest beneficiaries of the demand for crack in the United States. Originally formed as strong-arm political street gangs in Kingston, Jamaica, the posses have spread. It is now estimated that there are more than 40 posses with at least 10,000 members in Jamaica, Great Britain, and the United States. Incredibly brutal (some of their members were trained by Cuban guerrilla warfare specialists), the posses have been implicated in over 2,000 drug-related murders since 1985.

The power of the posses in the United States is such that they not only buy and fortify "crack houses" as bases for the retail distribution of drugs, they also buy other houses for wholesale distribution of crack to their own retail outlets, with local black juveniles running the supplies. Sometimes they buy whole sections of neighborhoods in order to shelter their operating facilities. By these methods, they control almost half the crack market in America.

"The most grievous of all the organized crime developments in the 1980s relate directly to cocaine traffic."

Though many in the top leadership of the posses are Jamaican nationals who have been legal residents of the United States for years, most of the rank and file are illegal aliens. They are provided with false identification documents and can change locations and identities virtually at will, both within the United States and abroad.

This advantage against law enforcement penetration is increased by two other dimensions of posse operations. First, the posses' record of reprisal when betrayed makes police efforts to enlist informants and to persuade witnesses to testify against them extremely difficult, just as in the case of the Colombian traffickers. Second, the posses communicate in a corrupted dialect with French roots that complicates law-enforcement infiltration and poses a language barrier to gathering evidence similar to problems encountered in investigating Asian organized crime.

Los Angeles-based Gangs

By 1989, the United States had become home to more than 100,000 street gangs with a combined membership of over 1 million youths and adults. Los Angeles County alone is the base for some 750 of these gangs, with a total membership of roughly 70,000.

Law enforcement officials in the Los Angeles area estimate that long-standing Hispanic gangs have about 30,000 members. These "Home Boys" ("cholos") are known for heroin trafficking, high levels of deadly violence in defense of neighborhood turf, and more recently for crack sales, primarily to black users.

But the most dramatic change in Los Angeles crime organizations in the 1980s took place within the black gangs. With a total of 15,000-20,000 members, these gangs are no longer neighborhood street gangs. Their entry into the crack trade has enabled them to expand violent criminal operations into every area of the country, and they have been directly linked to crack distribution in 46 states. They may market as much as one-third of all the crack sold in America, after purchasing cocaine wholesale from Colombian traffickers.

Crips and Bloods

The most infamous of these gangs are the Crips and the Bloods. Each of these is a rough association of smaller gangs; by 1988, there were 189 distinct "sets" of Crips and 72 Bloods. Though these two super-factions are endlessly at war with each other, they also fight among themselves, and they account for most of the 1,026 gang-related killings in Los Angeles County since the beginning of 1988. An uncertain number of the victims—estimates run as high as 50 percent—were innocent bystanders.

A particularly heinous practice of the LA-based Crips and Bloods, like many similar gangs in Chicago, is their active recruitment of children, sometimes only seven or eight years old, as new members. The gangs recruit them by a combination of terror and seduction. They threaten reprisals for refusing to join, while they promise the rewards of wealth, sex, thrills, mutual loyalty, and the safety of numbers. The children who are forced, or drawn, into the gangs are known as "wanna-bes" or "baby gangsters." They serve in a variety of criminal roles: some act as lookouts and carry drugs and guns to older members; some commit burglaries, particularly to steal

weapons. These children, along with older juvenile gang members, are largely immune to criminal sanction. If they are apprehended in criminal acts, police often have no choice but to release them to the custody of their parents—many of whom exercise no parental control in any situation.

> ## "Jamaican posses may be the greatest beneficiaries of the demand for crack in the United States."

Indeed, it is the extent to which organized criminal groups are staking claim to the next generation of our nation's children by selling them drugs and by recruiting them into gangs that is the most serious of all their threats. They would remorselessly condemn the young to lives as blighted by ignorance and cruelty as their own—barren, corrupt, violent, and often short. This attack on the hopes, possibilities, and aspirations of the young violates the future, and its viciousness proves that legalization of narcotics promises no relief from the ravages of drugs or from organized crime itself. This is the irreducible element in current disputes about the merits of narcotics legalization.

Against Narcotics Legalization

Demand for illegal narcotics and criminally diverted prescription drugs is directly responsible for the strength of the criminal groups in the United States described above. Demand has promoted drug trafficking and nourished criminal empires. As drugs become more widely available, consumption tends to become contagious: users who can easily obtain drugs give them to friends, encourage use by companions, and belittle peers who do not use.

America has suffered for years through this cycle of demand that both increases supply and fuels greater demand. For too many of those years, we ineffectively opposed rising levels of drug consumption by concentrating primarily on hurling police into a breach they could not possibly close by themselves. . . .

The latest survey of the National Institute on Drug Abuse shows that drug consumption has declined by 37 percent since 1985, and cocaine use has been cut in half in the United States. Yet, according to a recent State Department report, the increase in worldwide drug production and the criminality associated with it has been dramatic. Opium production is up 187 percent since 1985, coca 143 percent, and marijuana 502 percent. In this climate, legalization would further exacerbate our drug problems. Many advocates of legalization admit that drug consumption would rise—perhaps dramatically—under legalization. The progress we have made against drug consumption and dependency would be erased.

"The present organized crime groups will not be driven from drug trafficking."

The victims of legalization would include countless children. First, if drugs were legal, an even greater number of women, including teenagers, could be expected to use them during pregnancy. Many of the infants who survived drug exposure would suffer severe lifelong mental and physical disabilities.

Second, legalization would have little power to make inroads into the adult black market. But if it did, organized crime would market drugs more intensively among youths and children.

As we have seen since the end of Prohibition, criminal organizations like La Cosa Nostra do not fade away just because substances are legalized. They must be unraveled by prudent modifications in antiracketeering and other laws and by unrelenting and extended application of those laws. The higher the stakes in money and power, the more these efforts will be evaded. The present organized crime groups will not be driven from drug trafficking and the rest of their criminal enterprises by narcotics laws. Legalize some drugs, and they will undersell the legal distributors with higher potency versions, market illegal drugs, and introduce new drugs. Legalize drugs for adults, and organized crime will sell to children by persuading them that what is all right for grownups is all right for them. This is the basic lesson their past and present treatment of children has already taught.

Critical Questions

Critical questions of law, policy, and ethics are being obscured by the debate over legalization. We could serve the interests of the public much more effectively by asking how to combat nontraditional organized crime and its causes and effects.

What should we do to prevent organized crime from thwarting investigations by using the Freedom of Information Act to identify and take reprisal against informants? How should we modify juvenile courts and law to handle juvenile involvement in organized crime drug trafficking, violence, and intimidation? How shall we intervene to prevent gang recruitment of children? What should we do about the collapse of the social and cultural order associated with gang-related crime and violence? Which kinds of neighborhood drug treatment and recovery programs should we publicize and provide with financial support?

How should we combat urban gang tyranny? How shall we modify bail and probation standards to safeguard the public?

All of these questions, and many more like them, are of inestimably greater importance than the question of whether we should legalize drugs. They demand answers. By contrast, legalization debates trivialize our gravest problems. Quick-fix "remedies" like legalization are irrelevant to facing and controlling the worst effects of human frailty as they reveal themselves in drug consumption and of human depravity and viciousness as they reveal themselves in organized crime.

Drug Trafficking Has Harmed America's Youth

Terry Williams

About the Author: *Terry Williams is a writer whose best known book is* The Cocaine Kids: The Inside Story of a Teenage Drug Ring, *from which this viewpoint was taken.*

This is a story about teenagers who move in a very fast lane, each one trying to be "the king, making crazy money for as long as I can, any way I can."

It focuses on the lives of eight young cocaine dealers in New York City. From 1982 to 1986, I spent some two hours a day, three days a week, hanging out with these kids in cocaine bars, after-hours spots, discos, restaurants, crack houses, on street corners, in their homes and at family gatherings and parties.

These studies took me to the Bronx, Harlem and Washington Heights—areas of high unemployment and diminishing resources, especially for young people. But while quality entry-level jobs were disappearing, illegal opportunities were emerging with considerable force because of the growth of a powerful and profitable multinational drug industry. . . .

My intention is to throw light on a major and complex social problem, but without blaming the victims and without placing teenagers in stereotypical roles. Every teen aspires to make good. In the cocaine hustle, that means to "get behind the scale"—to deal in significant quantities; it is like landing a top sales job in a major corporation, or being named a partner, after a long apprenticeship, in a brokerage firm with a seat on the Stock Exchange. The kids who get that far have some control over prices and selling techniques, direct the work of subordinates, and, above all else, make large amounts of money.

The teenagers in this story are sophisticated cocaine distributors, wholesalers and retail sellers. Their work has been essential to the growth of a major industry; they have helped establish an organizational structure that sustains a regular market and outwits law enforcement authorities. These teenagers have also found a way to make money in a society that offers them few constructive alternatives.

In many ways, these kids and others like them simply want respect: they are willing to risk their lives to attain those prized adult rewards of power, prestige and wealth. Theirs is a difficult and dangerous way of life, one closed to almost all outsiders. Because they must continually make tough decisions in trying circumstances, these young people grow to adulthood with little time to be young.

Everybody Has Cocaine

The apartment is crowded with teenagers, all wearing half-laced sneakers and necklace ropes of gold. Doorbells ring every few minutes, white powder dusts the table tops; jagged-edge matchbook covers and dollar bills seem to flow from hand to hand. The talk is frenetic, filled with masterful plans and false promises. Everybody has a girl. Everybody has cocaine. Everybody has a gun. . . .

> **"While quality entry-level jobs were disappearing, illegal opportunities were emerging."**

When I first came on the teenage cocaine scene, I was apprehensive, even fearful. I knew these young people were volatile and unpredictable, prone to violence, and not inclined to trust adults—or, for that matter, anyone outside their circumscribed world. Yet I wanted to find out about the kids who sold drugs. How did they get into the cocaine business, and how do they stay in it? How transient is their involvement—can they get out of the business? And where do they go if they do? What are the rewards for those who succeed?

> # "These young people were volatile and unpredictable, prone to violence, and not inclined to trust adults."

The only way to find the answers to these questions was to follow the kids over time, and that is what I did. For more than four years, I asked questions and recorded the answers without trying to find support for any particular thesis. In the process, I found that the truth was embedded in a complex, miniature society with institutions, laws, morality, language, codes of behavior all its own. I also found young people whose only shield against fear and uncertainty was a sense of their own immortality....

At the retail level, the distribution and sale of cocaine in New York City involves mostly African-American and Latino boys and girls under eighteen. In general, they come from families whose income is below the poverty line, and from neighborhoods where there is little chance to rise above that line. It is difficult to say how many young people are engaged in this trade, but certainly there are many thousands in the metropolitan area.

Many teenagers are drawn to work in the cocaine trade simply because they want jobs, full time or even as casual labor—the drug business is a "safety net" of sorts, a place where it is always possible to make a few dollars. Teens are also pulled by the flash and dazzle, and by the chance to make big money, and pushed by the desire to "be somebody."

Those who recruit teenagers are following a tradition that dates back almost twenty years, and was the direct effect of the harsh "Rockefeller laws" mandating a prison term for anyone over eighteen in possession of an illegal drug. This led heroin dealers to use kids as runners, and cocaine importers have followed this pattern: young people not only avoid the law but are, for the most part, quite trustworthy; they are also relatively easy to frighten and control.

Today, teenagers who work at the retail level are expected to sell cocaine and crack for cash in a way that generates repeat business—in other words, to act like sales people in any business. In addition, they are expected to limit their own consumption of the drug, keep accurate records, and avoid arrest. Most of the kids are users as well as dealers, and so cocaine rather than cash has often been the medium of exchange; the introduction of crack has changed this, as most dealers disdain the use of crack, so cash payment is now more common.

A Valuable Commodity

Cocaine is a highly valued commodity, especially among the middle class, but because distribution and sale must be clandestine, reaching users on a regular basis presents problems. Thus there are important roles in the network which do not directly involve selling at all. For instance, there are "runners"—messengers who take cocaine to buyers or let buyers know of a particular dealer; the runner earns a "p.c.," a part commission or percentage of the sale from the dealer. Where the drugs are sold from a fixed location there are "lookouts" and guards, and often "catchers" standing by in case a police raid or other emergency means drug stocks must be moved swiftly. At this level, there is considerable flexibility, and an individual may shift quickly and easily between several roles: today's lookout may be tomorrow's runner; a door guard may eventually move to a selling position....

Money and drugs are the obvious immediate rewards for kids in the cocaine trade. But there is another strong motivating force, and that is the desire to show family and friends that they can succeed at something. Moving up a career ladder and making money is especially important where there are few visible opportunities. . . .

Max was fourteen and already considered a "comer" in the cocaine business when I met him. We were introduced by a Dominican friend who knew of my interest in New York's underground cocaine culture and the teenagers who survive outside the regular economy. I assumed we would talk and then go our separate ways: he trusted my friend but he was shy; there was certainly no reason for him to talk with me about anything, and I was not about to press the issue. But there was something special about Max, and he became my friend and guide for nearly five years. I think we got along because I was an outsider and he had a story to tell and he chose me to tell it to. . . .

Over several years, Max assembled the crew called here the Cocaine Kids. He introduced me to them—Chillie, Masterrap, Charlie, Hector, Jake and Kitty—at *"la oficina,"* the office. This is an apartment, rented by Chillie (though not in his own name), where the Kids cut and mix cocaine, pick and pack crack; it is also the base from which they sell unpackaged cocaine to individual buyers.

"Young people not only avoid the law but are . . . quite trustworthy; they are also relatively easy to frighten and control."

In the summer of 1984, with Max's approval, I had a chance to observe the operation at *la oficina* which was run by Chillie, the crew boss and Max's first lieutenant. There was constant rivalry between all members of the crew, but I had to get along with each one, and that would not have been possible without Max to pave the way. They knew I was recording their lives and they accepted me and let me know their secrets, pro-

fessional and otherwise. I did have something to give them—functions to perform, roles to play; small things, but they meant a great deal to the kids: I was kind of a big brother, able to help with homework and even babysitting, but most of all a willing and sympathetic listener. . . .

The Teenage Labor Pool

Max runs part of his operation in a loosely organized way, hiring workers as needed to sell cocaine and crack in a variety of locations. He can draw from a sizeable labor pool of teenagers who have dropped out of high school and are unemployed. Like workers in the above-ground economy, the kids have a chance to be promoted and make more money; many can look to an eventual move up behind the scale. . . .

All the Kids snort cocaine regularly. This is accepted, but the use of crack is generally frowned upon: those who snort are thought to have more control and discipline than those who smoke crack or freebase. Most dealers see crack smokers as obsessive consumers who cannot take care of business; crack users, they say, tend to become agitated, quickly lose control and concentration, and take one dose after another at the expense of everything else. Snorters, however, can use the drug and still take care of business.

Yet the Kids who snort do so on almost any pretext: Chillie will sniff and ask Masterrap and Charlie to join him whenever he makes a sale of more than $100. One day they decided to celebrate because the New York Mets, their favorite baseball team, won a game. They called Max, began snorting and playing music, and called girls to join them. On less joyous occasions, cocaine serves a therapeutic purpose, as an antidote to stress, disappointment, and the problems of everyday life. . . .

The Cocaine Kids, and many of the kids coming behind them, are drawn to the underground economy because of the opportunities that exist there. The underground offers status and prestige—rewards they are unlikely to attain in the regular economy—and is the only real economy for many. Certainly, they have no illusions about the "quick" dollar. They know the work is hard and dangerous; there is no such thing as a quick dollar.

Any solution to "the drug problem" will be difficult, but any solution that does not consider the real world of the kids must fail. This [viewpoint] has tried to present a calm and uninflated look at that world, without using the language of problem-finding and without offering ready-made answers (like "build more prisons," "develop a pharmacological block" or "arrest all drug users"). Unless we begin to see the life as it is, to understand how the drug trade affects, and is affected by, children (and the adults around them) we will not be able to look for solutions in an open and creative way.

Today, as I walk through this city of fallen dreams and unquenchable hope, to the neighborhood where I first met Max and the Kids, I see a new generation of Cocaine Kids in faded jeans and unlaced sneakers, draped with gold chains, their arrow-pointed haircuts topping fresh faces and hard-edged frowns. These kids are grown before their time, wise before they leave home, smart before they go to school, worshippers before attending church, rule-breakers before they know the rules and lawbreakers after they know the law.

"Money and drugs are the obvious immediate rewards for kids in the cocaine trade."

On the corner of 162nd Street, three boys and two girls shout to me almost in unison, their outstretched hands revealing their wares, "got that coke, got that crack, got red caps, got blues, got yellow ones—you choose. What you want, my friend? What you need?"

The innocence of the young is lost in Washington Heights these days as a new generation of street corner boys and girls enters the shadowy world of dealing and prostitution. A new generation of Cocaine Kids is embarking on a voyage, searching for dreams that most will never find.

Drug Trafficking Has Harmed America's Economy

Jonathan Beaty and Richard Hornik

About the Authors: *Jonathan Beaty is a Los Angeles correspondent and Richard Hornik is the Southeast Asia correspondent for* Time, *a weekly newsmagazine.*

In Willemstad, the sunny Caribbean capital of the Netherlands Antilles, a banker ushers an American visitor through a hotel casino and into a dining room overlooking the harbor. During refreshments, the prospective customer says he expects a six-figure cash windfall soon and would like to bring the money "quietly" into the U.S. At first the banker responds cautiously. "This money isn't, ah, tainted, is it?" When the American assures him it is not, the officer of the Curacao branch of the French-owned Credit-Lyonnais Nederland smiles and orders another tonic water. In that case, says the banker, he can arrange a so-called Dutch sandwich.

Under this multilayered plan, the Paris bank would set up a corporation for the customer in Rotterdam, where he would deposit his cash in the bank's local branch. The American would control the newly created Dutch corporation through an Antilles trust company, but his identity as the owner would be protected by the island group's impenetrable secrecy laws. The Caribbean branch would then "lend" the American his own money held in Rotterdam.

If the American were questioned by the Internal Revenue Service [IRS] or other authorities about the source of his wealth, he could point to his loan from a respected international bank. "Many of your largest corporations, many of your movie stars, do much the same thing here," says the banker. "We wouldn't want to handle criminal money, of course. But if it's just a matter of taxes, that is of no concern to us."

When U.S. drug agents tallied up the amount of cocaine they seized during fiscal 1989, their haul totaled 89 tons, or 44% more than 1988's. The volume, which is believed to be only a small percentage of the tons flooding the country, is evidence of more than just a frighteningly effective drug-smuggling industry. The wholesale value of the coke, as much as $28 billion, is testimony to another kind of dark genius. This is the scandalous ability of the coke kingpins to launder billions of dollars in drug proceeds using many of the same financial services available to the FORTUNE 500. In a wash cycle that often takes less than 48 hours, the drug smugglers can turn coke-tinged $20 and $100 bills into such untraceable, squeaky-clean assets as money-market deposits, car dealerships and resort hotels.

> ## "Much is at stake as the powerful flow of narcodollars is recycled through the world's financial system."

The coke smugglers can accomplish this feat because they have plenty of help. They rely on a booming money-laundering industry that serves a clientele ranging from tax-avoiding corporations to the Iranscam schemers. The system depends on the collaboration, or often just the negligence, of bankers and other moneymen who can use electronic-funds networks and the secrecy laws of tax havens to shuffle assets with alacrity. The very institutions that could do the most to stop money laundering have the least incentive to do so. According to police and launderers, the basic fee for recycling money of dubious origin is 4%, while the rate for drug cash

Jonathan Beaty and Richard Hornick, "A Torrent of Dirty Dollars," *Time*, December 18, 1989. Copyright © 1989 The Time Inc. Magazine Company. Reprinted with permission.

and other hot money is 7% to 10%.

Much is at stake as the powerful flow of narcodollars is recycled through the world's financial system. Drug lords and other lawbreakers are believed to be buying valuable chunks of the American economy, but clever Dutch sandwiches and other subterfuges make it almost impossible for U.S. authorities to track foreign investors. A case in point: blind corporations based in the Netherlands Antilles control more than one-third of all foreign-owned U.S. farmland, many of the newest office towers in downtown Los Angeles and a substantial number of independent movie companies producing films like Sylvester Stallone's *Rambo* pictures.

While businesses and individuals may conceal their assets for purposes that are completely legal, or dubious at worst, the systems set up for their convenience can be perversely efficient at helping drug barons launder as much as $100 billion a year in U.S. proceeds. "It is hard to understand why we failed for so long to institute adequate controls," says Massachusetts Democrat John Kerry, chairman of the Senate's Subcommittee on Terrorism, Narcotics and International Operations. The state of regulation is "so lackadaisical," says Kerry, "it's almost damnable."

President Bush, for his part, has declared money launderers a critical target in the war on drugs, allocating $15 million to launch a counteroffensive. While the sum is minuscule for the task, the declaration signals a change in philosophy for the Administration, which had resisted calls for tighter banking regulations. Only hours after Bush unveiled his antidrug offensive in September 1989, a federal task force began taking shape. The Financial Crimes Enforcement Network (FINCEN) hopes to zero in on money launderers with computer programs capable of spotting suspicious movements of electronic money.

In a high-tech game of cat and mouse, the Justice Department said that it had found and triggered the freezing of $60.1 million in bank accounts in five countries that contained the personal income of Jose Gonzalo Rodriguez

Gacha, a leader of the Medellín cartel. Using financial records and computer disks captured by the Colombian government, U.S. agents traced Rodriguez's money to accounts in the U.S., Luxembourg, Switzerland, Austria and Britain.

"Drug barons launder as much as $100 billion a year in U.S. proceeds."

Drug Enforcement Administration officials told *Time* that one of Rodriguez's purported financial advisers, Panama-based Mauricio Vives, tried desperately to keep moving the money one step ahead of the agents. Vives called a British banker and told him to move several million dollars, fast, to an account in Luxembourg. If the bank were to delay, his Colombian client would kill him, Vives pleaded. The banker refused, and British authorities cooperating with the DEA froze the account. Not all countries were as helpful. U.S. agents said they tracked Rodriguez's money to the Cayman Islands, Spain and Montserrat, but local authorities said they could not cooperate, citing rigid bank-secrecy laws as an excuse.

What makes enforcement so difficult is a financial murkiness that has long frustrated tax collectors as they search for dirty money afloat in the world's oceans of legitimate payments. The multibillion-dollar flow of black money, the profits from criminal enterprise, moves through the world's financial institutions as part of a vastly larger quantity of gray money, as bankers call it. This dubious, laundered cash amounts to an estimated $1 trillion or more each year. Often legitimately earned, this money has an endless variety of sources: an Argentine businessman who dodges currency-control laws to get his savings out of the country; a multinational corporation that seeks to "minimize its tax burden" by dumping its profits in tax-free havens; a South African investor who wants to avoid economic sanctions; an East German Communist leader who stashed a personal nest egg in Swiss bank accounts; or even the CIA [Central Intelligence Agency] and KGB [Soviet Secret Police] when they need to finance espionage or covert activities overseas.

The world's prosperity depends on a fluid and unfettered financial system, yet the lack of supervision is producing a large shadow economy. The IRS estimates that tax cheats skim as much as $50 billion a year from legitimate cash-generating businesses and launder the money to avoid detection. Banking experts calculate that the private citizens of debt-choked Latin American countries have smuggled more than $200 billion of their savings abroad in the past decade.

The money-laundering process, especially in the drug trade, begins with greenbacks. Much of the cash simply leaves the U.S. in luggage, since departing travelers are rarely searched. Larger shipments are flown out on private planes or packed in seagoing freight containers, which are almost never inspected. That explains, in part, why U.S. officials are unable to locate fully 80% of all the bills printed by the Treasury. Once overseas, the cash is easy to funnel into black markets, especially in unstable economies where the dollar is the favored underground currency.

"Once the money is in a financial institution, it can be moved with blinding speed."

But hauling cash out of the U.S. has its drawbacks. The interest revenue lost while cash is in transit pains a drug dealer as much as it would a corporate financial officer. And since narcotraffickers see America as a safe and profitable haven for their assets, they often launder and invest their cash in the U.S. The first and trickiest step is depositing the hot cash in a U.S. financial institution. Reason: the IRS requires all banks to file Currency Transaction Reports [CTRs] for deposits of $10,000 or more. During the early

1980s, launderers got around this scrutiny by employing couriers called Smurfs, named for the restless cartoon characters, who would fan out and make multiple deposits of slightly less than $10,000.

The Government now requires banks to keep an eye out for Smurfs, but launderers have developed new techniques. Since retail businesses that collect large amounts of cash are often exempt from the $10,000 rule, launderers have created front companies or collaborated with employees of such outlets as 7-Elevens and ComputerLand stores. To drug dealers, "an exempt rating is like gold," says a Wells Fargo Bank vice president. A restaurant that accepts no checks or credit cards can be an ideal laundering machine. Even a front business with no exemption is valuable because launderers can file the CTRs in the knowledge that they are unlikely to attract scrutiny, since the Government is swamped with 7 million such reports a year, up from fewer than 100,000 a decade ago. Other places where drug dealers can often dump their cash include the currency-exchange houses along the Southwest border and urban check-cashing and money-transmittal stores.

Once the money is in a financial institution, it can be moved with blinding speed. Communicating with the bank via fax machine or personal computer, a launderer can have wire transfers sent around the world without ever speaking to a banking officer. The goal of many launderers is to get their money into the maelstrom of global money movements, where the volume is so great that no regulators can really monitor it all. Such traffic has exploded because of the globalization of the world economy, which has multiplied the volume of international trade and currency trading. On an average working day, the Manhattan-based Clearing House for Interbank Payments System handles 145,500 transactions worth more than $700 billion, a 40% increase in just two years.

Much of the electronic money zips into a secret banking industry that got its start in Switzerland in the 1930s as worried Europeans began shifting their savings beyond the reach of Hitler's Third Reich. Later the country's infamous numbered accounts became a hugely profitable business. Chiasso, a quaint Swiss town of 8,700 inhabitants on the Italian border, has 18 banking offices. But during the past few years, Swiss secrecy has been weakened by a series of cases involving money laundering. Switzerland is now preparing a new law that will make money laundering a crime punishable by prison terms. Explains Jean-Paul Chapuis, executive director of the Swiss Bankers Association: "Our hope is that the criminals will go to another country."

They apparently are, since many small countries have successfully attracted banking business by creating discreet, tax-free havens. In Luxembourg total bank deposits have grown from $40 billion in 1984 to more than $100 billion in 1988. In the wake of a drug-money scandal involving the Florida operations of Luxembourg-based Bank of Credit and Commerce International, the country has tried to burnish its public image by declaring money laundering a criminal offense, even while it has fortified its bank-secrecy rules.

The most inventive havens allow investors to set up shell corporations with invisible owners, which means that high rollers can secretly stash their money in real estate, corporate stock and other assets. The Netherlands Antilles, with cash flowing steadily from banking centers in Amsterdam and Rotterdam, is a favorite financial center for investors seeking a low profile. Many Hollywood filmmakers love the arrangement, since movie profits can be diverted to a nearly tax-free setting. Many actors, producers and directors set up so-called personal-service companies in the Antilles so they can collect their paychecks through such corporations and avoid U.S. taxes. "It has to be structured very carefully, since the rules are tortuously complicated, but it is legal," says a top entertainment lawyer. "However, the IRS may take a closer look after your story comes out."

Just as Hollywood paychecks pour into these havens to avoid taxes, mystery money flows out in search of well-paying investments. "The man I'm working with now," says a prominent screenwriter, "is an American representing vaguely described movie and cable interests in Europe who seem to have a waterfall of money from banks in Luxembourg and Amsterdam. He's all over town offering unlimited financing, but he won't show up himself at any of the meetings with the networks or studios."

"Once the money is in a financial institution, it can be moved with blinding speed."

Dozens of islands, from Britain's chilly Isle of Man to Vanuatu in the South Pacific, have boosted their economies by turning into havens for money. While narcotics traffickers launder their dollars through so-called brass-plate companies on these islands, the main business of the tax-free offshore havens is servicing some of the world's largest multinational corporations. "The idea is to put profits where there are the least taxes. Everybody does it," explains the president of a major U.S. corporation's foreign subsidiary.

One technique for minimizing taxes is a quasi-legal fabrication called reinvoicing, a paper shuffle that enables companies to re-book sales and profits into tax havens. For example, one FORTUNE 500 corporation imports raw materials through an offshore dummy company, which buys shipments at the lowest possible price and resells the material to the parent firm at a high markup. This dumps profits in the tax haven, while the U.S.-based company can boost its apparent costs to reduce taxes on the mainland. The profits can then be repatriated in the form of tax-free "loans" from offshore entities to the U.S. parent corporation.

While the IRS tolerates such schemes up to a point, the U.S. Government has tried to choke the river of drug money flowing through the same channels. Yet laundering hot spots tend to be moving targets. After the U.S. negotiated new treaties with Bermuda and Cayman authorities to allow limited access to banking records in narcotics cases, many of the launderers found new havens.

As the financial center of gravity in the world has shifted toward the Pacific Rim, new tax and secrecy havens have multiplied on such remote islands as Nauru in the western Pacific and Palau and Truk in Micronesia. Citizens of Vanuatu, a volcanic archipelago of some 80 islands formerly known as the New Hebrides, have found that international finance beats coconut and taro farming. In Port Vila, the capital, it is not unusual for a $100 million transaction between major international banks to take place on any given day.

Still, Hong Kong remains the pre-eminent laundering center in the Pacific. Almost everyone there does it, usually legitimately, at least according to the laws of Hong Kong, where even insider trading is no crime. By the puritan standards of the U.S., says one American banker, "the lack of public disclosure here is scandalous." The city is a mecca for arms dealers, drug traffickers and business pirates of every description. "Where else could I broker a deal that involves machine guns from China, gold from Taiwan and shipments traded in Panama City?" says a Brazilian arms merchant who maintains an apartment in Hong Kong.

In the U.S. a money-laundering center can be spotted by the huge surplus of cash that flows into the local branch of the Federal Reserve System. In 1985 the Miami branch posted a $6 billion excess. But after several years of intense federal probes of South Florida banks, Miami's cash glut fell to $4.5 billion in 1988. Much of the business went to Los Angeles, where the cash surplus ballooned from $166 million in 1985 to $3.8 billion. Despite such rocketing growth, the staffing of federal law-enforcement offices in L.A. still lags far behind the levels in Miami or New York City.

Both in the U.S. and abroad, financial businesses and even governments are often reluctant to impose regulations to keep out launderers.

One reason is that a thriving financial industry brings jobs and income. South Florida's 100 international banks employ 3,500 workers and pump $800 million into the local economy. Even more appealing is the inflow of foreign capital. During the spend-and-borrow era of the 1980s, the gusher of flight capital into the U.S. from Latin America helped finance America's deficits. As in Hollywood, not many politicians were concerned about where the money was coming from. Alarmed by the tide, House Democrat John Bryant of Texas has long pushed for legislation to require disclosure of the identity of foreign investors. But for years, the Reagan Administration refused to go along, claiming that such openness might scare away capital.

"The U.S. Government has tried to choke the river of drug money."

Now that a consensus is building that the U.S. must pick out the black money from the gray, the tools at hand seem minimal for the task. Says Jaime Chavez, an international banking consultant: "The people who will probably be searching for it have a very limited knowledge of what money movement is all about. How is a third-rate employee of the Justice Department going to dissect the entire financial system to pinpoint the drug money correctly?" During the Reagan years, the budgets of agencies in charge of catching financial cheats failed to keep pace with the changing world of money manipulation. Even IRS agents are largely unprepared for the task of tracking transactions that can involve four or five banks, several shell companies and two or more currencies.

Few agents can be spared because IRS employees are working overtime to contain an explosion of smaller-time money-laundering cases involving car salesmen, ordinary investors, real estate agents and other entrepreneurs. In Florida undercover IRS agents operating a sting operation that they touted as a "full-service financial investment corporation" have nabbed 50 would-be money launderers in 1989. "Some are lawyers and businessmen who are skimming cash from their businesses, and they've heard about what you can do through an offshore bank," says Tampa IRS supervisor Morris Dittman. "Others have cash that rolls out of the drug trade. When a druggie buys a big home and car for cash, you have a real estate agent and a salesman with sudden cash, and they begin wondering if they have to share it with the Government."

Such amateurs are running afoul of laws that professionals have already discovered. The statutes began tightening in 1986, when money laundering became a specific crime. Later it became illegal to evade the $10,000 currency-reporting requirements by making groups of smaller deposits. Banks have begun to exercise more internal supervision as well, prodded by a series of investigations in the mid-1980s in which such institutions as Bank of America and Bank of Boston were forced to pay hefty fines for their involvement in laundering schemes. Yet many major banks are still participants, witting or not, in ever more sophisticated laundering operations.

To close the gap, Bush's offensive against drug-cash handlers is being placed in the hands of a task force that includes the CIA, the National Security Agency and the Pentagon, as well as a team of drug, tax and customs agents. FINCEN is already at work in a crowded Virginia office littered with discarded coffee cups, overflowing ashtrays, computer terminals and maps of the world. "We're going to be a financial think tank to help train cops who are deluged in financial data," says Gene Weinschenk, acting director of FINCEN's research-and-development division. "We're looking for money, not dope."

The biggest problem may be in deciding how to handle all the borderline illegality the task force will find. "How do you separate drug money from capital-flight money?" asks one of the mavens. "It will be more than drug money

we come up with, and what happens when we stumble over a really major company and hold up its dirty linen? Maybe the banks will start turning in the narcotics people rather than lose their biggest customers."

To make a dent in the money-laundering trade, authorities will need more support from the financial community. "They're now willing to tell us about people coming in with bags of cash," says a regulator, "but as far as anything else goes, you can forget it." Yet many bankers think the feds have become indiscriminate in their crackdown. "They are characterizing traditional, ordinary, international banking transactions as money laundering," gripes Gerald Houlihan, a Miami attorney who represents financial institutions in money-laundering and forfeiture cases. "They are not going after money launderers, but are attempting to terrorize banks in an effort to give the impression they are doing something about drugs."

"Many major banks are still participants, witting or not, in ever more sophisticated laundering operations."

U.S. bankers rightly point out that they must abide by relatively strict currency-reporting laws, while their counterparts in other countries play fast and loose. That discrepancy has prompted Washington to try to persuade the rest of the banking world to adopt the record-keeping system used by American institutions.

The biggest push could come from the provisions of the Kerry Amendment to the 1988 anti-drug abuse act. The law requires the Treasury Secretary to negotiate bilateral agreements on money-laundering detection and prevention with all U.S. trading partners. Countries that refuse to participate or that negotiate in bad faith could conceivably be excluded from the U.S. banking network and clearinghouses. Yet Assistant Treasury Secretary Salvatore Martoche indicated that the Bush Administration is reluctant to enforce the law zealously for fear of hampering the U.S. banking industry.

"Many experts believe the financial stability and national security of whole countries will be in jeopardy."

But there is more at risk than the dislocation of business as usual. Many experts believe the financial stability and national security of whole countries will be in jeopardy until the problem is solved. Says the head of the Italian treasury police, General Luigi Ramponi: "Now that they are too rich, the drug lords will start investing everywhere: in industry, in the stock market." In the U.S. some lawmakers have begun worrying about the impact of billions of drug dollars invested in U.S. institutions and wonder what influence the drug barons might eventually exert. . . .

Financial experts are beginning to recognize that Washington will be unable to control drug money unless the U.S. compels offshore financial institutions to make their books "transparent" enough to show the true owners of the money. In the end, the Colombian drug cartels are about to force the world to re-examine the international financial system that has developed haphazardly over the 60 years since the Swiss first popularized secret banking. Countries may not yet be willing to make their banking transactions fully "transparent," but some light must be shed on everyone's books. Says Kerry: "It will take significant leverage and leadership. The President has to have the top bankers in and say, 'Unless you are part of the solution, you are part of the problem.' "

Yet there is still a deep-seated reluctance to take drastic measures. Briefing reporters after a Paris conclave on money laundering in September 1989, a senior U.S. official declared that global efforts to trace drug money will have to be balanced against the freedom from unnecessary red tape. Too many controls, he declared, could "constipate" the financial exchanges. That is the kind of attitude that has brought the system to its current state, in which drug money freely mingles with the life force of the world economy, like a virus in the bloodstream.

Drug Trafficking Has Damaged Minority Communities

William Bennett

About the Author: *William Bennett is the former director of the Office of National Drug Control Policy. He is now a senior editor at* National Review, *a conservative weekly journal of news and opinion.*

Ralph Ellison's classic novel, *Invisible Man,* begins with this passage: "I am an invisible man . . . simply because people refuse to see me . . . it is as though I have been surrounded by mirrors of hard, distorting glass. When [people] approach me they see only my surroundings, themselves, or figments of their imagination—indeed, everything and anything except me."

Invisible Man is the story of a young black man's passage from the deep South to the streets of Harlem. Ellison's task was to illuminate the plight of those who were both black and American at a time when our country was not committed fully to the proposition that all men are created equal. That was what made the book so powerful. Through it, he taught us that there are men and women—living, breathing children of God—who are invisible to us.

We are witnessing the emergence of a new "invisible man" in contemporary American society—a new man or woman many do not see. This new invisible man is the black urban citizen who doesn't use drugs. In fact, significant numbers of inner-city residents do not commit themselves to the drug world, but that doesn't mean anyone sees them.

William Bennett, "Drugs and the Black Community." Reprinted, with permission, from *USA Today* magazine, © July 1990 by the Society for the Advancement of Education.

Everyone knows that drugs are a serious problem in the black community. Crack in particular is taking a terrible toll on blacks in our cities. Drug violence is rending the social fabric. A disproportionately high percentage of blacks are IV [intravenous] drug users, emergency-room admissions, and are involved in drug-related deaths. Yet, the point that needs to be made is that most blacks in our inner cities are law-abiding citizens who lead decent lives and disdain drugs. Most black Americans are victims, not perpetrators, of drug crimes. Many are fighting to save their families and neighborhoods from the ravages of drugs. Unfortunately, they are almost invisible so far as much of public opinion is concerned.

Instead of the law-abiding black men and women, we've seen the emergence of a new, all too "visible man"—the black predator; the young, inner-city black male who terrorizes communities, preys on innocent victims, or is arrested in drug busts. This image is given wide currency through the hard glass of the camera lens. One television report after another sears images in our sensibilities—drugs, violence, the inner city, and blacks. These images and associations perpetuate a racial stereotype. We need to confront it now, immediately, directly, before this myth and these images harden into dogma.

> ## "Everyone knows that drugs are a serious problem in the black community."

The problem is not so much that what's being reported in the newspapers and on television is false. Blacks—particularly young black males—are responsible for much of the drug-related violence in the cities of America. That story is true and needs to be told—as do some of the whys and wherefores of that use and violence. According to Calvin Rolark, president of the United Black Fund, drug-related homicides in Washington, D.C., are "a black problem, and we in the black community must stop it, if it is to be stopped. We can't lay this on racism, because it's black on black." Benjamin Hooks, executive director of the NAACP [National Association for the Advancement of Colored People], has warned that "drugs are doing to us what the Ku Klux Klan could never do—destroy our families."

The problem is that the image that's being presented is partial and incomplete. Throughout our inner cities are examples of ordinary citizens—hard-pressed and in the midst of adversity—who rise to magnificent heights of self-sacrifice, courage, and devotion to ideals. These Americans are being tested by the fire and keeping shape. They are rising to the defense of their children and communities. They are working to reclaim their streets. They are modern-day heroes. Yet, their stories—while being told in some quarters—are not being done so often enough or loudly enough, for the things they affirm are one of the great lessons of our time. Let me cite some of the heroes I'm referring to.

"There is no immutable law that dooms disadvantaged minorities to a life of drugs."

• LaShon Randolph is a single parent of four children, living in Washington, D.C. She often works 12 hours a day to support her family. LaShon Randolph's children have inherited her affection for family, faith in God, determination to get a better education, and healthy sense of self-esteem. In a neighborhood where sharp-eyed youths stand on street corners selling drugs, LaShon Randolph's children have never been in trouble.

"My mother set us on the right path and all we had to do was follow it," says her son William, 19. "I hung out with friends, but when they started doing wrong I had an incentive to come home—my mother."

"We did what we did because we loved her, and so things wouldn't be so hard for her," explains her son Anthony, 20. "What is peer pressure compared to the pain we could have caused her if we had gotten into trouble? When I got out there [in the street], I could hear her voice."

"I try to listen to my mom, play sports, and follow my older brothers and sister because they are my role models," says Quincy Randolph, 15.

A Good Example

A lawyer once asked Mrs. Randolph how she could raise such healthy children while living in the middle of the drug market. She told him that she believes children imitate their parents, and so she's tried to set a good example. Indeed she has.

• Five years ago, Frank Parks, the athletic director and a 26-year veteran at Washington, D.C.'s Spingarn High School, created a peer counseling group called SAND—Student Activities, Not Drugs. This year, 40 students are participating as peer counselors. The students receive classroom training, work with youngsters in the summer, and then confront their peers who are having problems. "They can't operate under the positive peer pressure we put on them," Parks says.

According to a former counselor, "When young people start to take a strong stand, others see that it's the popular thing to do." Spingarn has a separate "Rap Room" for students to discuss their problems openly and in confidence. What else is necessary? Former counselor Eric Abraham says: "Having your own mind. Knowing what you want to do. Not following the crowd." When President Bush honored Spingarn in 1989 for its efforts to eliminate drugs, it was a bright moment in a tough year for the city.

Parks is also president of the National High School Coaches Association and is expanding coaches' roles beyond the playing fields. "We do a lot of [diagramming plays on the chalkboard], but we also have seminars [on social issues] and we are primarily concerned with the drug prevention program. We want to tell the coaches, 'You are the role model. You are who the kids depend on.' We want them to be able to defend themselves with material and information. It has to be more than just telling the kids to 'say no.'"

• After nearly a dozen unsolved murders, Alvin Brooks formed the Ad Hoc Group Against Crime in 1977 to prevent further drug-related violence in Kansas City, Mo. His group, joined by the police, spends weekends knocking on doors. "If we come to a place that's been reported as a drug house, we tell the people they should move along. Then we take a bullhorn and announce to everyone that we want the drug dealers out of here," says Brooks, a former police detective. Working with other community groups, police, and prosecutors, 54 crackhouses were shut down between February and May, 1989.

• Benjamin Edwards, Sr., the chairman of the Third Shiloh Baptist Church on New Orleans' Piety Street, decided to buy out the drug dealers, rather than shout at them. Drug dealers worked out of two abandoned houses across the street from the church. In April 1989, the church bought the two houses, five other houses nearby, and a plot of land where it hopes to build homes for elderly church members. Other churches should do the same, Edwards says: "The black churches should have been involved a long time ago. Nobody else is going to have an impact like the church because the people have confidence in their spiritual leaders."

"Drug dealers are teachers— malevolent ones."

• In Houston, Teresa Spencer, a resident of the Huntington Forest Apartments, helped mobilize other residents in a housing area that at one time was overrun by drugs. Her efforts largely have succeeded. Today, the Huntington Forest Apartments residents are safer, the area has been reclaimed, and the drug dealers have been pushed aside. One woman with grit and courage made a difference.

These stories serve as a source of hope. They demonstrate that there is no immutable law that dooms disadvantaged minorities to a life of drugs simply because they are disadvantaged, or minorities, or both.

Conventional Wisdom

I know it is fashionable among some circles—primarily among some elites—to wonder how, for example, we can expect any child of the inner city not to succumb to the lure of drugs. After all, their reasoning goes, jobs paying the minimum wage don't hold much of an appeal when youngsters have the opportunity to make $300 or $500 or $1,000 a day. Drugs are so pervasive, their allure so strong, the money so easily obtained, the draw of evil so powerful—and the power to resist evil so feeble—that we simply should face reality and surrender any quaint notion we continue to harbor about children resisting drugs.

However, it violates everything a civil society stands for simply to throw in the towel and say, "Okay, we give up. It's not right that children use drugs, but we adults can't seem to do anything about it." Of course, drugs exert a tremendous pull. Nevertheless, responsible adults are supposed to be better, do better, point to a better way, and pull back. Inner-city parents who are trying to do right by their children, who are trying to shape their children's character, need allies. Those far-away commentators who excuse these children trample on the parents who are trying to teach good lessons.

Again, those who argue that efforts to shape character are doomed to failure should realize that the number of children who obey their parents and the law give witness to the lie. Many inner-city youth—including those living in or near drug markets—refuse to serve as "mules," lookouts, runners, or assassins. We should give those youngsters honor, support, and reinforcement. At the very time when they need to affirm things like individual responsibility, civic duty, and obligations to parents and God, too many segments of society are equivocating and sending mixed messages. This sort of moral enervation must be renounced in the strongest terms.

We know that, when adults don't teach children how to live responsible lives, these youngsters often become cynical and go astray. As a resident of New York's Covenant House (a home for youth who once were involved with drugs, prostitution, and crime) told Pres. Bush on a recent visit, "I'm not working for $125, $110, there's no way. For a whole week and sitting over a hot oven flipping hamburgers? One hundred dollars a week, that ain't no money. I can make $100 in 15 minutes by dealing drugs." Maybe he can, but it's the responsibility of adults and civil society to see to it that he won't, and to punish him if he does.

"We need to tell what really is happening in communities throughout the country."

It's not surprising to discover that, left to their own devices, children often will act like children. They will want everything, and they will want it all at once. One of the tasks of adults is to tell children, "You can't have everything, all at once," and then explain why. That used to be part of education; it still needs to be.

Drug dealers are teachers—malevolent ones. They are teaching our children the terrible lesson that you can get it all at once—money, cars, gold chains, fancy clothes, and all the rest—and it doesn't matter the means by which you attain it. That is one more compelling reason why we need to remove drug dealers from the presence of our children. They are teachers of a wicked lesson.

The stories that I've highlighted remind us of the resiliency and importance of nurturing institutions like the family, church, school, and neighborhood. The last two decades have seen a draining away of legitimacy from our existing institutions and prevailing cultural values, beliefs, and responsibilities. In many places, the fabric of support which Americans traditionally could find in the culture at large became worn, torn, and unraveled. We now see the human cost. It is one we should resolve to bear no longer. That means society must commit itself to a reinvigoration of our institutions and a resumption of their basic responsibilities. That is surely a long-term task. Let it begin; let's get to it. . . .

If we are to win the war on drugs, it seems to me that we have two choices. We either can restore the moral authority of families, schools, and churches, or we can increase the police authority of the state. I expect that, in the short run, we may have to do both. In the long run, however, the solution lies with these critical, nurturing institutions. One's first moral lesson should come from parents, not from a police officer.

This is not to absolve government of responsibility. Government has much to do if we are to win the war on drugs—in the areas of law enforcement, treatment, education, interdiction, and supply. Vigorous leadership by government *is* necessary, but it is not sufficient.

Our teaching and nurturing institutions are the hinge of civil society. They have sustained and advanced our best ideals as a culture and as a civilization. This country must not lose or remain indifferent to them.

So, let me end where I began, by quoting the words of Ralph Ellison's *Invisible Man:* "Being invisible and without substance, a disembodied voice, as it were, what else could I do? What else but try to tell you what was really happening when your eyes were looking through?"

We need to tell what really is happening in communities throughout the country. We need to make the invisible man visible again. We need to do more to attend to the institutions that will make him visible—and protect and nurture him. Every day in every U.S. city, we see our families, schools, churches, and communities work. We see them work for Americans of all races, and we see in them the face of the invisible man—the good men and women trying to do the right thing. It is in that recognition that we see our duty and our common destiny.

Drug Trafficking Harms America's Inner Cities

Ishmael Reed

About the Author: *Ishmael Reed is an author, playwright, and poet. Reed has written several novels, including his most recent work,* The Terrible Threes. *He has contributed articles to the* Washington Post, The New York Times, *and* Spin.

In June 1986 I returned to my house in Oakland from teaching at Harvard University to discover that a crack operation had changed my neighborhood. I became angry, disgusted, and frustrated. At the end of that November, I was optimistic that the downtown Oakland establishment would put down what amounts to a criminal uprising on the part of the drug intermediaries. As I'm writing this, several years later, nothing has been done, and now the problem is getting still worse.

My experience tells me this: It's the black working class—people who've put in time at stupid, dull jobs all of their lives and suffered all manner of degradation so that their children might become achievers—that is bearing the brunt of the brutal crack fascists. Members of the black working class are the victims of the drive-by shootings, the burglaries, rapes, and assaults committed by the crack dealers and their clients.

Attitudes toward the drug problem seem to be based upon distance from Ground Zero. The farther away from the situation, the more likely that people's response is to be abstract and

philosophical, and the more they're inclined to insist upon the constitutional rights of some of the most vicious enemies of black people. Conversely, the closer to Ground Zero the more heat they're likely to feel, and to advocate primitive solutions such as vigilantism.

Both positions are understandable.

In 1986 there were signs that the situation, once limited to East Oakland, as far away from your neighborhood in North Oakland as a Third World country, was moving closer to home—signs that you chose to ignore because you shared the lenient attitude of your generation toward drugs. In Cambridge, you live the life of a Harvard professor, residing in a condominium in the Chester Kingsley mansion, a rambling Queen Anne landmark whose picture and history appear in a coffee-table book. In June, when you return to Ground Zero, you discover that what was once a tranquil North Oakland zone is occupied by a deadly army.

You discover that living in an area in which a crack den, smokehouse, or—in the language of the police—"problem house" is in operation is like living under military rule. Your neighborhood is invaded at all times of the day and night by armed men and women—death squads—who carry the kinds of weapons that are employed in small wars all over the world. People are trapped in their homes, intimidated by rival drug armies who on more than one occasion have murdered innocent men, women, and children as they fight over the spoils.

> **"Members of the black working class are the victims of the drive-by shootings . . . committed by the crack dealers."**

The retired people, single-parent families, and widows who used to take so much pride in the neighborhood stay indoors. The lawns are still kept up and the repairs done, but the mood is one of trepidation. You dread coming home because you never know when a car full of unsavory characters might be parked in front of your house, or a drug dealer's pit bull, a "dangerous weapon," might be running up and down the street unleashed and terrorizing the neighborhood children. The streets are quiet during the day—an improvement—but at night it sounds like troop movements. You think of the song "The Freaks Come at Night." This must be how it is in Haiti under the Duvaliers, which is the kind of regime that comes to mind when you see the hoodlums milling about on your street. They have all the charm of the TonTon Macoutes and wear the same kind of sunglasses. Robberies occur; within one month, four auto break-ins and four burglaries, as the Living Dead attempt to steal radios or anything that will finance their habit.

> ## "Your neighborhood is invaded at all times of the day and night by armed men and women—death squads."

The horror movie metaphor is apt because the customers for this brain-scrambling stuff resemble cadavers as they wander zombielike, some barefoot and wearing pajamas under overcoats. Some are obviously into prostitution to support their habit, and you read that in Chicago a woman sold her child for cocaine. In Oakland, another woman hid in the closet so her mother wouldn't share her profits. She was making $100 per day. So that her child wouldn't cry and her position be given away, she smothered the child to death.

This scene is spreading throughout Oakland. No matter what the people in the Junior League and the Lakeview Club, the ballet and symphony boosters, may say about image, Oakland is in a state of war against drug fascists, and for the time being the drug fascists have gained the upper hand.

When you hear that the Oakland cocaine operation is a sort of take-out center for people in some of the more exclusive neighborhoods of Berkeley and Oakland, you wonder how many of the people in these exclusive neighborhoods have "Out of Nicaragua" bumper stickers on their Volvos but are perfectly willing to tolerate drug fascists who prey on the decent citizens of Oakland. You wonder how many agreed with an alternative East Bay newspaper reporter who just about drooled on his copy as he recorded the lurid activities of a heroin street dealer, making out as though this man were Robin Hood. Anybody who praises a person who is trafficking in cocaine and heroin, when intravenous drug use may wipe out one-third of the black population—something that even the segregated regimes of the South and all of the American racists combined haven't been able to accomplish—must be sick, and the admiration that some blacks have for these people must be the kind of twisted, perverted affection that a dog feels toward a master who sadistically tortures him.

The Rev. Fred Shuttleworth, in the acclaimed PBS series "Eyes on the Prize," says that you can't walk away from either physical or psychological oppression. And for those who believe that you can't do anything about crack because it's so prevalent, a comment that you hear often, you think of the young martyrs whose lives we celebrate. Suppose John F. Kennedy, Martin Luther King Jr., Robert Kennedy—all of whom could have chosen lives of ease and comfort—had taken that attitude? You can't deal with a problem like racism because it's so prevalent. We'd still be in the back of the bus and eating at segregated lunch counters.

Choices

Crackers have to realize that people are not going to stand by as they destroy working-class America and that if it comes to a choice between their survival and the people who form the incubator that produces black excellence, then most people will choose the latter without a moment's hesitation.

You finish your last essay as the *San Francisco Examiner*'s 13th writer-in-residence in an apartment the *Examiner* provides for the writers who are part of their series on the drug problem. From the window you can see the crowds visiting the bustling Fisherman's Wharf. You put the final touches on one of the most depressing pieces you've written.

If you were a drinking man you'd fetch some George Dickel whiskey, the concoction that kept you in a daze during your mid-20s. Instead you walk down to the Exploratorium, and, coincidentally, the first exhibit shows that for you, there seems to be no escaping from Ground Zero. It reads: "Radioactivity spreads out just like light. The farther you move from a light source the dimmer it looks. When you move farther away from radioactive particles, fewer particles hit you."

Drug Trafficking Has Corrupted American Foreign Policy

Alfred McCoy, interviewed by David Barsamian

About the Author: *Alfred McCoy is the author of* The Politics of Heroin in Southeast Asia *and* Drug Traffic: Narcotics and Organized Crime in Australia. *He is professor of history at the University of Wisconsin at Madison. David Barsamian interviewed McCoy for Alternative Radio in Boulder, Colorado.*

Barsamian: In your book The Politics of Heroin in Southeast Asia *you state that the United States was poised at the end of World War II to terminate the problem of drug addiction in this country and could have done so. Because of forces I'd like you to discuss, it wasn't able to.*

McCoy: America's failure to reduce if not eliminate drugs as a major problem was the result of a contradiction between the needs of domestic policy and demands of the national security state. After World War II, the United States became a global power and set up a number of agencies to exercise this power, most importantly, the executive agency known as the U.S. Central Intelligence Agency. Formed in 1948, the CIA was willing to ally with anybody and everybody that could provide strength and support in this global struggle against communism. In Europe and in Asia the CIA allied themselves with major drug brokers and other crime syndicates. In sum, what they did was to sanction the start of a flow of narcotics from the Middle East

Excerpted, with permission, from "The Politics of Drugs," an interview of Alfred McCoy by David Barsamian. For a complete transcript of this interview and/or a catalog, please write to David Barsamian, 1814 Spruce, Boulder, CO 80302.

through Europe to the United States which dominated America's drug markets until the 1960s. At the same time that the CIA was forging alliances and protecting the traffickers in Europe, they also formed similar alliances in Asia which were actually deeper and had much more profound and lasting impact on the Asian drug trade. As the European trade began to diminish in the 1960s or 1970s, this secondary flow of Asian drugs came into the United States and supplemented the old Turkey-Marseilles heroin connection. Ultimately, when you look at the source of supply and the politics that provided drugs to America in the post-war era, you come down to this contradiction between a vague commitment to "do something about drugs" versus a very high-profile effort to contain communism. In this balance between an inarticulated, poorly formed, weak narcotics policy and a very clear national goal of containing communism, the narcotics policy was barely considered. So the fact that the CIA was dealing with governments, intelligence chiefs, war lords, gangsters, traffickers of all sorts, was not considered matter of any a moment. The main U.S. foreign policy priority from the late 1940s and through the 1980s was containing communism. . . .

"America's failure to reduce if not eliminate drugs . . . was the result of a contradiction."

The recolonization of Indochina by the French at the end of World War II and in 1946 led to the "first Indochina war" and the establishment of a major international narcotics trade in which French intelligence was very much involved.

. . . . In Indochina, you have to understand first of all that the extensive opium trade, mass consumption, particularly in the cities, was a result of European colonial policy. This didn't occur anywhere else in the world. Asia, Africa, and Latin America were at one time entirely colonized. It's only in Southeast Asia that colonial governments paid for their very dynamic development: irrigation, massive road networks, rail networks by direct taxes upon indigenous consumers, taxes on alcohol, salt, and particularly opium. In British Malaya 40 percent of colonial taxes came from opium. In French Indochina it ranged about 15 percent from the period from the 1870s up through the 1950s, when as a result of UN [United Nations] pressure, all of these governments abolished the state opium trade. Thailand was the next to last to do it. It didn't abolish its state opium monopoly, rather like an alcohol beverage control that a lot of states have, until 1957. Laos didn't abolish theirs until 1961. So you had mass opium consumption in Southeast Asia as a result of the colonial policy of making the colony pay with opium. That was the policy.

Opium Production

Most of the opium was not produced in Southeast Asia. It came from abroad, either southern China or India. The thing that changes significantly after World War II is not the emergence of Southeast Asia as a major area of opiate consumption. It had been so for a century and even more. What is significant is the emergence of the mountain areas of Southeast Asia as major areas of global opium production. Indeed, by the early 1960s, the largest single source of opium anywhere in the world is the so-called Golden Triangle region of Southeast Asia. How did this come about? Two ways. Most importantly, we have to look at northeastern Burma. That's the bulk of the Golden Triangle. In fact, most of that imaginary geographical construct is in Burma, northeastern Burma in particular. So where did opium come from? Look at the British colonial records for Burma. You find opium production until 1945 in northeastern Burma was almost insignificant. There was very little grown. Most of the opium consumed in northeastern Burma came from India. Burma, after all, was a province of India under the British. So they just brought it in and sold it legally. Where the opium came from was a major

CIA operation. The biggest, the only one I know of its scale that has yet to be exposed by journalists or muckrakers of any sort. This is the attempt to overthrow the People's Republic of China. . . .

"Where the opium came from was a major CIA operation."

Baptist missionaries who told me, and they were in the area, that peasants who did not deliver their opium quota suffered the loss of limbs. Fingers would be cut. Hands would be taken. You and your family. So people produced. Under this forced occupation, where you had the Nationalist Chinese forces backed by the CIA occupying the prime opium-growing areas in northeastern Burma, Burma went from seven or eight tons of opium production per annum to anywhere up to 1,000 tons by the time the CIA's mercenaries were driven out in 1961. One thousand tons would have been in any given year up to 60 percent or 70 percent of the world's total illicit opium production. It came from this one area as a result of a decade of CIA-backed Nationalist Chinese occupation.

The other Southeast Asian era was as you described. Until 1950 France had an opium monopoly in Indochina and they were under pressure from the United Nations as well as the United States to clean up. They signed the UN Convention on narcotic drugs and they abolished the opium monopoly. But it didn't disappear. The opium dens were simply transferred from the French Ministry of Finance to French military intelligence. The military turned the dens over to a criminal syndicate that was running Saigon for the French, using their funds to buy daily intelligence and ferret out communist terrorists in the streets of Saigon. The communists were running a terror campaign that the French were powerless to control. They set up a very elaborate intelligence apparatus to try to stop that terror. Money was the fuel that drove that engine and the money came from drugs. Moreover, there were Corsican syndicates that dominated the illicit economy of Indochina in Saigon, and they began exporting morphine to Europe. In fact part of the so-called Marseilles connection came from Saigon. So as a result of French counterinsurgency efforts in Indochina, but primarily as a result of CIA operations in Burma, the so-called Golden Triangle goes into high-scale production. The Americans moved into Indochina after the French departure in 1955. We picked up the same tribes, the Hmong, the same politics of narcotics, that the French had established. By the 1960s the CIA is operating in collusion with the major traffickers exporting drugs from the mountains to meet the consumption needs of Southeast Asia itself, American combat forces fighting in Vietnam, and, ultimately, the world market. Southeast Asia, by the way, is now the number-one source of American heroin. So it's those very mountains of Burma, those very fields that were cleared and planted to the poppy as a result of this Nationalist Chinese/CIA counterinsurgency policy, that's supplying American addicts today with illicit heroin.

"The CIA was complicitous in the Laotian drug trade at a number of levels."

Was the anti-communist ideology so powerful and so strong that the CIA would risk the worldwide opprobrium of being linked with drug trafficking? Why would they take that risk?

It's easy. It worked. It was effective. I interviewed a guy named Lt. Col. Lucien Conein, and I asked him why they worked with the Corsicans in Saigon, for example. He said that there aren't very many groups that know the clandestine arts. When you think about what it takes to run an extralegal operation, to have somebody killed, to mobilize a crowd, to overthrow a government and put a new one in who does this?

Accountants? They go to a little office every day. Students? They go to classes. Where do you get people that have this kind of skill? You have your own operatives, and they're limited, particularly if you're foreigners. Sometimes you can turn to a state intelligence agency in a country you're working with, but most effectively you can turn to the underworld. That's why the CIA has worked with the warlords of the Golden Triangle, with Corsican syndicates in Europe, and continuously with the American Mafia because they practice the same clandestine arts. They operate with the same techniques. They have the same kind of immorality. They're natural allies. . . .

Drugs and Communism

One thing that has perplexed me on this particular issue of the CIA being involved in drug trafficking in Southeast Asia is the heroin flowing into the veins of the American GI's who are putatively there to defeat the communists. That's kind of bizarre, to say the least.

When I published my book I got a lot of flak from people on the Left who said I was probably a CIA agent because I was so moderate in my analysis. The thesis in the heated political times in the 1970s about drugs was this: The CIA, or the American ruling class, whoever these invisibles are that control this complex, uncontrollable country, had two problems. One was insurgency among minorities, particularly black uprisings in the cities of America. Another was the winning the war in Vietnam. So people on the Left put one and one together and they came up with two, the Southeast Asian drug trade. Their vision was of the CIA deputy director in charge of global narcotics, telling the Hmong caravans to get moving out of the highlands of Southeast Asia. Let's get that caravan down to the lab. OK, let's get that heroin loaded onto the aircraft. OK, now we've got it into Harlem. Get that kid. Kid, step forward, buy the bag. OK, that's it. A potential insurgent has been narcotized. Write him off for black power. I didn't see things operating quite so comprehensibly, and for this I was accused by people on the Left of being moderate and cowardly in my analysis. . . .

In effect, the CIA's involvement in narcotics was regionally specific. It didn't get much beyond Laos. The agency in Laos, just like the agency globally in the 1940s and 1950s, was myopic, short-sighted. It was fighting a war. It was trying to stop the Ho Chi Minh trail from operating. In order to do so it had a 30,000-man mercenary army made up largely of Hmong hill tribespeople who lived in the area and were opium growers. The CIA operatives just weren't interested in consequences of their complicity in the narcotics traffic. From 1960 to 1975 they ran this secret war with a massive army of 30,000 men, an operation of unequalled duration and size. The CIA had never run as big an operation.

What about Afghanistan in the 1980s?

That didn't last 15 years. It started in about 1981, and it's already over. It didn't make it. It lasted eight years. I don't think the Mujahiddin were as integrated with the CIA. They were just rebels that the CIA was backing. Laos had a 30,000 man army that the CIA *ran*. It was their army. They bought every bullet. They trained every soldier. They had a mercenary officer corps under General Vang Pao that they ran. It wasn't a hands-off operation. It was their army. That's why we've got all these Hmong in Los Angeles and Minnesota and Wisconsin. We're looking after our loyal tribe that fought and died for us. That's why we have all these mountain peasants trying desperately to adapt to life in this country.

The CIA was complicitious in the Laotian drug trade at a number of levels. . . .

The legacy of Laos, I think, is something that nobody's really thought about. For ten years the CIA's biggest operation was completely integrated with the structure of the Indochina opium trade. The capacity of that Hmong army to fight, to move, the capacity of these people to survive, to keep replacing soldiers who were killed by the tens of thousands was integrated with the opium trade. The secret war apparatus was part of the opium trade. We ran that war through Vang Pao. He is now living in the United States. He was a general in the Laotian army, but more importantly he was the CIA's general. Vang Pao was not from a traditional elite family. He was not very popular with the Hmong, certainly not at that time. His capacity to get recruits out of the villages once the war started taking heavy casualties and people seeing one and two and three sons dying, his capacity to extract more and more recruits to keep that war going relied upon him being able to put pressure on those villagers. I was in a village in Laos that had stopped sending recruits, and the CIA cut off the rice supply. The people were pushed to the brink of starvation. Because they had lost all the males down to the 14-year-olds. The village district leader didn't want to send the 14-year-olds. He said, "This is the next generation. If we send these kids, we will disappear. We won't produce another generation. We can't do this." He said, "No. We've been doing this for six, seven years, now we've lost everybody. We're not going to do it any more." So they cut off his rice.

Opium and Cash

The other pressure point that Vang Pao had was the opium. The Hmong have two products: rice to survive and opium for cash to buy the things that they need. So Vang Pao became the opium broker for the Hmong. As such, he gained extraordinary power over their economy and thus over their lives. So that by controlling those two products Vang Pao controlled those villages and could force them to support him, even after the casualties began to mount.

"You get a policy and personnel which integrates covert action with narcotics."

My metaphor for Vang Pao is kind of like a Judas goat. You know what a Judas goat is? In the stockyards there's a goat that will lead the sheep through the maze of the stockyards. As they're heading into the chute the Judas goat jumps aside and the flock of sheep go pelting through to be slaughtered. That's Vang Pao, like a tribal Judas goat, leading the Hmong to the slaughter. Except the Hmong are not like sheep. They know what's going on. They know that they're being slaughtered. It's not like they're being slaughtered in one room at one time. They're being slaughtered slowly over a decade. How does he get to keep leading them? Through the control of these two products. So you've got then a CIA secret war which in an essential, fundamental way, is linked with the opium traffic. More than that, it appears that a number of CIA operatives as individuals got involved. They started smuggling, wheeling and dealing, doing a couple of bags here. We know, for example, a famous case of a CIA global money-moving bank called the Nugen Hand bank, which was established in Australia. The founder of that was Michael John Hand, who was a Green Beret and a contract CIA operative in Laos. When he first came to Australia in 1969-70, Australian federal police got intelligence on him—I've seen the files—saying that he was bringing down light aircraft that are flying from Thailand to northern Australia into those abandoned airstrips that were left over from World War II and he is dealing heroin. That's what Michael John Hand, according to Australian police intelligence, was doing. So individual CIA operatives were getting involved. What you've got then, as a result of Laos, is the policy of integrating intelligence and covert action operations with narcotics. You get an entire generation of covert action warriors used to dealing with narcotics as a matter of policy. In short, you get a policy and personnel which integrates covert action with narcotics. This manifests itself in a number of ways. First of all, the Nugen Hand bank. Not only was it moving money globally for the CIA, but it was the major money laundering conduit that was shunting funds up to Southeast Asia from Australia and linking the Golden Triangle heroin trade of Southeast Asia with the urban drug markets of Australia. In Afghanistan as well, the same disturbing pattern that we saw in Laos emerges.

This is one case that hasn't been well studied. I've spoken to one correspondent for the *Far East Economic Review*, Mr. Lawrence Lifshulz, a friend of mine. What he found was something of a similar pattern to what I found in Laos. He was a correspondent in Pakistan and Afghanistan during the Mujahiddin campaign, and he wrote articles in the *Nation* and elsewhere describing a similar pattern. You've got Pakistani government officials very heavily involved in narcotics, Mujahiddin manufacturing heroin, exporting it to Europe and the United States. They're using it to support their guerrilla campaign, and the Pakistanis and the CIA are complicitious either not doing anything, or actually getting involved, in the case of some of the Pakistani elite. The Mujahiddin operation was integrated with the narcotics trade. And the CIA was fully informed of the integration and doesn't do anything about it.

Iran-Contra Operations

Moving on to our fourth instance of CIA complicity, one closer to home is the whole Iran/Contra operation. First of all, I think the Laos parallel is very strong in the Iran/Contra operation, even in the formal outlines of the policy. You get the contras on the border of Nicaragua, a mercenary army supported through humanitarian operations. They're given U.S. logistic support, U.S. equipment, and U.S. air power to deliver the equipment and logistic support.

"The CIA policy of integrating covert-action operations with narcotics . . . has gotten worse."

All the personnel that are involved in that operation are Laos veterans: Ted Shackley, Thomas Clines, Oliver North, Richard Secord—they all served in Laos during this ten-year war. They all experienced that policy of being complicitious in the narcotics trade for furtherance of covert action. In this case, it's not just the same. It's not just simply that the CIA was complicitious in allowing the contras to deal in cocaine, to serve as a link between the Andes across the Caribbean to the United States. I think you can see that the situation has gotten worse here. In Laos, as I said, the CIA was hands-off. Once heroin got beyond their secret base, they wouldn't touch it. They gave Vang Pao their aircraft, and once it got any further they didn't really know about it. They didn't want to know about it. They remained knowingly ignorant about it. Ultimately what you're looking at was a traffic in a remote region that wound up serving American combat forces fighting in Vietnam in a way that the CIA did not see was going to happen.

"There are instances of minor traffickers being arrested . . . and the CIA will actually go . . . and get them off."

The level of cynicism in Central America is even worse. We're not talking about original traffic or moving the raw product. We're talking about taking finished cocaine, providing aircraft, moreover, providing protection for these traffickers as they fly across the Caribbean with these massive loads of cocaine. Can one estimate what percentage of the cocaine was politically protected by these intelligence operations? Until there is a full investigation, which there's not likely to be, it's difficult to say. If you look at the drug flow in the United States in the 1960s, when this Laos operation was going, there was probably a much smaller percentage of narcotics entering the United States from politically protected brokers than there is today. In other words, the CIA policy of integrating covert-action operations with narcotics, just turning a blind eye to the fact that our allies are drug brokers, has gotten worse. It's closer to home. It's not moving the raw material out in the jungles. It's actually bringing the finished narcotic, co-caine, into the United States. . . .

One of the things that will happen as a result of the Bush war, I expect, will be another major expansion of the DEA [Drug Enforcement Administration]. Working against that is the CIA. Because they have a political covert-action mandate, they have found it convenient to ally themselves with the very drug brokers the DEA is trying to put in jail. When you are working for the CIA you are untouchable. The CIA backs you up. There are instances of minor traffickers being arrested in the United States for importing drugs and the CIA will actually go to the local police and courts and get them off. Because the accused threaten to talk and make trouble. The CIA just gets them out. What the CIA does in these known instances it does more broadly. I, for example, had reasonable evidence based on talking to American officials and my own inquiry, that the Chief of Staff of the Royal Laotian Army and the commander of the CIA's secret army are involved in drugs. What happened when I made those allegations? The CIA did everything to discredit my allegations. They attacked me. They didn't attack Vang Pao, who was operating heroin laboratories. They didn't go after General Ouane Rattikone, who had the world's biggest heroin operation. They went after *me*. They tried to suppress my book. They threatened to murder my sources. They spent $1.75 million staging a massive opium burning by the Nationalist Chinese forces in northern Thailand announcing that they were retiring from the drug trade. They went through all kinds of hoops to discredit me and my allegations. They protect these guys. While you're working with the agency, you are protected. So the DEA is going to go up against the CIA as well? No.

U.S. Intervention

Do you think that the current war on drugs might be used as a vehicle of U.S. intervention in foreign countries?

That is something I can't answer. But I'll speculate. The evidence brought out by Jonathan

Marshall, who's preparing a book on cocaine in Central America, raises real questions about the Panama operation. [Manuel] Noriega was portrayed as this desperate drug lord, this satanic figure that had to be knocked out for the drug war to go ahead. We knocked out this evil man, Noriega, and put him on trial. We put in a government which, according to the *New York Times*, is in fact linked, personally, with the Panamanian banking industry. Why is there a big banking industry in Panama? Panama is a little tiny country that was once formerly a province of Colombia. The United States separated it and built the canal. So if you're a Colombian cocaine merchant, the Medellin cartel or the Cali cartel, where do you do your banking? You don't go to Bogota, you do it in Panama City. You do it through these big Panamanian banks. If you've noticed the photographs of the financial district of Panama City, it looks like a mini-Wall Street or a mini-downtown Los Angeles. Why in this poor economy do you have this elaborate banking structure? It was built from money laundering. And the Endara government as individuals—one of his vice-presidents, several of his cabinet ministers—are on the boards of banks that have been big in the money laundering industry. Moreover, one of Endara's key cabinet people was actually a lawyer for one of the big drug lords of Colombia. So we have replaced Manuel Noriega, who is supposedly this evil drug dealer who made $4 million protecting the Medellin cartel, with people who represent the Panamanian money laundering industry, which is moving the money from the United States to Colombia. We got rid of some petty thug, some tough guy in the street who was stealing hubcaps, and we put the Mafia in power. Why? I don't know yet.

Influence in Panama

What it means to me is that the whole Panamanian operation didn't have anything to do with the drug war. I think it has to do with simply trying to maintain influence in Panama. And Noriega, whatever else he was, was a nationalist who was very good at manipulating the United States. I think that infuriated us.

"We stigmatize him as a drug lord. We invade. We get rid of him."

Just to continue my speculative vein: My scenario, created by looking at Laos and then guessing what could be going on in Colombia and Panama, would be that the hidden history of Panama reads like this: You have a nationalist general who takes control of this colonial creation of the United States, a charismatic figure, General Omar Torrijos. The United States hated Torrijos. Why? Because Torrijos was a convincing nationalist. He mobilized the Panamanian people. He had some kind of prestige internationally, and he forced the United States to give up our greatest jewel of empire, the Canal. What India was to the British, what Indonesia was to Holland, the Panama Canal is to us. That's our empire, our great triumph. So Torrijos took away the canal. Reagan comes into office and Torrijos has an aircraft accident. Why? It's never been explained. Maybe he was killed. The CIA runs a lot of the maintenance and aircraft contract firms in the Caribbean. In any case, somebody kills Torrijos. So they're looking around for some new, pliable man to put in power to make sure they don't have trouble. So they install Noriega. They know Noriega's reliable because he's been doing drug operations in a small, petty way. They know they've got him. He's manageable. He does whatever the CIA wants. He's the CIA's liaison, very reliable. What does he do? He turns around and does exactly what Torrijos did. He plays to the nationalist crowd. He uses the drug money and the Panamanian economy to build up an independent political base. He's no longer controllable. So what do we do? We stigmatize him as a drug lord. We invade. We get rid of him. We put in an utterly pliable government. We got rid of a man who maybe made $4 million from drugs and replaced him with a cabinet which represents a multi-million dollar money-laundering industry. To me the logic is not so much to get rid of drugs but to maintain U.S. influence in a key strategic area at a time when the canal is about to be turned over. So my hunch, my uninformed opinion is that the Panamanian invasion has very little to do with drugs and everything to do with maintenance of U.S. power abroad. We dressed up our national strategic interest no longer in the ball gown of anti-communism but in the formal wear of anti-narcotics policy. But we're still just maintaining U.S. power. It's likely that the drug war is going to have other episodes like this. Whether or not the drug war will ultimately become a creation of U.S. global strategic interests, I don't know. It's too early to say. But in this particular instance, a major battle in the drug war looks very dubious.

Bibliography

Books

Joseph D. Douglass	*Red Cocaine: The Drugging of America.* Fort Collins, CO: Clarion House, 1990. *1995*
Kenneth R. Feinberg	"Drug Enforcement: Criminal Division." In *America's Transition: Blueprints for the 1990s,* edited by Mark Green and Mark Pinsky. New York: Democracy Project, Inc., 1989.
Guy Gugliatta and Jeff Leen	*Kings of Cocaine: Inside the Medellin Cartel—An Astonishing True Story of Murder, Money, and International Corruption.* Englewood Cliffs, NJ: Simon and Schuster, 1989.
Rensselaer W. Lee III	*The White Labyrinth: Cocaine and Political Power.* New Brunswick, NJ: Transaction Publishing, 1989.
Michael Levine	*Deep Cover.* New York: Delacorte Press, 1990.
Clarence Lusane	*Racism and the War on Drugs.* Boston: South End Press, 1991.
Michael D. Lyman	*Gangland: Drug Trafficking by Organized Criminals.* Springfield, IL: Charles C. Thomas, 1990.
Elaine Shannon	*Desperados: Latin Drug Lords, U.S. Lawmen, and the War America Can't Win.* New York: Viking, 1988.
Terry Williams	*The Cocaine Kids: The Inside Story of a Teenage Drug Ring.* Reading, MA: Addison-Wesley Publishing Co., 1989.

Periodicals

Bruce Alexander	"Snow Job," *Reason,* December 1990.
America	"Drugs—To Make War or Peace?" April 27, 1991.
John Barron	"Castro, Cocaine, and the A-Bomb Connection," *Reader's Digest,* March 1990.
Malcolm Byrne and Jefferson Morley	"The Drug War and National Security," *Dissent,* Winter 1989.
Richard B. Craig	"Are Drug Kingdoms South America's New Wave?" *The World & I,* November 1989.
James Der Derian	"Narco-Terrorism at Home and Abroad," *Radical American,* vol. 23, nos. 2-3, October 31, 1990.
Joseph D. Douglass	"Legalizing Drugs: Is It the Answer?" *Conservative Review,* June 1990.
Drug Abuse Update	Special Issue, Spring 1991. Available from National Families in Action, 2296 Henderson Mill Rd., Suite 203, Atlanta, GA 30345.
The Drug Policy Letter	Special Issue, November/December 1989. Available from the International Conference on Drug Policy Reform, 4801 Massachusetts Ave. NW, Suite 400, Washington, DC 20016-2087.
Maria Jimena Duzan	"Leave the Army Out of Colombian Anti-Drug Operations," *The Wall Street Journal,* May 18, 1990.
Ebony	"War! The Drug Crisis," special section, August 1989.
Barbara Ehrenreich	"The Usual Suspects," *Mother Jones,* September/October 1990.
Dennis Eisenberg	"The World's Largest Drug Field," *Commentary,* June 1990.
Don Feder	"A Moral War on Drugs Would Be the Answer," *Conservative Chronicle,* February 7, 1990.
John J. Fialka	"How a Big Drug Cartel Laundered $1.2 Billion with Aid of U.S. Firms," *The Wall Street Journal,* March 1, 1990.
Steve France	"Should We Fight or Switch?" *ABA Journal,* February 1990.

Jeff Gerth "CIA Shedding Its Reluctance to Aid in Fight Against Drugs," *The New York Times*, March 25, 1991.

Linda R. Gordon "Europe's Kinder, Gentler Approach," *The Nation*, February 4, 1991.

Gustavo Gorriti "How to Fight the Drug War," *The Atlantic*, July 1989.

Edward Grimsley "There Should Be No Apologies in the Drug War," *Conservative Chronicle*, February 7, 1990.

The Heritage Foundation "Drug Legalization: Myths vs. Reality," January 25, 1990. Available from The Heritage Foundation, 214 Massachusetts Ave. NE, Washington, DC 20002.

David Isenberg "Military Options in the War on Drugs," *USA Today*, July 1990.

Robert M. Kimmitt *International Law and the War on Narcotics*. Washington, DC: United States Department of State, Bureau of Public Affairs, 1990.

Ted Kleine "A Portrait of the Drug Dealer as a Young Man," *Utne Reader*, May/June 1991.

Mark Kram "The Betrayal of Michael Levine," *Esquire*, March 1991.

Lewis H. Lapham "A Political Opiate," *Harper's Magazine*, December 1989.

Kim A. Lawton "Churches Enlist in the War on Drugs," *Christianity Today*, February 11, 1991.

Rensselaer W. Lee III "Cocaine Mafia," *Society*, January/February 1990.

Penny Lernoux "Playing Golf While Drugs Flow," *The Nation*, February 13, 1989.

Melvyn Levitsky "One Year Later: Update on Andean Drug Strategy," *U.S. Department of State Dispatch*, October 29, 1990.

Lawrence Lifschultz "Inside the Kingdom of Heroin," *The Nation*, November 14, 1988.

Richard Mackenzie "Borderline Victories on Drug War's Front Line," *Insight*, January 14, 1991.

Kenneth Mano "Legalize Drugs," *National Review*, May 28, 1990.

Michael Massing "Can We Cope with Drugs?" *Dissent*, Spring 1991.

Michael Massing "In the Cocaine War . . . the Jungle Is Winning," *The New York Times Magazine*, March 4, 1990.

Jefferson Morley "The Great American High: Contradictions of Cocaine Capitalism," *The Nation*, October 2, 1989.

Salim Muwakkil "Drugs and the Black Community," *Utne Reader*, May/June 1991.

National Review "Mr. Bennett's War," September 15, 1989.

Daniel Porter "Just Say No to Giving Inner Cities a Bad Rap," *In These Times*, January 24-30, 1990.

Peter Ross Range "The Drug-Money Hunt," *U.S. News & World Report*, August 21, 1989.

Charles B. Rangel "USA 1991: One Year After Legalization," *USA Today*, July 1990.

Linda Robinson "Still a Cocaine Crossroads," *U.S. News & World Report*, April 15, 1991.

Kurt L. Schmoke "Back to the Future," *The Humanist*, September/October 1990.

Jacqueline Sharkey "The Contra-Drug Trade Off," *Common Cause Magazine*, September/October 1988.

Eric E. Sterling "The Bill of Rights: A Casualty of the War on Drugs," *Vital Speeches of the Day, November 1, 1990.*

Jacob Sullum "What's the Problem?" *Reason*, March 1991.

Rick Szykowny "A Funny, Dirty Little Drug War," *The Humanist*, September/October 1990.

Richard Thornburgh "Money Laundering: You Make It, We'll Take It," *Vital Speeches of the Day*, July 15, 1990.

Cesar Gaviria Trujillo "To Save Colombia from Cocaine, Buy Its Roses," *The Wall Street Journal*, November 2, 1990.

Signe Waller "The War on Drugs: A Substitute for the War on Communism," *New Politics*, Summer 1990, vol. 3, no. 1.

James Q. Wilson "Against the Legalization of Drugs," *Commentary*, February 1990.

Walter Wink "Biting the Bullet: The Case for Legalizing Drugs," *The Christian Century*, August 8-15, 1990.

Charles B. Wohlford "Off the Pot," *The New Republic*, December 3, 1990.

Marin Morse Wooster "The War over the War," *Reason*, August/September 1990.

Robert C. Yeager "Kids Who Can't Say No," *Reader's Digest*, February 1991.

Emily Yoffe "How to Legalize," *Mother Jones*, February/March 1990.

Organizations
to Contact

The editors have compiled the following list of organizations that are concerned with the issues debated in this book. All of them have publications or information available for interested readers. The descriptions are derived from materials provided by the organizations. This list was compiled upon the date of publication. Names and phone numbers of organizations are subject to change.

American Civil Liberties Union (ACLU)
132 W. 43rd St.
New York, NY 10036
(212) 944-9800

The ACLU champions the rights set forth in the Declaration of Independence and the Constitution. It objects to drug testing because it believes such testing violates the individual's right to privacy. The ACLU also objects to illegal searches and seizures in the course of narcotics investigations. It publishes a *Briefing Paper on Drug Testing* and also distributes a packet of materials on drug testing.

American Enterprise Institute
1150 17th St. NW
Washington, DC 20036
(202) 862-5800

The institute sponsors research on a wide range of national and international issues. The institute publishes the bimonthly journal *American Enterprise,* which frequently carries articles on the drug trade and drug trafficking.

Cato Institute
224 Second St. SE
Washington, DC 20005
(202) 789-7419

The institute is a public policy research foundation that supports limited government, and believes that the war on drugs threatens individual rights. It publishes *Cato Journal* three times a year, and the bimonthly *Cato Policy Report.*

Christic Institute
1324 N. Capitol St. NW
Washington, DC 20002
(202) 797-8106

The institute is an interfaith religious organization that works to expose business and government corruption. It takes credit for exposing the Contragate scandal in which the federal government was accused of sanctioning drug trafficking in Central America. The institute asserts that the U.S. government passes stringent drug laws at home but uses drugs for political ends abroad. Publications include the bimonthly *Contragate Alert* and the quarterly *Convergence.*

Committees of Correspondence, Inc.
57 Conant St.
Danvers, MA 01923
(508) 774-2641

The committees, a national coalition of community groups, fight drug abuse among youth by publishing data about drugs and drug abuse. The coalition opposes drug legalization and advocates treatment for drug abusers. Publications include the quarterly *Drug Abuse Newsletter,* the periodic *Drug Prevention Resource Manual,* and related pamphlets, brochures, and article reprints.

Drug Enforcement Administration (DEA)
1405 I St. NW
Washington, DC 20537
(202) 307-1000

The Drug Enforcement Administration is the branch of the federal government charged with enforcing the nation's drug laws. This agency concentrates on stopping high-level narcotics smuggling and distribution in the United States and abroad. It publishes *Drug Enforcement Magazine* quarterly.

Drug Policy Foundation
4801 Massachusetts Ave. NW, #400
Washington, DC 20537
(202) 895-1634

The foundation supports legalizing many drugs and increasing the number of treatment programs for addicts. It distributes material on legislation regarding drug legalization. The foundation's publications include the bimonthly *Drug Policy Letter* and the books *The Great Drug War* and *1989-1990, A Reformer's Catalogue.* It also distributes *Press*

Clips, an annual compilation of newspaper articles on drug legalization issues.

Drugs and Crime Data Center and Clearinghouse
1600 Research Blvd.
Rockville, MD 20850
(800) 666-3332

The clearinghouse, an office of the U.S. Department of Justice, compiles and distributes information on drug-related crime for use by policymakers and other researchers. Its publications include *Federal Drug Data for National Policy* and *State Drug Resources: A National Directory.*

Fraternal Order of Police
National Headquarters
6830 Laurel St. NW
Washington, DC 20012-9979
(800) 451-2711

The order distributes material related to criminal justice and law enforcement issues. It upholds the right of law enforcement agencies to administer drug tests to their officers and applicants. The order works to support national efforts in the war on drugs. It distributes copies of current periodical articles on drug laws and various police memos, including: "Drug Testing and Polygraphs" and "Law Enforcement Drug Screening Guidelines."

The Heritage Foundation
214 Massachusetts Ave. NE
Washington, DC 20002
(202) 546-4400

The Heritage Foundation is a conservative public policy research institute that opposes the legalization of drugs and advocates strengthening law enforcement to stop drug abuse. It publishes position papers on a broad range of topics, including drug issues. Its regular publications include the monthly *Policy Review,* the *Backgrounder* series of occasional papers, and the *Heritage Lecture* series.

International Narcotics Enforcement Officers Association (INEOA)
112 State St., Suite 1200
Albany, NY 12207
(518) 463-6232

INEOA examines national and international narcotics laws and seeks ways to improve those laws and prevent drug abuse. It also studies law enforcement methods to find the most effective ways to reduce illegal drug use. The association publishes *International Drug Report* and *Narc Officer,* both monthly journals, and a newsletter devoted to drug control issues.

Libertarian Party
1528 Pennsylvania Ave. SE
Washington, DC 20003
(202) 543-1988

The Libertarian Party's goal is to ensure respect for individual rights. It advocates the repeal of all laws prohibiting the production, sale, possession, or use of drugs. It publishes *Libertarian Party News,* many books, and distributes a compilation of articles supporting drug legalization.

National Clearinghouse for Alcohol and Drug Information
PO Box 2345
Rockville, MD 28052
(301) 468-2600

The clearinghouse provides educational literature and a reference and referral service on drug issues. It publishes a bimonthly newsletter, *Prevention Pipeline: An Alcohol and Drug Awareness Service,* to report the newest data on alcohol and drug abuse.

National Institute of Justice
PO Box 6000
Rockville, MD 20850
(800) 851-3420

The institute serves as a clearinghouse for information on the causes, prevention, and control of crime. Among the publications available are *Alcohol Use and Criminal Behavior* and *Probing the Links Between Drugs and Crime.*

National Organization for the Reform of Marijuana Laws (NORML)
1636 R St. NW
Washington, DC 20009
(202) 483-5500

NORML fights to legalize marijuana and to help those who have been convicted for possessing or selling marijuana. It publishes a newsletter, *Marijuana Highpoints,* on the progress of legislation concerning marijuana throughout the country.

Office of National Drug Control Policy
Executive Office of the President
Washington, DC 20500
(202) 467-9800

The Office of National Drug Control Policy, established by the National Narcotics Leadership Act of 1988, is responsible for the government's war on drugs. It formulates the government's policy on illegal drug trafficking and coordinates the federal agencies responsible for stopping drug trafficking. Drug policy studies are available upon request.

The RAND Corporation
Publications Department
1700 Main St.
Santa Monica, CA 90406-2138
(213) 393-0411

The RAND Corporation is a private research institution. It publishes material on the costs, prevention, and treatment of smoking, alcoholism, and drug abuse. The corporation believes the war on drugs is misdirected and must be refocused on reducing the demand for drugs. Its extensive list of publications includes the book *Sealing the Borders* by Peter Reuter.

Index